Teacher learning for educational change

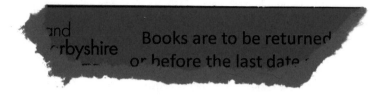

Professional Learning

Series Editors: Ivor Goodson and Andy Hargreaves

The work of teachers has changed significantly in recent years and now, more than ever, there is a pressing need for high-quality professional development. This timely new series examines the actual and possible forms of professional learning, professional knowledge, professional development and professional standards that are beginning to emerge and be debated at the beginning of the twenty-first century. The series will be important reading for teachers, teacher educators, staff developers and policy makers throughout the English-speaking world.

Published and forthcoming titles:

Ivor Goodson: *Professional Knowledge*
Andy Hargreaves: *The Learning Profession*
Alma Harris: *Improving Schools through Teacher Leadership*
Garry Hoban: *Teacher Learning for Educational Change*
Bob Lingard, Martin Mills, Debra Hayes and Pam Christie: *Leading Learning*
Judyth Sachs: *The Activist Teaching Profession*

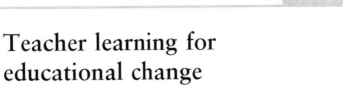

Teacher learning for educational change
A systems thinking approach

Garry F. Hoban

Open University Press

Open University Press
McGraw-Hill Education
McGraw-Hill House
Shoppenhangers Road
Maidenhead
Berkshire
SL6 2QL

email: enquiries@openup.co.uk
world wide web: www.openup.co.uk

and

Two Penn Plaza,
New York, NY 10121-2289, USA

First Published 2002
Reprinted 2010

A catalogue record of this book is available from the British Library

ISBN-10   0 335 20953 X (pb)   0 335 20954 8 (hb)
ISBN-13   978 0 335 20953 8 (pb)   978 0 335 20954 5 (hb)

Library of Congress Cataloging-in-Publication Data
Hoban, Garry F. (Garry Francis), 1953–
    Teacher learning for educational change : a systems thinking approach / Garry F. Hoban.
        p. cm. – (Professional learning)
    Includes bibliographical references and index.
    ISBN 0-335-20954-8 (hard) – ISBN 0-335-20953-X (pbk.)
        1. Teachers–In-service training. 2. Educational change. 3. Effective teaching. I. Title.
    II. Series.

    LB1731 .H55 2002
    370'.71'55–dc21

                                                                2002024607

 **Mixed Sources**
Product group from well-managed
forests and other controlled sources
www.fsc.org Cert no. TT-COC-002769
© 1996 Forest Stewardship Council

Typeset by Graphicraft Limited, Hong Kong
Printed in Great Britain by Bell & Bain Ltd., Glasgow

To my loving family, my wife Sharon, my son Christopher, and my daughter Ellena – may we always treasure our relationships and be best friends.

Contents

Series editors' preface

Teaching today is increasingly complex work, requiring the highest standards of professional practice to perform it well (Hargreaves and Goodson 1996). It is the core profession, the key agent of change in today's knowledge society. Teachers are the midwives of that knowledge society. Without them, or their competence, the future will be malformed and stillborn. In the United States, George W. Bush's educational slogan has been to leave no child behind. What is clear today in general, and in this book in particular, is that leaving no child behind means leaving no teacher or leader behind either. Yet, teaching too is also in crisis, staring tragedy in the face. There is a demographic exodus occuring in the profession as many teachers in the ageing cohort of the Boomer generation are retiring early because of stress, burnout or disillusionment with the impact of years of mandated reform on their lives and work. After a decade of relentless reform in a climate of shaming and blaming teachers for perpetuating poor standards, the attractiveness of teaching as a profession has faded fast among potential new recruits.

Teaching has to compete much harder against other professions for high calibre candidates than it did in the last period of mass recruitment – when able women were led to feel that only nursing and secretarial work were viable options. Teaching may not yet have reverted to being an occupation for 'unmarriageable women and unsaleable men' as Willard Waller described it in 1932, but many American inner cities now run their school systems on high numbers of uncertified teachers. The teacher recruitment crisis in England has led some schools to move to a four-day week; more and more schools are run on the increasingly casualized labour of temporary teachers from overseas, or endless supply teachers whose quality busy administrators do not always have time to monitor (Townsend 2001). Meanwhile in the Canadian province of Ontario, in 2001, hard-nosed and hard-headed reform strategies led in a single year to a decrease in applications to teacher education programmes in faculties of education by 20–25 per cent, and a drop in a whole grade level of accepted applicants.

Amid all this despair and danger though, there remains great hope and some reasons for optimism about a future of learning that is tied in its vision to an empowering, imaginative and inclusive vision for teaching as well. The educational standards movement is showing visible signs of over-reaching itself as people are starting to complain about teacher shortages in schools, and the loss of creativity and inspiration in classrooms (Hargreaves *et al.* 2001). There is growing international support for the resumption of more humane middle years philosophies in the early years of secondary school that put priority on community and engagement, alongside curriculum content and academic achievement. School districts in the United States are increasingly seeing that high quality professional development for teachers is absolutely indispensable to bringing about deep changes in student achievement (Fullan 2001). In England and Wales, policy documents and White Papers are similarly advocating for more 'earned autonomy', and freedom from curriculum constraints and inspection requirements, where schools and teachers are performing well (e.g. DfES 2001). Governments almost everywhere are beginning to speak more positively about teachers and teaching – bestowing honour and respect where blame and contempt had prevailed in the recent past.

The time has rarely been more opportune or more pressing to think more deeply about what professional learning, professional knowledge and professional status should look like for the new generation of teachers who will shape the next three decades of public education. Should professional learning accompany increased autonomy for teachers, or should its provision be linked to the evidence of demonstrated improvements in pupil achievement results? Do successful schools do better when the professional learning is self-guided, discretionary and intellectually challenging, while failing schools or schools in trouble benefit from required training in the skills that evidence shows can raise classroom achievement quickly? And does accommodating professional learning to the needs of different schools and their staffs constitute administrative sensitivity and flexibility (Hopkins) *et al.* 1997), or a kind of professional development apartheid (Hargreaves, forthcoming)? These are the kinds of questions and issues which this series on professional learning sets out to address.

In this book, Garry Hoban sets out to construct a deep conception of what professional learning for teachers looks like – not when it is packaged in courses, workshops and training sessions, but when it is embedded into the life, the very organization of an entire shcool. Hoban develops a highly sophisticated analysis of what professional learning looks like and should look like in rapidly changing, even complex systems. Indeed, he provides some of the most accessible writing on the relevance of complexity theory to schools that exists in the educational field. Hoban's message is that for teachers' professional learning to be effective, it must be an integral part of how the school as a whole 'learns' to improve and to cope with change over time.

After years of working in the classroom trenches in several different roles, Garry Hoban never falls into the trap of being an armchair theorist. Through his own wide ranging research and experience he demonstrates what learning, enquiry and networking look like for teachers in real school settings, casting vital new light on the nature of schools as complex learning communities. He provides clear cases of what these communities can come to look like in practice. And in an age when professional development is squarely back on the agenda of educational policy, Garry Hoban points a way forward that is both emotionally optimistic and strategically powerful.

Andy Hargreaves
Ivor Goodson

References

DfES (Department for Education and Skills) (2001) *Achieving Success*. London: HMSO.

Fullan, M. (2001) *Leading in a Culture of Change*. San Francisco: Jossey-Bass/Wiley.

Hargreaves, A. (forthcoming) *Teaching in the Knowledge Society*. New York: Teachers College Press.

Hargreaves, A. and Goodson, I. (1996) Teachers' professional lives: aspirations and actualities, in I. Goodson and A. Hargreaves (eds) *Teachers' Professional Lives*. New York: Falmer Press.

Hargreaves, A., Earl, L., Moore, S. and Manning, S. (2001) *Learning to Change: Beyond Teaching Subjects and Standards*. San Francisco: Jossey-Bass/Wiley.

Hopkins, D., Harris, A. and Jackson, D. (1997) Understanding the schools capacity for development: growth states and strategies, *School Leadership and Management*, 17(3): 401–11.

Townsend, J. (2001) It's bad – trust me, I teach there, Sunday Times, 2 December.

Waller, W. (1932) *The Sociology of Teaching*. New York: Russell & Russell.

List of figures and tables

Figures

Tables

Acknowledgements

I would like to thank the many people who supported me in different ways over the years and in a direct or indirect way contributed to the writing of this book:

My doctoral committee from The University of British Columbia (UBC), Gaalen Erickson, Tony Clarke, Peter Sexias and Erminia Pedretti.

Shona Mullen from Open University Press and the series editors, Andy Hargreaves and Ivor Goodson, thanks for your encouragement.

Staff at the Centre for the Study of Teacher Education at UBC, especially Gaalen and Tony, who always model a sense of care and community.

My fellow students from UBC, especially Ed Robeck, Gary Hepburn and Gabbie Minnes Brandes, who challenged me and supported me.

My research buddies, John Loughran from Monash University and Tom Russell from Queen's University.

The teachers who allowed me to conduct research on their practice and gave me insights into how they learn, Geoff Hastings, David Lloyd, Craig Luccarda, Greg Auhl, Maureen Dickson, Sharon Hoban and Dee Petersen.

The two facilitators who wrote chapters for this book, Jan Turbill from the University of Wollongong and Rob Walker from Christchurch, New Zealand.

A special high school student, Loreena McMahon, who knew more about teaching than many teachers.

My colleagues from the University of Wollongong, especially members of the RILE (Research in Interactive Learning Environments) group.

My teaching buddies at the University of Wollongong, Brian Ferry and Barry Harper, who gave me confidence to pursue my ideas.

Brian Cambourne and Barry Harper from the University of Wollongong who supervised me at the beginning of my PhD and encouraged me to continue my studies in Canada.

The people who gave me feedback on different chapters, John Loughran, Kerry West, Tom Russell, Lyn Middleton, Brian Ferry, Barry Harper and Deslea Konza.

My colleagues at Charles Sturt University who gave me my start in academia, especially Bob Meyenn, Judith Parker, Doug Hill, Michael Arthur, Bob Ingle, Rod Francis, Robin Wills and Larry Antil.

Mark Schlager from SRI who gave me permission to feature TAPPED IN as an online community in Chapter 7.

Peter Keeble from Wollongong University who proof-read the manuscript.

William Doll from Louisiana State University who helped me clarify the distinction between chaos theory and complexity theory.

The Carnegie Foundation for the Advancement of Teaching for displaying materials from their Knowledge Media Laboratory.

Carfax Publishing Company for Figure 4.1 from Huberman, M. (1995) Networks that alter teaching: concepualizing exchanges and experiments, *Teachers and Teaching: Theory and Practice*, 1(2), October, p. 202.

Introduction

I had an awakening in 1990. For the previous 14 years, I had taught science in five different high schools in Australia and overseas believing that I was a very good teacher. My self-perception was based on several achievements – I passed a rigorous two-day inspection for promotion, was selected from over 100 applicants for a prestigious overseas appointment and was promoted to be a department head when I returned to Australia. In 1989, I was appointed as a K-12 Science Consultant to share my wisdom with teachers in elementary and secondary schools across New South Wales. At that time I believed I had 'mastered' teaching, because I knew my science content as well as having accumulated a large repertoire of teaching strategies and hands-on activities. After one year as a consultant, I felt that I needed some more challenges and so I applied for a position as a teacher-educator at a university in rural New South Wales, Australia. My academic qualifications were inadequate (no higher degree), but I had a wealth of teaching experiences and argued that I should be employed on the basis of my expertise, as long as I commenced my Master of Education (Honours) degree.

Over time, my self-perception as having 'mastered' teaching slowly dissolved. As part of my new role as a teacher-educator, I supervised trainee elementary and early childhood teachers on practicum. This involved visiting classes in different schools and watching lessons being taught in a variety of ways and settings. I progressively became aware that my teaching of high school science over 14 years was rather mundane when compared to the exciting teaching being demonstrated in many elementary and early childhood settings. I saw classrooms decorated with a range of creative work, teachers interacting with children in different ways, children working in small groups, learning in context and having fun at the same time! What really impressed me was the variety of strategies used for the teaching of literacy, such as using big books, process writing, role plays, pictures, posters, word games and hands-on activities. This was far removed from my practice as a science teacher – working in a classroom with several posters on the walls, equipment scattered in cupboards and a pile of textbooks in the front corner. There was not much problem solving by students in my lessons as I prescribed the experiments; even so, most did not work perfectly anyway. Besides, the curriculum was so packed we never had enough time to be flexible or to repeat experiments to check our results.

In 1990, I commenced my Master of Education degree and started reading about the nature of social conditions to support children's learning. From seeing different classrooms and reading a variety of educational literature, I became aware of social influences on learning and the importance of making children's learning an adventure rather than a routine. And I now understood more about how to incorporate these influences into my teaching. Upon reflection, I realized that, as a secondary science teacher for 14 years, I knew my science content but very little about how children learn. In essence, my teaching was driven by my knowledge of subject matter, not my understanding of children's learning. Hence, it became clear to me that mastering subject matter does not mean mastering teaching. In particular, I underestimated the importance of developing a rapport with children in a class and building up their self-esteem by showing a personal interest in them as people. Thus began my awakening about understanding the complex relationships between teaching and learning that is still evolving today.

In retrospect, I often thought about why I had such a simplistic conception of teaching during those first 14 years; it is a little embarrassing that I believed I had mastered the job. I finished my teacher training – I had a Bachelor of Arts degree (Biology major), I had completed a postgraduate Diploma of Education and had attended several inservice courses every year. Yet, in hindsight, I knew rather little about the dynamic relationship between teaching and learning. I also believe that many teachers, especially those in secondary schools, were just like me. Our perceived role was to get the content across to children in small chunks so that they could build their own knowledge of science. After I completed my Master of Education degree in 1992, I wanted to find out about how teachers learn about their practice and, in 1993, I commenced my PhD with that purpose in mind at The University of British Columbia in Vancouver.

I completed my degree in 1996 and the title of my thesis was 'A Professional Development Model Based on Interrelated Principles of Teacher Learning'. What surprised me at the time was the lack of a coherent theoretical framework in the educational literature to guide long-term teacher learning to support educational change. I attempted to address this in my thesis, but I only scratched the surface. Since graduating with my doctorate, I have been reading more widely, mostly in the business literature, to give me different perspectives about learning in the workplace and change. The business literature embraces complexity theory as a world view and uses systems thinking as a way of understanding complexity. After five years of extra reading, this book has evolved using a blend of literatures from education, science, business and philosophy. I now believe that complexity theory provides us with a more useful world view than mechanistic ways of thinking for understanding educational change and teacher learning.

When viewed from a conventional mechanistic paradigm, educational change is a linear event supported by a one-step approach to teacher learning. What is new in this book is that educational change is viewed as a complex system assuming that change is a non-linear process that needs to be supported by a framework for long-term teacher learning. The central question of this book, therefore, is 'What conditions will help to establish a framework for long-term teacher learning to support educational change?' To address this question, I use a systems thinking approach to draw together ideas from existing learning perspectives into a new theoretical framework to guide long-term teacher learning. This framework is not a formula, but a new mindset; it is an approach that helps us to understand the non-linear dynamics of the change process and encourages us to think creatively about how a framework for teacher learning can support it.

Finally, in writing this book I would like to thank the two authors who each contributed a chapter in Part 2 and who were facilitators in their respective teacher learning projects. Chapter 5 was written by Jan Turbill, who is a senior lecturer in the Faculty of Education at the University of Wollongong, Australia. She was one of the main authors of the 'Frameworks' project as well as being a facilitator. These professional learning projects were run in the USA for over 10 years to support the teaching of literacy in grades 3–8. Chapter 6 was written by Rob Walker, who was a facilitator for the Christchurch cluster of schools involving a long-term project to support the teaching of ICT (Information and Communication Technologies) in New Zealand.

Part 1

Thinking differently about educational change

There is a paradox embedded in our teaching profession – in a rapidly chang-ing society, teachers are often reluctant to change their practices. After being presented with a multitude of ideas in preservice and inservice programmes, many teachers fall into a repetitive pattern of teaching in the conventional way in which they were taught when they were at school (Lortie 1975). This pattern is based on the assumption that their students will learn in the same way as the teachers did and there are several influences that reinforce this pattern. First, there are social influences on teachers that encourage them to conform to the way colleagues around them teach. To 'fit in', new teachers are likely to match the practices that already exist in schools, especially if these are driven by rigid school policies. Second, teaching in innovative ways often requires extra resources and time, which may be lacking for those who are just coping in their job. Third, teachers are often under pressure to cover a prescribed curriculum that is reinforced by the requirements of external exams, leaving little flexibility to explore new strategies. This reluctance for teachers to change is often reinforced by the existing structure and organization of schools, as many are not designed to be learning environments for teachers:

> When we turn to the school level (particularly the high school), the most logical venue for day-to-day community, we run into a series of structural, cultural, and vocational impediments. The simple fact is that in the typical American high school the structures for on-going intellectual community do not exist.
>
> (Grossman and Wineburg 2000: 10)

I believe that another reason educational change is difficult to achieve is because many stakeholders in the educational community, including teachers,

administrators, policy-makers and researchers, underestimate the difficulties of changing classroom practice. Also, many have a simplistic view of
the nature of teaching and teacher learning that does not complement the
complexity of educational change. This simplistic view assumes that teaching is a craft that can be mastered by learning one element at a time, similar
to a 'stimulus–response' reaction. For example, many still believe that change
in classroom practice will occur if teachers gather together for a day or for
a brief after-school workshop, receive a new policy, curriculum or set of
instructional strategies, and return to their classrooms with little back-up
support. Naively, it is thought that teacher learning is a linear step-by-step
process, independent of who teachers are, the culture in their schools and
the experiences they bring to a request for change. Sometimes teachers try
new ideas after attending a brief workshop, but efforts often fade or teachers
adapt the ideas to their existing classroom practices. Rarely does a one-off
workshop promote change, as it does not take into account the existing
complexity of a classroom context or have a framework to support teacher
learning through the non-linear process of change.

What is turning up the heat in schools on top of this simplistic approach
to teaching and teacher learning is the increasing pace of attempts for change.
With the myriad of innovations introduced over the last 10 years from the
standards movement, new curriculums, devolved decision making and technology, schools are like pressure cookers with change continually being
expected of teachers. Hargreaves (1994) described this social context as 'an
increasingly postindustrial, postmodern world, characterized by accelerating change, intense compression of time and space, cultural diversity, technological complexity, national insecurity and scientific uncertainty' (p. 3). If
policy-makers feel compelled to push for rapid change in schools, they need
to think about *how* and *why* change should occur if they really expect it to
happen. According to Cuban (1990), most efforts for reform are adopted
as policy, but are not implemented in practice:

> Most get implemented in word rather than deed, especially in class-
> rooms. What often ends up in districts and schools are signs of reform
> in new rules, different tests, revised organizational charts and new
> equipment. Seldom are the deepest structures of schooling that are
> embedded in the school's use of time and space, teaching practices,
> and classroom routines fundamentally altered even at those historical
> moments when reforms seek those alterations as the goal.
>
> (Cuban 1990: 9)

In short, efforts for change need to be supported with a framework for
long-term teacher learning because most attempts at educational change
involve learning how to do something new in a classroom that often has consequences for other aspects of classroom practice. Also, if teachers understand

how they learn in the workplace, they may begin to manage their own change that will help them to maintain interest in their job as well as coping with the rapid pace of change swirling around them.

In this book, I argue that existing educational literature on teacher learning is fragmented and inadequately theorized such that there does not exist a coherent theoretical framework to guide long-term teacher learning through the non-linear process of change. I believe that this is one reason why many efforts for educational change produce disappointing results. Instead, I use complexity theory as a new mindset to view schools and classrooms as complex systems, which helps us to understand the uncertainty of teaching and the non-linear process of educational change. I use the approach of systems thinking, which complements complexity theory, to pull together ideas from existing learning perspectives in educational literature to propose a new theoretical framework for long-term teacher learning. This framework is based on the existence of multiple conditions that need to interrelate as a system to increase the possibilities for managing educational change.

There are three parts in this book. Part 1 presents a theoretical platform for why we need to rethink our beliefs about educational change. Chapter 1 proposes that one reason why educational change is difficult to achieve is because of commonly held mechanistic views about the nature of teaching, teacher learning and the process of educational change. Chapter 2 puts forward a new mindset based on complexity theory and shows how educational change can be viewed as a complex system. Chapter 3 uses systems thinking as an approach to propose a new unit of analysis for teacher learning that links key features of existing learning perspectives. Part 2 of the book uses this unit of analysis as the basis for a new theoretical framework to underpin long-term teacher learning called a Professional Learning System (PLS). Chapters 4, 5 and 6 demonstrate the practical application of this framework with three case studies of long-term teacher learning projects. Part 3 reviews the main ideas in this book and outlines new possibilities for professional learning using information and communication technologies. Chapter 7 discusses the role of online technologies in teacher learning and Chapter 8 discusses how to design a professional learning system as a framework to support educational change.

one

A mechanistic view of educational change

To be accepted as a paradigm, a theory must seem
better than its competitors, but it need not, and in fact
never does, explain all the facts with which it can be
confronted.

(Kuhn 1970: 17)

Educational change is a tricky business. Testament to this statement is the number of failed efforts at educational reform over the last 30 years. Banathy (1991) suggested five reasons why most attempts at educational reform have produced disappointing results: (1) the piecemeal or bits-and-pieces approach to change; (2) the failure to integrate new ideas from research; (3) the fragmented discipline-by-discipline study of education; (4) reductionist approaches; and (5) thinking within existing boundaries. Collectively, these reasons are symptomatic of a mechanistic paradigm for educational change that is characterized by thinking about independent components of change in isolation to other influences. This chapter explains what this paradigm means and the implications for beliefs about educational change, the nature of teaching and teacher learning.

When comparing change efforts in industry and education, Wilson and Daviss (1995) concluded that industry acts as a 'community of learners', with researchers and practitioners sharing ideas and generating innovations that build upon each other. In contrast, change is difficult to achieve in education because various stakeholders often do not share ideas and work together as a professional community as they do in industry:

Technical cultures are shaped and driven by such a community of learners. In essence, they are webs that link research, development, evaluation, and dissemination into a single, synergistic, supportive system that increases the effectiveness and efficiency of creator, user, and process alike. In contrast, the teaching profession is marked by a series of missing links – separations between areas within the profession that, if joined, could create the technical culture necessary to sustain progressive innovation in education.

(Wilson and Daviss 1995: 92)

Wilson and Daviss (1995) argued that education needs to be more like industry with a 'systems design approach' that links researchers and practitioners interacting as a community of learners to generate a progressive discourse. But this is easier said than done. Historically, teachers and university researchers do not have a common language to share ideas. The discourse of university researchers is embedded in the theoretical divisions of educational research, mainly for the purpose of publishing articles in internationally refereed journals. In contrast, the discourse of teachers is embedded in their school experiences, pragmatically focusing on 'what works' in classroom practice – different discourses for different purposes.

Other authors have also supported a more integrated approach to encourage educational change. In *The Dynamics of Educational Change,* Goodlad (1975) stated that the main cause of failed change efforts is that they are often driven by a mechanistic approach that tries to change independent components of schooling, such as teaching, curriculum, budgeting, governance or resources, in isolation from other components. He contended that change efforts need to be holistic and proposed an ecological model of education whereby 'ecological thinking embraces the whole: the impact of pupils on teachers as well as the reverse; the impact of teachers on teachers; the use of resources; the relationship among all of these' (Goodlad 1975: 206). Similarly, Sarason (1971) stated in *The Culture of School and the Problem of Change* that influencing school culture was like trying to change an ecosystem with many aspects of the school affecting each other. Later, in *The Predictable Failure of Educational Reform,* Sarason (1990) noted that change in schools needs to occur simultaneously in several areas. First, change efforts must acknowledge the complex nature of teaching and how this acts as a form of resistance to change in schools. Second, change efforts need to address power relationships in schools as well as establish an environment that is conducive to teacher learning, 'because teachers cannot create and sustain the conditions for the productive development of children if those conditions do not exist for teachers' (Sarason 1990: xiv). What, then, is the paradigm, or set of beliefs, that underpins traditional thinking and reinforces a mechanistic approach to educational change?

The meaning of 'paradigm'

The word 'paradigm' comes from the Greek word *paradeigma*, meaning 'pattern'. It was made popular by Kuhn (1970) when describing the conceptual framework of a scientific community who are committed to the 'same rules and standards for scientific practice' (p. 11). These researchers often think in similar ways, as it is publishing research articles consistent with these beliefs that gains them acceptance within their community. When discoveries are made that conflict with an existing paradigm and anomalies emerge to challenge existing beliefs, a paradigm shift occurs:

> Discovery commences with the awareness of an anomaly, i.e., with the recognition that nature has somehow violated the paradigm-induced expectations that govern normal science. It then continues with a more or less extended exploration of the area of anomaly. And it closes only when the paradigm theory has been adjusted so that the anomalous has become the expected.
>
> (Kuhn 1970: 52–3)

Capra (1988) also used the word 'paradigm' when describing world views that influence society, which are 'the thoughts, perceptions and values that form a particular vision of reality, a vision that is a basis of the way a society organizes itself' (p. 11). In essence, a paradigm is a mindset that influences thinking and hence action within a community. It is much like a religion with its different traditions and explains why Catholics, Hindus and Buddhists have a different view of the world.

A mechanistic paradigm in education

Doll (1986) contends that the history of western thought can be placed into three broad paradigms or world views: (1) a classical Christian view developed by Aristotle, Ptolemy and Thomas Aquinas; (2) a scientific or mechanistic world view; and (3) a postmodern world view. The classical Christian view dominated thinking up until the sixteenth century and was controlled by monks who occasionally produced doctrines of faith that described 'truth' about the world. As an example, for centuries the Church promoted the idea that the earth was at the centre of the solar system. The genesis of mechanistic thinking occurred during the sixteenth and seventeenth centuries with the mathematical and scientific discoveries of Copernicus, Kepler, Galileo and Brahe. Many of these new theories conflicted with existing church doctrines and challenged their authority as the sole source of knowledge about how the world worked. Sir Isaac Newton cemented the importance of mechanistic ways of thinking when he presented his famous paper, *Philosophia Naturalis Principia Mathematica,* to the Royal Society of London in 1729, which outlined principles of physics and how the world worked. In this presentation, he contradicted the commonly held Christian view of the earth as the centre of the solar system and proposed that the planets were like cogs in a large machine (the solar system) whose movement could be predicted with great accuracy. Later, he put forward his three laws of motion explaining the role of gravity, suggesting that every force on earth has a direct cause and effect that can be measured.

As a result of the predominance of these mechanistic views in the sixteenth and seventeenth centuries, science was enshrined as the discipline for explaining what is an objective reality and established as a methodology for researching how this reality worked. Central to this approach is an emphasis on analysis to identify independent elements or parts that equate to variables in scientific experiments. This world view underpinned a positivist view of knowledge and has dominated western thought right through to the twentieth century. It has only been in the last 20–30 years that another paradigm, postmodernism, has become a popular way of thought contradicting the notion of an objective reality and instead promoting 'pragmatic doubt' (Doll 1993: 61) by emphasizing the uncertainty and unpredictability of our world. Of these three paradigms, the most dominant for educational thought over the last century has been mechanistic ways of thinking influencing ideas about the nature of teaching, teacher learning and educational change.

Epistemology

A scientific or mechanistic world view assumes that reality can be observed, explained and predicted. The widespread influence of this way of thinking is well summarized by Clarke (1996), who stated that 'our society is founded on the view that there is a single solid reality, that truth is a matter of agreement with reality, and that science is a procedure for determining the nature of reality and for judging the truth of factual statements' (p. 21). Two key features of a mechanistic world view are empirical measurement and positivism, which are approaches to problems that together are called 'logical positivism'. This means that priority is given to empirical knowledge that is measurable and privileges a positivist methodology of logical analysis (Carnap 1966). From a philosophical perspective, this classical scientific view of the world has been called 'realism' (Rorty 1991), based on the acceptance of an objective reality that seeks truth to equate to reality. Consistent with this view, there are clearly defined procedures (according to scientific conventions) for justification of a belief to knowledge so, 'to be truly rational, procedures of justification *must* lead to the truth, to correspondence to reality, to the intrinsic nature of things' (Rorty 1991: p. 22; emphasis in original). The opposite of realism is 'relativism', which refers to a world view that assumes there is no objective reality.

A mechanistic world view based on the truth of scientific knowledge has had a profound influence on the organization of schools, especially when designing school curriculums. According to Doll (1993), the legacy of a Newtonian or mechanistic world view is a narrow-minded methodology for conducting research that produces prescriptive knowledge to be sub-divided and sequenced to construct rigid school curriculums:

> It is Newton's metaphysical and cosmological views – not his scientific ones – that have dominated modern thought for so long, providing a foundation in the social sciences for causative predictability, linear ordering, and a closed (or discovery) methodology. These, in turn, are the conceptual underpinnings of scientific (really scientistic) curriculum making.
>
> (Doll 1993: 34)

Cynically, Doll (1993) mentions that the only places in education where there is not a 'serial, graduated order' of knowledge in a curriculum are in kindergarten classes and in doctoral seminars. Moreover, the identification of an objective knowledge base to explain reality has established a system of privileging what counts as knowledge. Schön (1983) called this way of thinking 'Technical Rationality' and described it as 'instrumental problem solving made rigorous by the application of scientific theory and technique' (p. 21). He claimed that this way of thinking evolved from Positivism, the dominant philosophy of the nineteenth century, calling it a 'Positivist epistemology of practice' (p. 31), which he claimed is evident in much of the professional knowledge generated by conventional research at universities.

In terms of teacher education, formal knowledge produced by university researchers is often perceived to have a higher status than practical know-ledge generated by teachers in schools (Cochran-Smith and Lytle 1993; Cochran-Smith 1994). Schön (1983, 1987) called for a new epistemology based on reflection to resolve the dichotomy between formal knowledge, produced by researchers who strive for rigour, and practical knowledge that is experientially driven but has relevance for those who are working in the 'swamp' of practice:

> The dilemma of rigor or relevance may be dissolved if we can develop an epistemology of practice which places technical problem solving within a broader context of reflective inquiry, shows how reflection-in-action may be rigorous in its own right, and links the art of practice in uncertainty and uniqueness to the scientist's art of research.
>
> (Schön 1983: 69)

Schön (1983) contends that university researchers need to acknowledge the 'complexity, uncertainty, instability, uniqueness, and value-conflict' (p. 39) of work settings that make it difficult to apply formal knowledge directly without consideration of a changing context.

Conceptions of teaching

Consistent with a mechanistic paradigm emphasizing analysis to identify independent parts, what we know about teaching tends to be itemized into discrete sets of knowledge and skills. This is evident in how the curricula of teacher preparation courses are often organized for preservice students. In many teacher education programmes, courses focus independently on pedagogy, sociology, learning, assessment, classroom management, technology, evaluation or discipline knowledge. These courses are often taught to students in isolation to each other because they can study a discrete topic in depth as it is easier for instructors to organize and assess. Packaging educational knowledge into discrete courses, however, presents the curriculum as a jigsaw puzzle and often leaves it to the students to make their own connections between the courses so that they can construct their own big picture of education. The tendency, however, is that discrete courses present a technical view of education and does not encourage a way of thinking that considers how aspects of education have a dynamic effect on one another. Also, presenting educational knowledge in discrete packages can lead to a misrepresentation of the complexity evident in real schools and classrooms.

Research by Wise *et al.* (1984) in 32 US cities concluded that teachers usually hold one of four conceptions of teaching – as a craft, labour, profession or art. These four conceptions are ideal forms, but nevertheless do indicate different approaches to teaching. When conceived as a *craft*, teaching is believed to be a repertoire of skills or competencies that are accrued over time. Knowledge about these techniques also means having generalized rules for when and how to apply them, as 'this view of teaching assumes that general rules for applying specific techniques can be developed and that proper use of the rules combined with knowledge of the techniques will produce the desired outcomes' (Wise *et al.* 1984: 7). Similarly, when conceived as a *labour*, teaching is a set of goals, lesson plans and skills that others have designed and the role of the teacher is to implement these. Both of these conceptions are underpinned by a mechanistic approach that atomizes teaching into technical skills that need to be 'mastered' over time. Even the commonly used term 'master teacher' implies that a person is an expert because he or she has accumulated a stockpile of strategies and knowledge over many years.

When I reflect on my own life history as a high school science teacher from 1976 to 1989, I believe that I had a conception of teaching as a craft. I worked very hard in my first few years of teaching learning science content, instructional strategies and classroom management techniques. Having acquired this expertise, I usually taught in the same way year after year with only slight modifications, because I perceived that I had 'mastered' science teaching. I still liked the job because I enjoyed interacting with high school students and I did not have to put as much time into preparing lessons. Upon reflection, however, the problem with this conception is that I only perceived teaching from my own point of view. My lens for viewing classroom practice was one-way – I taught a subject, not children. When things went wrong, I thought it must be the students' fault because the lesson had worked last year with another class and the year before. The legacy of my mechanistic conception of teaching as a craft was that I did not have a perceived need to rethink constantly how to improve my practice; rather, I thought about how to consolidate it. I went to many workshops over the 14 years, but either ignored ideas that were too hard to implement or adapted them to fit into my view of teaching as a craft. In contrast, a conception of teaching as a *profession* or an *art* implies that teaching is more than the development of a repertoire of techniques, but also includes personal judgements about when and how these techniques should be applied. To make an informed judgement means having a theoretical basis for making decisions as well as awareness of the 'unpredictable, personalized nature of teaching' (Day 1999: 94).

The process of teacher learning

If teaching is conceived to be a craft or labour to be mastered, then it is logical to assume that teacher learning involves attending workshops to gain additional knowledge and skills to increase that mastery. Consequently, teacher learning is perceived to be an 'additive' (Day 1999) process based on the accumulation of new knowledge or strategies to an existing repertoire. This view assumes that ideas presented in a workshop are transferable, as formal knowledge generated from research in one context is expected to work just as well in others. Workshop presenters who propose this view assume that a teacher's workplace is a static environment that will readily accommodate the introduction of an innovation. But often what happens is that teachers adapt parts of an innovation to complement their existing practice if it necessitates only a small change in how they teach (Hoban 1992).

Attempting to introduce major change, however, is another story. I can remember in my first year as a high school science teacher going to an afterschool workshop on mastery learning. This was similar to outcomes-based learning in which a curriculum is driven by the tasks that a student can master. I thought it was interesting at the time, but there was no way it was going to be a major influence on my practice. First, I was the only member of my department that went to the workshop and my colleagues did not care for it. Second, my teaching was driven by a mindset to pass on my knowledge to the students in small chunks, not by what the students could achieve based on their interests, culture or beliefs. Third, the courses I taught and related knowledge-based tests for assessment were already written for the science department, and we were expected to use them to produce marks for the term reports to parents. Fourth, I was struggling in my first year of teaching trying to learn the science content, designing lesson plans and coping with classroom management; I had no time or interest for any complicated ideas. So mastery learning presented to me in a one-off workshop was never going to get a start in my classrooms.

Attempts at change in elementary schools are similar. I have seen an example in Canada when parents of children at a school decided to spend C$10,000 on individual readers as part of a new reading scheme for the children. This involved the purchase of reading books with distinct levels to cater for the different reading abilities of young children. Some of the teachers used them because the new books complemented what the teachers already did in terms of listening to children read at their own level. But other teachers did not use the new resources as intended because it involved changing many aspects of their practice, such as how they used their existing reading schemes, the physical organization of the classroom, different assessment procedures and organizing the timetable so that teachers could listen to each child read once a week. Such holistic change is possible, but it involves adjusting many elements of an existing classroom system to replace it with a new one. A one-step change effort such as providing classrooms with new reading books without designing a learning environment for teachers to help them adjust other related areas of their practice is unlikely to succeed. But, if the teaching of reading is already perceived to be an art that differs from child to child, teachers will more readily use new resources that match their existing approach and will vary their teaching strategies to suit a particular child's needs:

> The best teacher will be he who has at his tongue's end the explanation of what it is that is bothering the pupil. These explanations give the teacher the knowledge of the greatest possible number of methods, the ability of inventing new methods and, above all, not a blind adherence to one method but the conviction that all methods are one-sided, and that the best method would be the one which would answer best to all the possible difficulties incurred by a pupil, that is, not a method but an art and talent.
>
> (Tolstoy 1967: 25)

When teachers perceive their work as a relationship with students, they think about it as a dynamic process – considering what the students know, their ways of preferred learning and what is the optimal strategy to bring the best out in each child. The way teaching is conceived is often related to the approach used for teacher learning to encourage educational change.

Educational change using a one-step approach for teacher learning

During the 1960s and 1970s, there were many examples of innovations being presented to teachers for implementation with little infrastructure to sustain their change. At this time, there were large amounts of public money invested in educational reform, resulting in wave after wave of classroom innovations. Initiated by an American perception that they had to catch up with the Russians after Sputnik was launched in 1957, millions upon millions of dollars were poured into the development of curriculum innovations for schools with the expectation that teachers would implement them. Calhoun and Joyce (1998) called this the 'Research and Development' or 'Outside-in' approach, stating that enormous funding was provided with the intention of educating the youth of America to be more knowledgeable and progressive. Many of the innovations developed were also used in other western countries, including Britain, New Zealand and Australia. Educational administrators often used a top-down or workshop model to introduce the innovation to teachers as a one-step approach for teacher learning. For example, teaching materials were delivered to a school with a set of instructions, and sometimes additional assistance was provided with a one-shot inservice course, as shown in Figure 1.1.

Innovation arrival ⎯⎯⎯⎯⎯► Teacher use ⎯⎯⎯⎯⎯► Teacher change

Figure 1.1 A one-step linear approach for educational change.

The beliefs that underpin this approach are that teacher learning is a linear process and that educational change is a natural consequence of receiving well-written and comprehensive instructional materials. However, disseminating an innovation assumes that it is context-independent and ignores the complex system of teaching that already exists in school classrooms.

Introducing new ideas in one-off workshops without a framework to support long-term teacher learning tends to reinforce existing practice and maintain the *status quo*. According to Sachs and Logan (1990), this type of teacher learning is consistent with a mechanistic view of the world and promotes a sense of control over teachers by focusing efforts for change on the presentation of independent skills and knowledge:

> Rather than developing reflective practitioners who are able to understand, challenge and transform their practice, inservice education in its current form encourages the development of teachers who see their world in terms of instrumental ends achievable through the recipes of

'tried and true' practices legitimated by unexamined experience or uncritically accepted research findings.

(Sachs and Logan 1990: 479)

This technical view of professional development is similar to Argyris and Schön's (1994: 19) notion of 'single-loop learning'. In this approach, the participant controls the activity such as how they teach and at a workshop considers how new ideas can fit into their existing practice. Participants still learn, because the workshop gives them a deeper understanding about what they already know, but tends to keep them within their zone of comfort by thinking 'inside the square' they teach in. Argyris (1993) provided an analogy for single-loop learning when describing how a thermostat controls room temperature. When it is preset to turn on the heat at a specific temperature, say 68 degrees, it will self-regulate to keep the room at that temperature. This is similar to a person who always teaches in the same way because it 'worked in the past'. In this situation, the teacher does have personal theories of action, but prefers to keep them private for fear of being vulnerable to the criticism of others. Hence, learning occurs in a workshop, but rarely do teachers think 'outside the square', as there is little testing of theories publicly and so this type of learning is 'self-sealing' (Argyris and Schön 1994: 68). There have been many types of professional development programmes over the last 30 years that have been designed on the basis that educational change is mainly about presenting teachers with new ideas to implement in their classroom.

Large-scale public funding of innovations for schools in the 1960s and 1970s was highlighted in the development of new curriculum materials for school science. When the Russians launched Sputnik, it caused various American authorities to question the quality of the science programmes being taught in their schools (Cain and Evans 1984). Consequently, new curriculum materials were developed for both elementary and high school science. For high schools, new projects were developed for the different disciplines, including the Physical Science Study (PSS) for high school physics, the Biological Sciences Curriculum Study (BSCS) for high school biology and the Chemical Bonds Approach Project (CBAP) for high school chemistry.

Elementary science also received a major funding boost with the development of comprehensive new curriculums, which included texts, equipment kits, student workbooks and teacher guides. These curriculums embraced the teaching philosophy of discovery learning and produced innovations that encouraged students to learn science through first-hand experimentation (Cain and Evans 1984; James and Hord 1988). Three of the innovations funded by the National Science Foundation (NSF) in the 1960s proved to be more popular than others. Between 1962 and 1974, a team from the University of California produced the Science Curriculum Improvement Study (SCIS) that was published by Rand McNally. This was a sequential programme of 12 units and required teachers to implement two units per grade each year. There were 10 major concepts, which were related to the skills of observing and questioning, with an emphasis on applying concepts and scientific literacy. The SCIS programme was underpinned by a learning cycle that encouraged students to explore, invent and discover for themselves.

Other innovations played down the importance of scientific concepts in favour of the development of 'process skills' (Fensham 1988). The Educational Development Center designed the Elementary Science Study (ESS) that was published by McGraw-Hill from 1961 to 1971. The three goals of the ESS were to involve the students in science, to have an intrinsic, aesthetic appeal and to incorporate the positive effect of play (Butts 1973). The 56-module programme offered teachers flexibility with non-sequential and independently constructed modules. The modules encouraged students to explore natural phenomena using skills of enquiry. Between 1963 and 1974, another programme called Science: A Process Approach (SAPA) was produced by the American Association for the Advancement of Science. This programme was highly structured and focused on the development of reasoning skills. There were eight basic and six advanced skills modules developed to teach students to use these specific skills (Bredderman 1983; Cain and Evans 1984).

Although each of the three NSF-funded innovations was organized differently, they had a common philosophy that encouraged the teacher to be a facilitator of student learning rather than a dispenser of knowledge. It was reported that the teams that developed these programmes contained the most recognized science educators in the USA and that the NSF supplied ample finance to produce quality innovations (James and Hord 1988). The developers believed that since elementary teachers had the instructional manuals, the equipment kits and associated programmes, the implementation of hands-on, enquiry-based science was assured. Evaluations, however, showed that many of the NSF programmes did not achieve their objectives in terms of the extent or method of use by elementary teachers, and that science remained a low priority in the elementary curriculum compared to other subjects (Shrigley 1983). Rudman (1978) claimed that, even at their peak time of implementation, no more than 20 percent of teachers used these innovations. This was attributed to the inadequate professional development procedures used to introduce the new curriculums to teachers (Berman and McLaughlin 1976; Shrigley 1983; James and Hord 1988). Although research showed that there were major problems in the dissemination of the new science curriculums (Calhoun and Joyce 1998), teachers who did use them reported that the new materials had positive effects on student learning (Bredderman 1983; Atwood and Howard 1990). The problem, therefore, was not the quality of the innovations, but *how* the innovations were introduced to teachers.

A similar professional development model based on a mechanistic paradigm is the traditional 'training staff development model'. The strengths of this approach are that new knowledge is presented to teachers that is often beyond their existing experiences and it can be presented in a convenient way. Programmes using this model are organized to disseminate new knowledge or skills to teachers in a short period of time with the presenter being the expert who controls the content and organization of the workshop. For example, the content of 'how to' workshops can focus on areas such as the acquisition of new disciplinary knowledge, strategies for a new curriculum, skills concerning conflict resolution, new technologies or cooperative learning (Hord and Boyd 1994). Sparks and Loucks-Horsley (1990) explained that workshops are beneficial because they promote practice deemed to be worth replicating that is beyond the regular experiences of teachers.

In summary, there are several strengths of professional development programmes based on a one-step approach to teacher learning. First, they provide new *content* about practice or theory that is often beyond the teachers' experiences. Second, they are a *convenient* and economical way to present new knowledge to teachers because they can gather at a venue and be provided with the new content over a brief period of time. This procedure may be appropriate to facilitate teacher learning, especially if the content is relatively simple. In addition, the topic of workshops may resonate with teachers' existing beliefs or focus on an area that the teachers are interested in learning more about. Moreover, training workshops provide opportunities for teachers to interact with colleagues from other schools, although this may not be their main intent.

There are several limitations, however, in using a one-step approach to teacher learning portrayed in both the 'Research and Development' and 'Training' professional development models. First, a workshop usually does not take into account the context of schools before the training and the resistance of teachers to ideas that are not consistent with their regular beliefs (Fullan 1992). Also, the models assume that teachers will understand the knowledge being presented, such that it is meaningful to them and has value as an authoritative source of information for their practice. Furthermore, teachers often do not adopt complicated innovations in a linear fashion, but may use some parts and not others. They also assume that teachers have a desire to change, which may not be the case when an innovation conflicts with existing practices or with the resources and routines already established. Although a one-step approach to professional development does sometimes encourage teacher learning, it often does not lead to educational change because teachers adapt innovations to suit their existing practices, which tends to maintain the *status quo*. In short, a simplistic approach to teacher learning is unlikely to be a catalyst for complex educational change.

Educational change using a process for teacher learning

The main lesson learned from the 1960s and 1970s was that a one-step approach to teacher learning does not mean teacher change, as it is a *'process, not an event'* (Fullan 1982: 41; emphasis in original). One model that had some success was a multi-step framework for change called the Concerns Based Adoption Model (CBAM). It was proposed by Fuller (1969) and developed at the Research and Development Center for Teacher Education at the University of Texas, Austin. Seven assumptions underpinned this model:

(i) Change in schools and colleges is a *process*, not an event.
(ii) The *individual* needs to be the primary focus of intervention for change in the classroom.
(iii) Change is a highly *personal* process.
(iv) Full *description* of the *innovation* in operation is a key variable.
(v) There are identifiable *stages* and *levels* of the change process as experienced by individuals.
(vi) Inservice teacher training can be best *facilitated* for the individual by use of a client-centred diagnostic/prescriptive model.
(vii) The change facilitator needs to work in an *adaptive/systematic* way.

(Hall 1978: 5; emphasis in original)

The CBAM model proposed that teachers pass through three linear stages when implementing an innovation, each with a particular focus or concern. When receiving an innovation, an individual first experiences personal concerns related to themselves, then concerns related to the task to be implemented, followed by concerns about impact on pupils. This linear model for change is represented in Figure 1.2.

Personal concerns ⟶ Task concerns ⟶ Impact concerns

Figure 1.2 Linear process of the CBAM for educational change.

For example, teachers who have not adopted an innovation usually have self-oriented concerns indicating that they want to know more about it and how it is going to affect them (Hall 1978). Once these are addressed, the teacher progresses to task-oriented concerns about how they implement the innovation. When a teacher has confidence to use and manage the innovation, he or she then focuses on the impact of the innovation on his or her students. This model recommends the use of three diagnostic instruments to provide information to change agents when attempting to address the professional development needs of teachers (Loucks 1977; Leary 1983).

This model for change, however, assumes that innovations are relatively simple and that change is a linear process as teachers progress from one type of concern to another. When an innovation is multidimensional, however, teachers may have concerns about different aspects of the innovation at different times or even at the same time (Hoban 1992). Also, this model is individualistic and ignores the social, cultural and physical factors that influence learning and hence the chances of innovation adoption. With complicated innovations, it is likely that implementation is non-linear and involves adjustments to many elements of classroom teaching simultaneously.

Educational change using a multifaceted approach

In response to the lack of success of most efforts for educational change, researchers in the 1980s began to study the rare examples of successful efforts to identify the factors that made the process work. According to Guskey (1986), most staff development programmes failed 'because they do not take into account two critical factors: what motivates teachers to engage in staff development, and the process by which change in teachers typically takes place' (p. 6). He concluded that the process of teacher learning is developmental and that one of the main factors that encourages teacher change is to observe evidence of positive outcomes for students as a result of using an innovation.

In *Improving Schools from Within*, Barth (1990) noted that there was an increasing trend in the 1980s for researchers to construct lists of effective characteristics of schools, teachers, classrooms, pupils, competencies, regulations and performance indicators. In many cases, administrators used these lists as goals in an attempt to change schools through planned interventions targeting such specific features. For example, in a study of 160 schools, Mortimer (1998) identified features that make them effective, including professional leadership, shared vision and goals, a learning environment, concentration on teaching and learning, purposeful teaching, high expectations, positive reinforcement, monitoring progress, pupil rights and responsibilities, home–school partnerships and a learning organization.

Administrators who list characteristics of effective schools and try to impose them on other schools are also falling into the 'parts' or mechanistic view of educational change. This view assumes that change involves more than the delivery of an innovation, as it also involves many independent factors or elements that work together like a 'machine'. This reductionist approach to educational change assumes that complicated phenomena can be understood by analysing and identifying all the parts or components that make up the phenomena. The view of reality proposed by a mechanistic paradigm is one of a static context which assumes that teachers and classrooms are similar from place to place. The assumption, therefore, is that the same factors or conditions that operate in one context will work the same way in another. This is like disassembling a complicated machine that has been purposely designed for a specific location and putting it back together in a different context, expecting it to work in exactly the same way.

According to Fink and Stoll (1998), the term 'school effectiveness' is vague and offers few ideas in relation to changing teaching and learning. Holmes (1998) argued that such efforts to change schools are not based on a clear rationale of what schools are for and how students will benefit from the change process. In support, Hargreaves (1998) criticized such a linear approach to educational change that did not consider the shifting context:

> Significant educational change can no longer be achieved (if ever it really could!) in a step-by-step, linear process. School improvement processes are not implemented smoothly through locked-in five year development plans. Schools do not have the luxury of being able to focus on a singular goal and go through stages of achieving it over several years while the rest of their world stands still.
>
> (Hargreaves 1998: 283)

A mechanistic approach to change that identifies and manipulates factors in an attempt to 'control' change is consistent with a scientific method that attempts to control variables in an experiment to get a desired outcome (Capra 1982). Schön (1983, 1987) called this type of thinking 'technical rationality', whereby a scientific method is used to analyse a phenomenon into independent factors or variables and then propose a linear cause and effect relationship that ignores the dynamic interactions of a particular context.

In his classic book, *The Meaning of Educational Change*, Fullan (1982) stated that one-dimensional theories of change were doomed to failure and that the only chance for 'planned' change to be successful was to have a combination of factors to create supportive conditions:

> Even well-intentioned change initiatives can create havoc among those who are on the firing line, if support for implementation has been neglected. On the other hand, careful attention to a small number of key details during the implementation process can lead to the experience of success, the satisfaction of mastering some new practice which benefits students . . . Confronting the isolationism and privatism of educational systems and establishing mechanisms for stimulating, adding to, and acting on these solutions and energies represent untapped resources which we can no longer afford to ignore.
>
> (Fullan 1982: xi)

From an extensive review of the literature, Fullan (1982) identified four main phases of the change process: initiation, implementation, continuation and outcome. Importantly, he noted that this four-phase process was not linear with change in one phase influencing another and that there were many factors operating at each phase. In the adoption phase, Fullan identified 10 supporting factors: existence and quality of the innovation; access to the innovation; advocacy from central administration; teacher pressure/support; consultants and change agents; community pressure; availability of federal funds; new government policy; problem-solving incentives; and bureaucratic incentives. In the implementation phase, he identified 15 supporting factors in four main categories that influenced the implementation of an innovation. These categories include: (1) characteristics of the change (need for the change as perceived by the users, explicitness of the change, complexity of the change and the degree of difficulty of use, completeness, organization, comprehensiveness and practicality of the change); (2) characteristics of the school district (district, community, principal and teacher); (3) characteristics of the school; and (4) characteristics external to the local system. In all, Fullan identified 25 factors that influenced the change process during adoption and implementation.

What are the relationships?

Although the identification of all these factors for educational change was valuable research, it became apparent over time that they do not always interact in the same way to produce the same result. In short, identifying features of effective schools and factors for planned change is also consistent with mechanistic thinking that focuses on analysing the elements of educational change, but ignores the relationships between them as well as the uniqueness of each context. In some cases, factors do not relate in the same way in different contexts or there are other unpredictable contextual factors that can come into play to cause teacher resistance to a change effort. For instance, a plan for change may provide teachers with factors such as a 'quality innovation', 'consultants and change agents' and 'advocacy from central administrators', but these may not relate to each other. The advocacy from administrators may be for their own political gain, the consultants may present themselves as experts and not collaborate with teachers, and the teachers may not value the innovation. What is more influential are the relationships between these factors so that the values and purposes held by the teachers, consultants and administrators with respect to the innovation are congruent. So it is not just the 'factors' or parts that need to be in place, but a coherent relationship between them is essential for the factors to interrelate as a support system for educational change.

Conclusion

Views about educational change have been dominated by a mechanistic paradigm that focuses on identifying independent components of educational knowledge and skills. These views promote a conception of teaching as a 'craft' or 'labour' with a sense of 'mastery' resulting from the progressive accumulation of knowledge and skills. The assumption is that educational change will result from the presentation of new ideas or resources to teachers in one-off workshops or on professional development days. Some professional development programmes have been a catalyst for change and teacher learning has occurred, but such learning usually reinforces existing practices rather than assist teachers to reconceptualize teaching and learning. Research has also identified key elements or factors that have contributed to successful efforts for planned change, but these are not readily transferable because of the unique context of each school and the different ways in which the factors can interrelate. Clearly we need a new way of thinking about educational change that takes into account the complex nature of teaching, teacher learning and the change process.

two

A complexity view of educational change

That the theory of development and of life in general must be a 'system theory' – that is no more to be doubted or disputed. The question only remains what relation there is between this 'system theory' and physics.

(von Bertalanffy 1933: 180)

It was not until the 1990s that a more dynamic paradigm for educational change emerged based on complexity theory. It did not, however, start in education. Ironically, it was scientific work in quantum physics by Einstein, Bohr and Heisenberg in the 1910s and 1920s that planted a seed for the emergence of a new world view highlighting the uncertainty of traditional scientific knowledge. More recently, complexity theory was featured in *Exploring Complexity* by Nicolis and Prigogine (1989) and in *Chaos: Making a New Science* by Gleick (1987). According to Nicolis and Prigogine (1989), scientific communities at the beginning of this century believed that 'fundamental laws of the universe were deterministic and reversible' (p. 3). Towards the end of the twentieth century, however, a new vision of matter was emerging because 'many fundamental processes shaping nature are irreversible and stochastic; that the deterministic and reversible laws describing the elementary interactions may not be telling the whole story' (Nicolis and Prigogine 1989: 3). In this chapter, a world view based on complexity theory will be presented together with systems thinking, which is a mindset focusing on interrelationships that helps us to understand the dynamics of complexity. The implications for educational change will be discussed, focusing on what this means for a conception of teaching, teacher learning and the change process.

A world view based on complexity theory

Several terms have been used to describe multiple elements that interact as a system in our rapidly moving society – 'chaos', 'complexity', 'holistic' and 'ecological'. Each of these terms represents the antithesis of mechanistic thinking, which focuses on linear step-by-step change, but there are subtle differences between the terms. Both chaos and complexity have been used to describe interactions among multiple elements that act collectively as a system to produce ripple or 'butterfly effects' across related networks (Gleick 1987; Waldrop 1992; Sullivan 1993). Common to both terms is the notion that the behaviour of a system is not due to linear cause and effect relationships between independent elements, instead, the behaviour of a system is caused by *non-linear* interactions because of the interrelationships that exist among a combination of elements and groups of elements. Because of this dynamism, the behaviour of a system is difficult and sometimes impossible to predict.

There are differences, however, between chaotic systems and complex systems. Marion (1999) contends that chaos theory is more appropriate for physical systems such as weather, fluid turbulence and soil percolation, whereas complexity theory is more appropriate for social systems such as population dynamics, ecological niches, body functions and social interactions that carry with them some information about themselves, enabling an ability to self-organize. It is this ability to more readily self-organize that distinguishes complexity from chaos, 'Complexity, therefore, has to do with the interrelatedness and interdependence of components as well as their freedom to interact, align, and organize into related configurations' (Eve *et al.* 1997: 20). Whereas chaos usually refers to disorder and randomness of movement that can produce 'weirdly, unpredictable gyrations' (Waldrop 1992: 12), complexity implies more equilibrium or order that can lead to productive change (Brown and Eisenhardt 1998). According to Waldrop (1992), complexity can be self-regulating, meaning that a complex system can have more balance than a chaotic system:

> These interactions allows the system as a whole to undergo *spontaneous self-organization* . . . these complex, self-organizing systems are *adaptive* . . . they actively try to turn whatever happens to their advantage . . . every one of these complex, self-organizing, adaptive systems possesses a kind of dynamism that makes them qualitatively different from static objects such as computer chips or snowflakes, which are merely complicated.
>
> (Waldrop 1992: 11–12; emphasis in original)

Change in a complex system results in dynamic interactions because of a special balance point between chaos and order that has been called the *edge of chaos*, 'where new ideas and innovative genotypes are forever nibbling away at the edges of the status quo' (Waldrop 1992: 12). According to Stacey (1996), the edge of chaos is when creativity occurs as people experiment with ideas and attempt to change the balance of a complex system. In sum, both chaotic and complex systems display non-linear interactions due to their interrelationships, but a complex system is more likely to develop a sense of order because it carries information within it, although this is not always the case. This does not mean, however, that complex systems can be controlled, rather, they are more inclined to be influenced and managed than chaotic systems.

Recently, the notion of complexity was popularized in business literature in *The Fifth Discipline* by Peter Senge (1990). He contended that efforts for planned change in business rarely worked because of a phenomenon he called 'dynamic complexity' (p. 71). This term means that factors interacting for change may work differently in various settings or over different time frames. It is simplistic, therefore, for businesses to focus on independent elements of the marketplace to improve output and profit. The key to studying complex interactions is to focus on the interrelationships between multiple elements and to reflect upon patterns that emerge to gain a 'big picture' of the change process.

According to Mainzer (1994), the way social systems behave is consistent with complexity theory as 'the principles of complex systems suggest that the physical, social, and mental world is nonlinear and complex. This essential result of epistemology has important consequences for our present and future behavior' (p. 305). Because of the interactions among elements of a complex system, behaviour or patterns of change are difficult but not impossible to predict. When explaining how complex systems work, Marion (1999) refers to the work of MIT meteorologist Edward Lorenz, who argued that systems such as the weather display non-linear change for three reasons:

1 non-linear systems respond to minor changes and display 'sensitive dependence' to initial conditions causing a ripple effect through a weather system;
2 every particle has a level of kinetic energy as well as potential energy and particles create a 'resonance' when they are close to each other, releasing energy in unpredictable ways; and
3 particles in close proximity display a 'correlation' such that the behaviour of one particle influences the other.

Marion (1999) contends that the characteristics of 'sensitive dependence', 'resonance', and 'correlation' are also applicable to human behaviour in complex systems. Input into these systems may cause minor change, major change or no change at all depending on the degree of interactions involved. In social systems, people have different priorities and the way they respond to change and each other influences the change effort itself. For example, social movements such as fads, collegial networks and teenage cults evolve because of the dynamics among members of a social group. In addition, complex systems often display a form of self-order called 'social homeostasis' (Marion 1999: 59), meaning that change tends to balance itself and return to a state of equilibrium. Self-order evolves because of energy transfer and adjustments from positive or negative feedback until an equilibrium or balance is again established.

Implications of complexity theory for education

In an educational context, the terms 'complexity', 'chaos' and 'ecologicial' have been used to describe change, but they are sometimes confused and understood as meaning the same thing. I believe that a world view based on complexity theory is the most appropriate to help us understand the dynamics of educational change because it highlights the multidimensional nature of change as well as acknowledging that non-linear interactions can result in a sense of order or balance. This is not a chaotic perspective suggesting randomness and unpredictability, but maintains that educational change can be better understood and hence managed by thinking about it as a complex system. Hargreaves (1998) contends that comparing educational change to chaos theory can be taken to extremes, as it suggests that schools are totally unique and cannot be managed. There are, however, implications for educational knowledge, the nature of teaching, teacher learning and educational change when viewed through the lens of complexity theory.

Epistemology

A paradigm or world view based on complexity theory questions the certainty and objectivity of knowledge that is central to a mechanistic view of the world. Nicolis and Prigogine (1989) argue that we can no longer assume the permanency of knowledge because we live in a world characterized by instability and fluctuations. Complexity theory does not deny the existence of reality, but assumes that reality is dynamic and ever changing. Because reality is never static or one-dimensional, the best we can do in predicting reality is to guess and hope that we make a closer approximation to it (Marion 1999). There is value, therefore, in theorizing in an attempt to understand reality, but any ideas or 'truth' are an approximation or best guess that may need to be modified later. This is not a relativist perspective, suggesting that all points of view are equally valid, rather that 'truth' may change according to the dynamics of a particular context. Knowledge, therefore, is never set in concrete, but is changeable and modern science is the pursuit of approximate knowledge, as 'science can never provide any complete and definitive understanding' (Capra 1996: 41).

In the context of education, Doll (1993) claims that a positivist conception of educational knowledge portrayed by a mechanistic world view attempts to be objective by falsely separating the knower from the known and ignores personal experience. Instead, he argues for an 'epistemology of experience' that does not separate the knower from the known but encourages a 'back-and-forth interplay between that known and the local knower' (Doll 1993: 126). In planning for change, we must assume that reality is fluid and expect that any change effort may produce unintended outcomes based on interactions of the multiple elements involved. In short, knowledge based on a complexity paradigm or world view lies somewhere between realism and relativism, as 'we may never arrive at absolute and total reality, and even if we did our blindness would likely prevent us from being able to confirm our arrival' (Marion 1999: 12).

Conceptions of teaching

In contrast to a mechanistic view of teaching as a 'craft' or 'labour' that can be mastered, a conception of teaching based on complexity theory acknowledges the dynamic context of each classroom and accepts that there is no such thing as fail-proof teaching strategies. This means that teaching is more than the delivery of prescribed knowledge using a repertoire of strategies, but is 'a dynamic relationship that changes with different students and contexts' (Hoban 2000b: 165). In this respect, what a teacher does in a classroom is influenced by a combination of elements, including the curriculum, the context and how students respond to instruction at any particular time. This interpretation is consistent with a conception of teaching as an *art* or *profession* (Wise *et al.* 1984); that is, characterized by 'holistic judgement' (Day 1999) about what, when and how to teach in relation to a particular context. Having a conception of teaching as an art means developing a repertoire of strategies as well as understanding that their application depends on making judgements about unique contexts and unpredictable classroom moments, as 'the teacher must draw upon not only a body of professional knowledge and skill, but also a set of personal resources that are uniquely defined and expressed by the personality of the teacher, and his or her individual and collective interactions with students' (Wise *et al.* 1984: 8).

One common feature that I have noticed about teachers who consider their practice to be an art is that they do not believe they can master teaching because they are aware of how complex classroom teaching really is. I recently asked an elementary teacher, who I think is reflective about her practice, to send me an email explaining whether she could ever master teaching. This was her reply:

The word 'mastery' to me conjures up the notion of having control over something that is fairly static or predictable such as a craft. Teaching is dynamic, it isn't static at all. Each class that I have taught has been composed of 25 or more complex individuals, all with their own needs, emotions, strengths, concerns, predilections and dislikes – and they are all placed together with me in a room to learn. Numerous factors can affect the success of teaching such as the language that I use to explain something, even the use of a few words, the emphasis placed on a term or the tone used can effect the level of a student's understanding. Other considerations are how receptive is the student? Did they have an argument in the playground? Are they tired? Do they have a negative attitude to the lesson content? Do the activities chosen support the child's preferred learning style? An activity or explanation that one child finds engaging and motivating will be boring or daunting to another child. No, I don't believe that teaching can be mastered! Being a teacher means that I am learning alongside my students. In fact I have used the adage, 'Everyone is a teacher and everyone is a learner' with my classes. I do believe though that I am developing into a better teacher, but only through continually examining my own practice and being willing to step outside of my 'comfort zone' and preferred teaching style to meet the needs of my students. Teaching for me is a profession of life-long learning. If I ever thought that I had it mastered, I would have to question whether the learning of each student was still the paramount focus of my teaching.

(Dee Petersen, email sent to Garry Hoban, 20 August 2001)

Each class, therefore, represents a unique complex system because of the range of students with varying background knowledge, culture, interests and gender. Because of the interrelationships among these elements, it is imperative that teachers are professionals who have some autonomy and are self-directed so that they can make discretionary judgements about the changing context. According to Goodson (2001b), this is more akin to the role of what he called the 'old professionals', who were autonomous as well as self-directed, and contrasts with 'new professionals', who are technically competent and compliant with government regulations. Hence, there needs to be public debate about the current role of teachers, as it is questionable whether they can keep pace with a changing world unless they have a significant degree of autonomy:

Unless governments, administrators and teachers together can address and resolve these challenges of restructuring teachers' work with openness, commitment and flexibility, it is unlikely that complex professionalism – the professionalism that comes with increasing work complexity – will simply become a synonym for teacher exploitation and burnout.

(Hargreaves and Goodson 1996: 19)

Hargreaves and Goodson's (1996) notion of a 'complex professional' raises the issue as to whether classrooms and schools have always been complex systems or whether this has emerged in the last 10 years with the prominence of complexity theory. I contend that classroom interactions have always been consistent with the notion of a complex system, but mechanistic ways of thinking, which dominated educational thought during the twentieth century, have promoted a simplistic and reductionist way of looking at these complex events. One way this has occurred is that educational research often focuses on curriculum, teaching or learning, but does not consider them as a dynamic relationship that is mutually influential (Hoban 2000b). It could be argued, however, that classrooms are becoming more complex with the rapid pace of change that has permeated schools in the last 20 years and has increased the need to view classrooms and educational change through a new lens.

In the context of university teaching, Biggs (1993) argued that every university class is a 'set of interacting ecosystems' (p. 74) made up of students, teachers, teaching contexts and curriculum. Changing one element, like a curriculum, means changing other aspects of the classroom, such as teaching strategies and assessment. He claims that these factors are often in equilibrium or 'alignment' and have evolved over time so that there is a balance or order between the curriculum, resources and assessment requirements like a system. Even a conventional teacher has a pedagogical system based on an alignment between the transmission of facts, rote learning by students and individual knowledge-based assessment. Biggs (1993) concluded that these elements interact with each other in a type of equilibrium and called each university class an 'ecosystem of the educational swamp' (p. 74). Where the balance exists in a teacher's instruction, be it in the transmission of knowledge or in the facilitation of student learning, depends on how teaching is conceived:

> We have to adjust our teaching decisions to suit our subject matter, available resourcing, our students and our own individual strengths and weaknesses as a teacher. It depends on how we *conceive* the process of teaching, and through reflection come to some conclusion about how we may do our particular job better.
>
> (Biggs 1999: 2; emphasis in original)

I believe that teaching in a school context is similar, which involves developing a balance among many elements, such as curriculum, teaching strategies, assessment, different children, parents and community expectations, and resources, that interact as a system (Hoban 2000b). If a proposed change is a simple one, like teachers using a whiteboard instead of a blackboard, then the chance of implementation is strong, because this does not require changing the balance or equilibrium of the existing classroom system. But proposals for major change in teaching practices is a much more difficult process.

In sum, a classroom can be thought of as a complex system with many interacting elements that can generate an inertia to resist change, especially when change is presented in a fragmented way or can respond dynamically to change. For instance, a new instructional strategy such as problem-based learning will not work if a teacher is reluctant to let children cooperate in groups and to redesign the assessment scheme from one that emphasizes the recall of facts in exams to the processes of solving a problem and monitoring outcomes. Existing teaching practices, therefore, create an inertia to resist change because the dynamics of the existing system are often stronger than the influences from a technical innovation introduced at a one-off workshop. To successfully implement a change such as problem-based learning into regular classroom practice, means adjusting many elements of the classroom system and this requires a framework to support teachers to learn to do something differently over time.

Educational change

A recurring theme in the 1990s has been that educational change is a complex process involving many interconnected elements that have a dynamic effect on each other (Fullan 1993, 1999; Banathy 1996; Fink 2000). Bascia and Hargreaves (2000) state that the educational landscape is not static, as 'the context of change operates as a complex and interrelated system where everything depends on (or undermines) everything else' (p. 18). Similarly, Goodson (2001a) recently defined segments of the change process as internal, being the change agents within schools; external, being the outside forces that mandate change such as a new curriculum; and personal, being the individual beliefs and experiences that are brought to the change process. He concluded that change is more likely to occur when these segments are 'integrated and harmonized', leading to a new balance to promote a social movement for change.

To cope with multiple influences on change in an integrated way, Fullan (1999) proposed that there needs to be an infrastructure for 'developing the capacity of the multilevel system to manage complex change on a continuous basis' (p. 74). He used complexity theory to recast many of his earlier ideas about educational change, stating that there had been a paradigm breakthrough since the 1980s, as 'the pursuit of planned change is a mug's game because reality under conditions of dynamic complexity is fundamentally non-linear. Most change in unplanned' (Fullan 1993: 138). He argued that attempting to put factors in place for planned change did not work as intended because it did not cater for the dynamics or the holistic nature of the change process:

> It is no longer sufficient to study factors associated with the success or failure of the latest innovation or policy. It is no longer acceptable to separate planned change from seemingly spontaneous or naturally occurring change. It is only by raising our consciousness and insights about the totality of educational change that we can do something about it.
>
> (Fullan 1993: vii)

Hargreaves (1998) also argued that factors for educational change should not be thought of as independent elements because 'managing change becomes a collective process, not an individual one' (p. 285).

Understanding complexity with a systems thinking approach

If educational change is viewed through the lens of complexity theory, then using a mindset or way of thought such as 'systems thinking' can be useful to help us understand the dynamic and interrelated nature of the change process. Banathy (1996: 74) called systems thinking the 'science of complexity' because it is an approach that transcends conventional disciplines and is a mindset that focuses on the interdependence of the world. According to Senge (1990: 69), 'systems thinking is a discipline for seeing the "structures" that underlie complex situations . . . systems thinking offers a language that begins by restructuring how we think'. In contrast to a mechanistic paradigm, which focuses on independent elements that have a linear cause and effect relationship, complexity theory is a world view focusing on multiple interdependent elements and the non-linear interactions that emerge. Systems thinking, therefore, is a mindset or lens that complements complexity theory by focusing on interrelationships and helps us understand the dynamic interactions indicative of complex systems.

In a system, the whole is greater than the sum of its parts because of the cumulative influence of the relationships among the elements as well as the elements themselves. Flood and Carson (1988) summarized the main terms used in systems thinking. A *system* is an assembly of related elements that act together as an integrated whole. An *element* is a part of the system that has some attributes which contribute to the system as a whole. A *relationship* exists between elements in a system if the behaviour of either one is influenced by the other. *Feedback* occurs when an element impacts on the overall system through a series of relationships. A *closed system* is where the relationships that influence a system are defined by a boundary around the system with no external influences. An *open system* is where there are external influences on the system itself beyond the operation of the system.

Over the last 100 years, the notion of systems thinking has emerged in different disciplines in opposition to beliefs underpinned by mechanistic thinking. One of the earliest and most detailed descriptions of systems thinking occurred in science in Ludwig von Bertalanffy's (1933) *Modern Theories of Development*. He strongly argued against mechanistic views held in the biological community that attempted to analyse living things into independent parts, instead contending that life has a 'systems-property':

> The fundamental error of 'classical mechanism' lay in its application of the additive point of view to the interpretation of living organisms. It attempted to analyse the vital process into particular occurrences proceeding in single parts or mechanisms independently of one another ... We believe now that the solution of this antithesis in biology is to be sought in an *organismic* or *system theory* of the organism which, on the one hand, in opposition to machine theory, sees the essence of the organism in the harmony and coordination of the processes among one another.
>
> (von Bertalanffy 1933: 177; emphasis in original)

In another area of biology, ecology, the focus was also changing from studying animals and plants independently to studying the relationships between them. The word 'ecology' comes from a combination of two words – the Greek words *oekos* meaning household or home and *logos* meaning the study of; and so ecology is the study of natural areas or natural households. The word was first used in 1869 by the German zoologist, Ernst Haeckel, who described relationships between organisms and their surroundings; later the term 'ecosystem' was used by the English botanist, A.G. Tansley (Sirotnik 1998).

In 1968, von Bertalanffy reiterated his holistic world views in a book called *General System Theory*, noting how systems thinking was emerging in other branches of science besides biology. In physics, Boltzmann's second principle of thermodynamics concerned 'laws of disorder' and equilibrium within a dynamic heating system. In quantum physics, properties of materials could not be explained by the features of independent subatomic particles alone, but sometimes needed to be explained by wave-like properties generated by interrelationships between particles. Heisenberg's uncertainty principle is also based on a web of connections between particles and highlights the limitations of trying to accurately measure atomic particles. In chemistry, the behaviour of gases is similar to a dynamic system of 'unorganized and individually untraceable movements of innumerable molecules' (von Bertalanffy 1968: 33). In mathematics and economics as well, von Bertalanffy noted that systems thinking was prevalent in several theories, including information theory, cybernetics, game theory and stochastic models.

As a result of this prevalence of systems thinking across the sciences, von Bertalanffy (1968) proposed a new discipline for science called 'general systems theory', describing it as 'a general science of wholeness' (p. 36). He defined systems as 'sets of elements standing in interrelation' (p. 37), claiming that this new discipline would integrate the natural and social sciences with five major aims:

(i)   There is a general tendency towards integration in the various sciences, natural and social.
(ii) Such integration seems to be centered in a general theory of systems.
(iii) Such theory may be an important means of aiming at exact theory in the nonphysical fields of science.
(iv) Developing unifying principles running 'vertically' through the universe of the individual sciences, this theory brings us nearer to the goal of the unity of science.
(v)   This can lead to a much-needed integration in scientific education.

(von Bertalanffy 1968: 37)

Although von Bertalanffy's vision of a unified science based on systems thinking did not eventuate, his ideas are still relevant today when referring to holistic thinking across various areas of science.

In another discipline, psychology, Bronfenbrenner (1979) proposed a new theoretical perspective for child development based on a 'theory of environmental interconnections and their impact on the forces directly affecting pyschological growth' (p. 8). He contended that existing psychological models of human development were limited, as they did not take into account the interconnections that influence development. This is because of a mechanistic paradigm that underpins conventional psychology with a 'scientific lens that restricts, darkens, and even blinds the researcher's vision of environmental obstacles and opportunities' (p. 7). For example, many psychological studies are conducted on individuals in laboratories and attempt to control variables or independent factors to seek cause and effect. This methodology disregards influences that the sociocultural environment has on individuals and does not consider how development is a product of the interactions between groups of humans and their surroundings.

Bronfenbrenner (1979) argued that human development should not be studied in isolation from its context, as 'environments are not distinguished by reference to linear variables but are analyzed in systems terms' (p. 5). He proposed that a unit of analysis for research should not be the individual, but should be the relationship or dyad between two individuals, or a triad between three individuals, depending on the number of elements in a system. Influences within a dyad or triad are bi-directional with reciprocity, such that each element affects the others. For this reason, children and adults often behave differently in the laboratory when compared to real-life settings because of different social interconnections between the setting and participants. In his ecological model of human development, Bronfenbrenner (1979) proposed a set of nested structures as a way of studying human development with four levels represented as concentric circles:

1 At the centre of the model is the child surrounded by a microsystem, which is the setting that interacts directly with the child such as family and peers.
2 The second layer is the mesosystem, including the home, school and neighbourhood.
3 The third layer is the exosystem, including the social setting and the backgrounds of parents and relatives.
4 The fourth layer is the macrosystem, which includes the values, laws and customs of a culture.

Central to Bronfenbrenner's ecological model is that human development is not controlled by the individual or the environment alone, but that one influences the other in a reciprocal dynamic relationship.

More recently, the notion of systems thinking emerged as a conceptual framework for understanding change in business management. Senge (1990) argued that modern businesses could not afford to think simplistically when the world is changing so quickly. Instead, a business needs to become a 'learning organization' to respond to an ever-changing dynamic world. He proposed five key features of a learning organization:

1 personal mastery, meaning that employees and employers need to have a vision and to see their work as continual learning;
2 mental models that suggest an awareness of assumptions that underpin practice;
3 shared vision, which is a belief in a company's purpose and a vision for the future;
4 team learning, such that employees need to work in groups that have clear communication channels; and
5 systems thinking.

The last of these is what he called 'the fifth discipline' because it links the other four and is the 'conceptual cornerstone' that holds a learning organization together. He defined systems thinking as 'a paradigm for seeing the world as a connected ecosystem. It is a framework for seeing interrelationships rather than things, for seeing patterns of change rather than static snap-shots' (Senge 1990: 68). To gain a big picture on why the business world works the way it does, employers need to consider the whole landscape – markets, customers, employees, resources, manufacturing and sales – simultaneously. Importantly, they need to be thought about collectively not individually, because independently they are snapshots representing elements of causality, not the patterns of causality.

Capra (1982, 1988) took a broader social science view and summarized the key ideas on systems thinking, arguing for its value as a way of under-standing how the world works. He identified key *interdependent* criteria of this approach:

- a change of emphasis on thinking from independent parts to wholes, meaning a shift from objects to relationships;
- the living world is an interconnected web of relationships;
- an ability to move attention back and forth between system levels; and
- knowledge as a network of concepts and models.

His view of knowledge as a changing network of relationships is consistent with the assumption of a complexity paradigm explained earlier in this chapter, which states that knowledge is never static or objective, but rather is always an approximation to reality.

A systems thinking approach in education

Although systems thinking has been prevalent in various disciplines, includ-ing science, psychology and economics, it is yet to be a major influence in educational literature because it is 'underconceptualized and underutilized, and is often manifested in misdirected applications' (Banathy 1996: 83). Banathy (1991) claimed that a fragmented, mechanistic world view under-pinned the failure of many efforts for educational reform in the 1970s and 1980s. He stated that such a piecemeal approach to educational change 'cannot possibly cope with complexity, mutual causality, purpose, intention, uncertainty, ambiguity, and ever accelerating dynamic changes that characterise our systems and the larger societal environment' (Banathy 1991: 10). Using the principles embodied in systems thinking, schools should encourage teachers to be proactive and make a collective commitment to a new vision for long-term change, rather than being reactive with quick-fix solutions. Similarly, Goodlad (1975) argued for a responsive model of educational change in which a school should consider the state of its own learning environment for it to respond to its own needs, as 'an eco-logical model of education goes far beyond schools in seeking to embrace people, things, and institutions in a systemic, interrelated whole' (p. 213).

Banathy (1996) suggested that educational change can be managed using a 'systems design approach' and proposed three models that portray education as a system with connected layers:

1 a system environment model that describes education in the context of its community and society;
2 a functions/structure model that focuses on snapshots of a system in terms of goals, functions, components and relations; and
3 a process/behavioural model that focuses on what an educational system is doing over time.

When using systems thinking to conceptualize holistic change, it is necessary to consider the three models collectively to gain a complete picture of education as a social system. In this respect, systems thinking has mostly been used in educational literature at a macro-level to describe the relationships among the layers and structures of education. However, systems thinking is also a useful mindset at a micro-level, as it helps us to understand the dynamics of educational change in a school and classroom setting.

Educational change as a complex system

Many theories about educational change have emerged in the 1990s and it is acknowledged that change, or the lack of it, is not due to one theory alone, as they are interrelated (Bascia and Hargreaves 2000). One way to think about how these theories are interconnected is through the notion of 'change frames', which are multiple foci or lenses for understanding the dynamic and interrelated nature of the change process (Hargreaves *et al.* 1997; Fink 2000; Moore and Shaw 2000; Retallick and Fink 2000). Importantly, change frames are not mutually exclusive and do not act in isolation to each other, but are interrelated, as 'the idea of "framing change" enables change agents to understand the multidimensionality and therefore the complexity of change in schools' (Fink 2000: 6). I will not dwell on individual change frames, as they have been explained by others; however, they include such influences as:

- *School leadership*: how principals can promote a shared vision for change as well as instigating and supporting the process (Fullan 1982, 1993; Leithwood 1992; Leithwood *et al.* 1999).
- *Teachers' lives and their work*: teachers are often more receptive to change up to the age of 40 but then tend to resist change or even become disenchanted due to teacher burnout (Sikes 1985; Huberman 1993; Acker 1995).
- *School culture*: shared beliefs and values are important in terms of establishing a collaborative relationship among teachers; however, this may

be difficult to sustain when different subcultures exist within a school (Fullan 1993; Hargreaves 1994; Stoll and Fink 1996; Fink 2000).

- *Structure*: changes within a school organization, including decisions about time, space, school timetables as well as jobs and role descriptions (Hargreaves 1994; Stoll and Fink 1996; Fink 2000).
- *Politics*: includes those external to a school, such as government and district policies, as well as those internal to a school, such as how power is distributed and gender politics (Acker 1983; Smyth 1992; Seashore Louis *et al.* 1999; Datnow 2000).
- *Context*: the broad composition and background of the school, including the pupils, location, subjects and departments, teachers, community, local and district educational bodies, teacher unions and national priorities (Bascia and Hargreaves 2000; Fink 2000).
- *Teacher learning*: any infrastructure provided to support teachers to cope with new ideas and the process of educational change (Baird 1992; McLaughlin 1993; Cochran-Smith and Lytle 1993; Bickel and Hattrup 1995; Quartz 1995; Clandinin and Connelly 1996; Calhoun and Joyce 1998; Day 1999; Moore and Shaw 2000; Putnam and Borko 2000).

What is important when thinking about educational change is that these frames act collectively, not individually, to influence the change process. Consequently, educational change behaves as a *complex system* with multiple frames or elements acting together as a *system* to produce non-linear interactions. Furthermore, these interactions are *complex*, meaning that the system can respond with an inertia to resist change and stay the same, or dynamically self-adjust to a new order or balance. For example, when a new curriculum is introduced, it may alter the relationships of the system and lead to significant change if there is positive leadership, a receptive political context, the school culture is consistent with the innovation and has a framework for teacher learning that supports teachers during the non-linear process of change. Conversely, the system may present an inertia to resist change if a new curriculum clashes with the existing culture, there is no political or leadership support, teachers are at the end of their career or there is no infrastructure for teacher learning. Alternatively, a curriculum may be implemented by some teachers and not others or to different extents because of the various ways in which elements or frames interact in the system. Consequently, change is difficult to predict because of the dynamics that exist between different change frames or elements that influence the change process itself. Importantly, attempts at managing change need to consider the multiple influences collectively and focus on the whole dynamics of the change process.

What is central to this non-linear process that encourages or resists change are the interrelationships among the multiple change frames. This

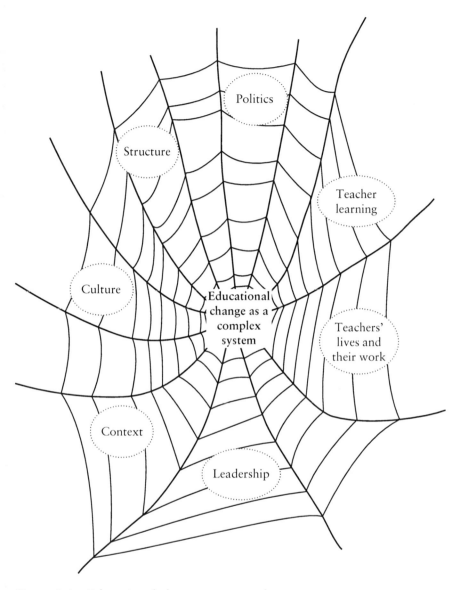

Figure 2.1   Educational change as a complex system.

conceptualization of educational change is represented in Figure 2.1 and shows that it is influenced by a combination of change frames; each frame is also a 'system' in its own right. The context of educational change can therefore be compared to a 'spider web', with each frame being interconnected so that change in one frame affects change in others. This metaphor

of a spider web is consistent with complexity theory, because it acknowledges the connectedness and dynamic nature of change that can self-
organize to a state of equilibrium.

Note that in Figure 2.1 educational change is dependent on the interrelationships among the elements as emphasized by the unbroken lines in
bold, because these interrelationships may enhance each other to support
change or undermine each other to block change. As well as highlighting
the connectedness of change, a representation such as a complex system
shows why change is so problematic and difficult to manage because of
the many influences and dynamics between them. Studying the process
of change in one high school over 25 years, Fink (2000) described this
uncertainty and acknowledged the complexity of change because it was so
interconnected:

> It seems clear that preventing, or at least minimizing, the attrition of
> change requires attention to a complex interrelationship of many fac-
> tors that influence purposes, structures, and cultures in schools . . . The
> complexity of the factors described, and their connections and rela-
> tionships, make it virtually impossible to determine exact pathways of
> causation, and therefore impossible to *predict* with certainty that
> attending to this factor or that will ensure a school's continuing growth
> and development. The best that can be said is that schools that become
> aware and attend to the factors I have listed will *be more likely* to
> retain their innovative edge and remain 'moving' schools over time.
>
> (Fink 2000: 153; emphasis in original)

Accordingly, to help understand how educational change behaves as a
complex system, it is necessary to develop a mindset that does not focus
on independent elements such as each change frame (as would occur in
a mechanistic view), but instead focus on the interrelationships that result
from the dynamic interactions among multiple elements in a complex
system.

Implications for teacher learning in a complex system

If educational change is conceptualized as a complex system, it becomes
clear why short-term approaches to teacher learning, as portrayed in 'training' or 'research and development' models of professional development, are
usually inadequate to promote change because they do not cater for the
long-term, non-linear nature of change. Yet, the most common approach to
teacher learning today is still the simplistic 'training' model, whereby teachers attend a workshop after school, or occasionally have a staff development day to listen to an 'expert' tell them how to teach or do a 'show and
tell' on a new curriculum. In a three-year study of change involving 45

teachers in four schools in Ontario, Canada, the most common type of professional learning experienced by them was still the one-step workshop model that 'takes place outside the workplace context focusing mainly on mandated innovations, theoretical and conceptual knowledge, involving use of an outside expert' (Moore and Shaw 2000: 6). They called this a 'transmission model of professional development' and found that teachers themselves expected to receive 'expert' help because they were unaware of alternative models for their own learning. In Chapter 1, I explained how this training model of teacher learning is consistent with a mechanistic paradigm that emphasizes a conception of teaching as a craft as well as a belief that teacher learning and educational change are a linear step-by-step event. Although learning does occur in these workshops, it tends to consolidate existing teaching, not transform it, as a one-off workshop does not support teachers during the non-linear, and sometimes erratic, process of change.

However, if educational change is viewed as a complex system, it emphasizes the need to accompany change with a framework for long-term teacher learning because change is, in essence, learning to do something differently, involving adjustments to many elements of classroom practice. At a classroom level, introducing a new curriculum may mean changing the instructional strategies, assessment and class organization, resulting in a new balance of the classroom system. At a school level, a new curriculum may mean devising a new policy, purchasing new resources and reallocating teaching duties. And all of this takes place in the ever-changing context of a school that is influenced by the combination of change frames identified in Figure 2.1, such as leadership, politics, teacher learning, context, culture, structure, teachers' lives and their work. The bottom line is that efforts for educational change need a long-term approach to support teachers through the non-linear process of change requiring the structure of schools to be reconceptualized as learning environments for their teachers.

Smylie (1995) contends that literature on workplace change for teachers has been 'virtually uninformed by theories of adult learning and change' (p. 93). When studying professional learning for three years in four schools in Ontario, Canada, Moore and Shaw (2000) found that there was no 'cohesive implementation design and action' (p. 3) in professional learning, rather that it was individualistic and haphazard. They concluded that teachers need to reconceptualize their own views on professional learning so that it begins with the sharing of their practical knowledge and then builds an infrastructure that is collaborative and focuses on the 'teacher as inquirer'. Accordingly, it appears that the literature on teachers' professional learning is inadequately theorized, as there is no clear framework to guide long-term teacher learning that is necessary when educational change is understood to behave as a complex system.

Conclusion

A world view based on complexity theory highlights the multidimensionality and hence problematic nature of educational change and has implications for thinking about the nature of teaching, teacher learning and the change process. Systems thinking is a useful lens or mindset for understanding complexity and gives us a way of thought to understand the change process. When considering how educational change behaves as a complex system, the chances for change are increased if there is a framework in place to support long-term teacher learning to help teachers cope with the non-linear process of changing classroom practice. But a theoretical framework to guide the design of such an infrastructure appears to be lacking in the educational literature. Moreover, much of the change literature tends to focus on cultural, structural and strategic influences on educational change (Hargreaves 1998) and under-theorizes the influence of teacher learning. For the rest of this book, I focus on developing a clearer theoretical framework for the change frame of teacher learning, but this is not intended to simplify or ignore the influence of other change frames in the complex process of educational change, rather, they already have been well theorized by others in the educational literature and will be revisited in the last chapter of this book.

three

A systems thinking approach to teacher learning

We are still a long way from having an integrated theoretical perspective that provides an adequate unified view of the ways we think and act.

(Schoenfeld 1999: 5)

If teaching is conceived to be an art or a profession in a complex world, then learning about it is more than an 'additive process' (Day 1999) involving the accumulation of knowledge and skills from one-off workshops. Efforts for teacher learning also need to take into account the unique context of each school and the difficulties of changing classroom practice. Because educational change involves adjusting many elements of class or school organization, a framework is needed to guide long-term teacher learning over time to support this non-linear process. But having such a framework is rare, often because the educational literature has historically been fragmented when it comes to teacher learning. This chapter explains why and uses an approach based on systems thinking to link existing learning perspectives into a coherent theoretical framework as a guide for long-term teacher learning.

Teacher learning in a complex world

When educational change is perceived to behave as a complex system, it is inconsistent to promote a simplistic one-step approach for teacher learning as proposed by a 'training' or 'research and development' model explained in Chapter 1. Alternatively, it has been shown that the most influential element of professional learning is the sharing of teachers' own experiences in groups that can operate as a learning community (Baird 1992; Cochran-Smith and Lytle 1993; McLaughlin 1993; Bickel and Hattrup 1995; Quartz 1995; Clandinin and Connelly 1996; Moore and Shaw 2000). Calhoun and Joyce (1998) called this type of teacher community a 'School-Based,

Faculty-Centred' or 'Inside-out' approach that takes into account the context of teachers' classrooms and schools. However, a limitation of these site-based programmes is that they often do not involve the injection of new ideas and may take several years to show any significant teacher change. Calhoun and Joyce (1998) stated that the success rate of these 'learning communities' for schools is no higher than the linear 'research and development' approach, as only *'ten percent of the schools have been able to generate initiatives that substantially changed the curricular, instructional, or technological dimensions of the school'* (pp. 1292–3; emphasis in original). I believe that both 'training' and 'learning community' models for teacher learning have strengths as well as limitations. The training model presents new ideas often as formal knowledge (Fenstermacher 1994) for teachers to implement in their practice, but ignores the existing classroom context and ways to sustain learning after the workshop. Conversely, the learning community model provides a framework to sustain learning by focusing on the sharing of practical knowledge (Fenstermacher 1994), but often ignores the importance of introducing new ideas to extend teachers' thinking.

There are, however, several models that integrate ideas from both 'training' and 'learning community' models. Richardson's (1994) staff development process includes the introduction of formal knowledge in context with discussions about teachers' classroom experiences using practical arguments. But this model has not been used extensively beyond reading instruction. Another integrated teacher learning model involved a three-year time frame in which teachers shared personal, social and professional experiences with each other, including inputs from educational research (Bell and Gilbert 1994). A different integrated model involved teachers and teacher educators working together in schools to share ideas about teaching and learning. In Australia, the Project for Enhancing Effective Learning (PEEL) featured teachers and teacher educators sharing ideas about strategies to support student learning (Baird and Mitchell 1987). In the USA, Cochran-Smith and Lytle (1993) have promoted the notion of teacher research with teachers and teacher educators engaging in collaborative action research to sustain teacher learning.

But these projects, which contain features of a learning community as well as including different ways to inject new ideas into group discussions, are rare and it is unclear as to what combination of conditions will encourage such long-term teacher learning. A question that is central to this book, therefore, is: 'What conditions will help to establish a framework for long-term teacher learning to support educational change?' Research has identified some conditions that encourage long-term teacher learning but these derive from a range of perspectives. Smylie (1995) outlined seven conditions for an optimal school learning environment based on an integration of social learning theory, incidental learning theory and organizational socialization theory:

1 teacher collaboration;
2 shared power and authority;
3 egalitarianism among teachers;
4 variation, challenge, autonomy and choice in teachers' work;
5 organizational goals and feedback mechanisms;
6 integration of work and learning; and
7 accessibility of external sources of learning.

He emphasized that these conditions do not act independently, but relate to each other in complex ways so that new knowledge is situated in the context of teachers' practice:

> To simply identify workplace conditions conducive to teacher learning is not the same thing as understanding in greater depth the complex, potentially interactive functional relationships of those conditions to learning. It does not shed light on the interactions between the work environment and individual cognition and psychological states in the learning process.
>
> (Smylie 1995: 107)

Placier and Hamilton (1994) described interactions in schools as a 'complex relationship' and identified several conditions that need to be in place to support teacher learning:

- positive working conditions such as flexibility and experimentation;
- autonomy to change their practice;
- motivation to change as supported by the school culture; and
- collegiality among the staff.

Richardson (1994) contended that classroom change starts with teachers examining their beliefs about their practices similar to a 'practical argument' that needs to be extended with other ideas presented in context with their beliefs. Many of these conditions support the formation of what has been termed a 'community of learners' for school improvement (Barth 1990). According to Pouravood (1997), learning communities assist teachers to change in a complex world. In particular, teacher networks enable the participants to negotiate knowledge according to their unique contexts. Thus, a structure such as a learning community, whereby knowledge is continually being generated and negotiated in a changing context, is consistent with a complexity world view. In such a community, teachers have a sense of managing their own growth, as opposed to conventional professional development programmes that usually involve someone outside the school attempting to control teacher learning. Barth (1990) identified the

characteristics of a learning community of teachers emphasizing the importance of interpersonal relationships:

- Schools have the capacity to improve themselves, if the conditions are
  right. A major responsibility of those outside the school is to help provide
  the conditions for those inside.
- When the need and purpose is there, when the conditions are right,
  adults and children alike learn and each energizes and contributes to the
  learning of the other.
- What needs to be improved about schools is their culture, the quality
  of interpersonal relationships, and the nature and quality of learning
  experiences.
- School improvement is an effort to determine and provide, from without
  and within, conditions under which the adults and youngsters who inhabit
  schools will promote and sustain learning among themselves.

(Barth 1990: 45)

It is no accident that these previously identified conditions, which promote and sustain teacher learning, are drawn from a variety of learning
perspectives – personal learning, social learning, adult learning, incidental
learning, organizational learning and situated learning. This range of perspectives shows that teachers can learn in many different ways and contexts. Yet, there is no theoretical framework in the education literature that
links these different learning perspectives and explains how a community
can sustain teacher learning. If a theoretical framework for long-term teacher
learning could be established, it would provide guidelines for designing
a supportive framework for educational change rather than relying on
'common sense' and 'the way we have always done it', which is usually the
case. However, historical traditions in education have actively encouraged
the fragmentation of learning theory, which is one reason for the absence of
a clear theoretical framework to sustain teacher learning.

Origins of a dichotomy in learning theory

Characterized by fragmentation, different theoretical perspectives on learning
have little in common because they are underpinned by different assumptions.
The key disagreement has centred on debates about the unit of analysis or
focus when examining learning processes. Arguments about this focus have
generated a dichotomy between a psychological perspective promoting a
unit of analysis as 'in the mind' (Cobb 1994) and a situated perspective
promoting a unit of analysis as the 'individual-in-social-action' (Minick
1989). This no-win debate has constrained the development of a coherent
theory as a basis for establishing a framework for long-term teacher learning.

Education is littered with many 'turf battles' regarding fundamental ideas about teaching and learning. Education is not a single, coherent discipline; rather, it is based upon many different perspectives that often conflict with one another (Lagemann 2000). Historically, the theoretical basis of educational literature evolved from several different disciplines leading to the development of a variety of perspectives:

> Neither singular in focus nor uniform in methods of investigation, education grew out of various combinations of philosophy, psychology, and the social sciences, including statistics. The variety that has characterized educational scholarship from the first, combined with the field's failure to develop a strong, self-regulating professional community, has meant that the field has never developed a high degree of internal coherence.
>
> (Lagemann 2000: ix)

This fragmentation of educational research originated in the late 1800s when schools of education were being established at universities with scholars from different disciplines (philosophy, psychology or history) and so 'research in education grew up in an *ad hoc*, essentially opportunistic fashion' (Lagemann 2000: 10). Another factor that added to the fragmentation was that education needed a research base to establish its status within universities. At the same time, the discipline of philosophy was evolving into several branches, including economics, sociology, political science and psychology (mental philosophy) and so there were debates as to whether education should be based on one discipline or remain multidisciplinary. Over time, many university educators began to use psychology as a core knowledge base, which included adopting what worked for the more established disciplines such as medicine and engineering – a methodology of research based on scientific principles. Opposing views on what discipline should underpin educational research was highlighted by approaches used by two well-known researchers in the USA.

In the early 1900s, two leading American educators, John Dewey and Edward L. Thorndike, promoted different views on the type of methodology that should underpin educational research. From 1894 to 1904, John Dewey, the chairman of the Department of Philosophy at the University of Chicago, pursued research in three areas – philosophy, psychology and education. He believed that philosophy should not be split into strands and that education should be an integrated discipline drawing upon psychology, philosophy and the social sciences (Lagemann 2000). To conduct research in education, Dewey set up his Laboratory School in 1896. The school reached its peak in 1902 with 140 students who were taught by 23 teachers and supported by 10 graduate students. Dewey had a clear educational philosophy underpinned by both psychological and sociological perspectives as expressed in his seminal article, *My Pedagogic Creed* (Dewey 1897), in which he described how children learn to talk in a family setting:

> I believe that this educational process has two sides – one psychological and one sociological; and that neither can be subordinated to the other or neglected without evil results following. Of these two sides, the psychological is the basis. The child's own instincts and powers furnish the material and give the starting point for all education ... Without insight into the psychological structure and activities of the individual, the educative process will, therefore, be haphazard and arbitrary ... I believe that knowledge of social conditions, of the present state of civilization, is necessary in order properly to interpret the child's powers.
>
> (Dewey 1897: 4)

This integrated approach to learning underpinned the curriculum of Dewey's Laboratory School at the University of Chicago. As director of the school, Dewey did not believe in a traditional structured curriculum based on independent subjects such as maths, science and literacy, because he thought that teachers would focus their instruction on subject matter in isolation to a context (Dewey 1902, 1916). Instead, he believed that subject matter should be introduced in context with individuals' experiences to extend their prior knowledge with the school curriculum focusing on 'occupations' in preference to 'studies' (Lagemann 2000). The implication was that pupils studied with teachers as a community, conducting everyday activities such as cooking, sewing, woodwork and agriculture. This integration of personal and social influences on learning was reiterated later in his book *Experience and Education* (Dewey 1938), in which he stated that the two criteria for learning through experience are 'continuity' (relevance to an individual's prior knowledge) and 'interaction' (social engagement with others to extend this knowledge). Dewey (1938) emphasized that these two criteria are not separate, as 'any normal experience is an interplay of these two sets of conditions. Taken together, or in their interaction, they form what we call a *situation*' (p. 42; emphasis in original). This interplay between personal and social influences on learning suggests that Dewey did not believe that the unit of analysis for learning was only 'in the mind', but also had a strong social and cultural influence:

> Experience does not go on simply inside a person ... In a word, we live from birth to death in a world of persons and things which is in a large measure what it is because of what has been done and transmitted from previous human activities. When this fact is ignored, experience is treated as if it were something which goes on exclusively inside an individual's body and mind. It ought not to be necessary to say that

experience does not occur in a vacuum. There are sources outside an individual which give rise to experience.

(Dewey 1938: 39)

When Dewey moved from the University of Chicago to the Philosophy Department at Columbia in 1904, his Laboratory School closed. This cut short much of Dewey's research in education, although he continued to write about it for another 40 years.

In contrast to John Dewey, Edward L. Thorndike believed that psychology should be a separate discipline from philosophy and was keen to establish the foundation for a new field called 'educational psychology' focusing on mental processes. In 1904, he was a professor at Teachers College and worked hard to establish a 'science of education'. In particular, he wanted to generate a research platform for education based on scientific experimentation, as this method had the highest status in established university research. To show the influence of science on education at this time, a yearbook summarizing educational research was published annually from 1902 to 1909 by the National Society for the *Scientific* Study of Education (my emphasis). In 1910, 'Scientific' was dropped from the title. In 1903, Thorndike wrote a book called *Educational Psychology* and, 10 years later, wrote three volumes that summarized empirical research in this evolving field. Consistent with a scientific method, Thorndike believed that educational research should be based on controlled experiments using individuals to monitor exact quantitative measurements of behavioural change. He believed that educational achievements are dependent on what an individual is 'by nature', which emphasizes an individualistic unit of analysis. Much of his research focused on cause and effect with studies that linked behaviour to independent variables. This deterministic and behaviouristic approach to learning was extremely influential at the time and encouraged teaching that was step-by-step and reductionist.

In the early 1900s, different perspectives on learning were also emerging in Europe (Cole and Engeström 1993). In 1921, the German psychologist, Wilhelm Wundt, outlined two complementary branches of psychology in his book *Elements of Folk Psychology*. One branch, called scientific or 'physiological psychology', used laboratory experiments to investigate the learning of simple language assuming that learning takes place inside an individual's head. The second branch, *Völkerpsychologie* (folkspsychology), focused on the learning of 'higher psychological functions', including reasoning and evaluation. Wundt (1921) argued that this higher-order learning could not be studied by doing traditional scientific experiments in a laboratory because learning was influenced by social and cultural factors:

A language can never be created by an individual. True, individuals have invented Esperanto and other artificial languages. Unless, however, language had already existed, these inventions would have been impossible. Moreover, none of these has been able to maintain itself, and most of them owe their existence solely to elements borrowed from natural languages.

(Wundt 1921: 3)

Researching complex educational processes, such as studying thinking skills, needed a more naturalistic method focusing on social interactions such as those embedded in sociology and anthropology. In short, Wundt argued that psychology needed two traditions for educational research – scientific experimental procedures to study simple learning processes for individual learning, and more open-ended procedures, such as ethnographies, to study higher-order learning processes in social contexts. Hugo Munsterberg concurred with Wundt that there should be two strands of psychology, one focusing on scientific methods called 'causal psychology' for individual learning and one focusing on social interactions of groups called 'purposeful psychology' (Munsterberg 1914). Although the popularity of Wundt's *Völkerpsychologie* and Munsterberg's purposeful psychology waned over the next 20 years, there were similar ideas about sociocultural influences on learning resonating in the writings of the Soviet psychologists Leont'ev, Luria and Vygotsky in the late 1920s and early 1930s that became popular later in the century (Cole and Engeström 1993). Throughout this time, different fields or perspectives on learning were evolving that focused primarily on individual learning or learning as a group in a social context.

Why do particular fields tend to maintain their assumptions over such long periods of time? Kuhn (1970) argued that researchers in the sciences often work with similar mindsets and solve 'puzzles' that are usually consistent with the beliefs of their research community and publish findings in academic journals that are controlled by members of that community. In this respect, most researchers solve 'puzzles' to fit an existing paradigm, not 'problems' that contradict commonly held beliefs. In the field of education, Seymour Sarason (1981) suggested that psychologists themselves are socialized into the assumptions of their discipline and conduct research with similar world views. The trend for most of this century, he argued, has been for psychology to focus on the individual and disregard the context: 'Psychology, at its core has been quintessentially a study of the individual organism unrelated to the history, structure, and unverbalized world views of the social order' (Sarason 1981: ix). He suggested that psychologists need to extend their world view beyond studying individual mental processes to include sociocultural influences on those processes.

The divisions in the learning landscape were exacerbated by another perspective that evolved because adult learning was perceived to be different to children's learning. The person who popularized this division was Malcolm Knowles, who in 1968, proposed the term *andragogy* as a theory of adult learning. He described andragogy as 'the art and science of helping adults learn'; that was different to *pedagogy*, which was 'the art and science of how children learn' (Knowles 1968: 351). He emphasized that pedagogy is controlled by school teachers who direct children's education by making all the decisions about what, how and when learning occurs. In contrast, andragogy shifts the emphasis of responsibility to adults who make their own decisions about learning because they are self-directed and not constrained by a school environment.

Knowles (1968) proposed five assumptions about how adults learn (the fifth was added after the first four):

1 Concept of the learner – as a person matures, his or her self-concept moves from that of a dependent personality towards one of a self-directing human being.
2 Role of learner's experience – an adult accumulates a growing reservoir of experience that is a rich resource for learning.
3 Readiness to learn – the readiness of an adult to learn is closely related to the developmental tasks of his or her social role.
4 Orientation to learning – there is a change in time perspective as people mature, from future application of knowledge to immediacy of application. Thus, an adult is more problem-centred than subject-centred in learning.

(Knowles 1980)

5 Motivation to learn – adults are motivated to learn by internal factors rather than external ones.

(Knowles and Associates 1984)

Although these assumptions have been the foundation for important notions such as 'self-directedness' in adult learning (Candy 1991), it has been debated as to whether they constitute a theory of learning (Elias 1979). Brookfield (1986) argued that andragogy is not a theory of learning so much as a set of desirable principles or characteristics of adults. He contended that the first three assumptions are problematic because not all experiences involve quality learning and are not unique to adults, as children also can be self-directed and use experience as the basis for learning (although children do not have the extent of experiences that adults have). In particular, andragogy has been criticized because it has a psychological emphasis focusing on characteristics of individual learners, with little consideration given to the social, political or cultural contexts that are always an influence on learning (Pratt 1993; Merriam and Caffarella 1999). It would appear, therefore, that andragogy is not a theory of learning, but instead highlights desirable characteristics of individual adult learners. In particular, Knowles's assumptions for andragogy are more related to the type of environment that adults usually learn in, which gives them responsibility for determining what, when and how they learn. It could be argued that children can also be responsible for their own learning, but this is more likely to occur in 'everyday settings' that have few constraints and encourage them to make their own decisions (Resnick 1987).

Other authors also have proposed that there is not a clear difference between adult and children's learning (Dewey 1901; Barth 1990; Sarason 1990; Huberman 1995). In *Psychology and Social Practice*, Dewey (1901) stated that the greatest obstacle to educational reform was the dependence of school organization on psychology in preference to social practice. He claimed that the conditions for children's learning were the same as for adult learning:

> Traced back to its psychological ultimates, there are two controlling bases of existing methods of instruction. One is the assumption of a fundamental distinction between child psychology and the adult psychology where in reality identity reigns, viz., in the region of the motives and conditions which make for mental power. The other is the assumption of likeness where marked difference is the feature most significant for educational purposes; I mean the specialization of aims and habits in the adult, compared with the absence of specialization in the child.
>
> (Dewey 1901: 10)

Later in his book, Dewey explained that the conditions for both child and adult learners should provide them with power and control to enable them to select personal problems and experiment to test ideas in a social context. In reference to teacher learning, Sarason (1990) contended that one of the fundamental conditions for teacher change was the provision of a learning environment that often exists for children, as 'teachers cannot create and sustain the conditions for the productive development of children if those conditions do not exist for teachers' (p. xiv). Although the processes of learning for adults and children may not be identical because there are different degrees of development and experience, I believe that they have a good deal in common, especially in the area of social and cultural influences. In support, Merriam and Caffarella (1999) contend that most writing on adult learning has an individual psychological emphasis and neglects a sociocultural emphasis, including the social, cultural and physical contexts. They argue that research needs to be more integrated and to use multiple lenses with biological, psychological and sociocultural perspectives to develop a richer understanding of learning. A similar point was recently made by Putnam and Borko (2000), who stated that much of the research on learning in the 1990s used the familiar cognitive and situated perspectives for children's learning, and that both perspectives have relevance for teacher learning.

The learning dichotomy continues

During the last 30 years, educational research has used a variety of qualitative and quantitative techniques to provide valuable insights into learning. Consistent with the trend of having different research perspectives, these insights have been generated from two main research communities, each underpinned by a different assumption concerning the unit of analysis or focus for learning (Cobb and Bowers 1999; Anderson *et al.* 2000). One community promotes a 'cognitive perspective' that is based on a psychological approach emphasizing the individual workings of the mind that evolved from the work of Piaget (Cobb 1994). Alternatively, a 'situated perspective' evolved from cultural-historical psychology, and is grounded in the work of Leont'ev, Luria and Vygotsky in the late 1920s and early 1930s (Cole and Engeström 1993). Recently, Schoenfeld (1999) contended that one of the main challenges for educational research in the twenty-first century is to heal the cognitive/social split, as 'we are still a long way from having an integrated theoretical perspective that provides an adequate unified view of the ways we think and act' (p. 5).

A cognitive perspective on learning

Cognitive learning theories evolved from a traditional psychological perspective in which the unit of analysis or focus for learning is in the mind of an individual. These theories originated from the work of Jean Piaget (1950), who believed that learning was a process of continually reworking an individual's knowledge based on personal experiences. He proposed the notion that thinking is about developing cognitive schemas and mental models that exist within an individual's mind. When learning occurs, an individual's schema becomes more complex, which Piaget (1950) called 'assimilation' and 'accommodation'. These schemes are modified with social interaction, but the process is a change 'in the head' of an individual. This cognitive perspective explains the process of personal knowledge construction and highlights the importance of an individual's prior knowledge as a major influence on learning. Putnam and Borko (1997) recently suggested that a cognitive perspective is also relevant for teacher learning, as teachers' prior beliefs and knowledge about classroom practices influence how they interpret new pedagogical ideas. A representation of this unit of analysis is shown in Figure 3.1 and suggests that the site of learning is like a 'box' in the head of an individual.

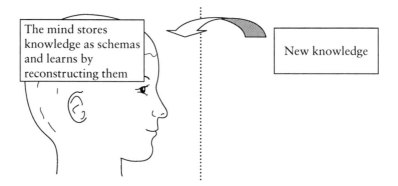

Figure 3.1   A representation of a cognitive unit of analysis as 'in the head'.

A cognitive learning perspective has been highlighted in views called 'constructivist' (von Glasersfeld 1984, 1987, 1989). A key element of a constructivist perspective is that knowledge is actively stored in the mind, as 'knowledge is not passively received but actively built up by the cogniz-ing subject; the function of cognition is adaptive and serves the organiza-tion of the experiential world, not the discovery of ontological reality' (von Glasersfeld 1987: 37). Constructivism has provided a strong research plat-form to explain children's learning, especially the influence of an individual's prior knowledge in making his or her own meaning. Research in science education has shown that, once children generate their own understandings about a concept, they tend to maintain their beliefs in spite of instruction from a teacher, leading to terms such as 'children's science', 'alternative conceptions' and 'misconceptions' (Erickson 1979; Osborne and Wittrock 1983; Osborne and Freyberg 1985; Driver and Oldham 1986; Faire and Cosgrove 1988; Gunstone 1990; Driver *et al.* 1994).

Constructivism has also played a role in teacher learning, as exemplified in the notion of reflection, which has become popular for teachers over the last 20 years. Dewey (1933) originally proposed reflection as a way of rethinking a problematic situation. Schön (1983, 1987) rejuvenated the term and distinguished between deliberate reflection after an experience (reflection-on-action) and reflection that is more spontaneous (reflection-in-action). Munby and Russell (1992) explained the difference between these two terms:

> Reflection-on-action refers to the systematic and deliberate thinking back over one's actions that characterizes much of what we do when we pause after an action and attend to what we believed has

occurred . . . Reflection-in-action is Schön's term for those interactions with experience that result in the often sudden and unanticipated ways in which we come to *see experience differently*.

(Munby and Russell 1992: 3; emphasis in original)

Reflection has been called the 'cornerstone of professional development' (Baird 1992) and has been a central element of many professional development programmes (Grimmett and Erickson 1988; Baird *et al.* 1991; Sparkes 1991; Barnes 1992; Brookfield 1995; Hoban 2000a). The action of reflection is consistent with a cognitive perspective, as it is the rethinking of experience that provides personal meaning and hence learning. In particular, one of the cornerstones of teachers' reflective learning is their existing knowledge and beliefs about classroom instruction:

Learning of all persons, including students and teachers, is highly influenced by their existing knowledge and beliefs because learning is an active process in which people interpret experiences through their existing conceptual structures to modify and expand their knowledge.

(Putnam and Borko 1997: 1240)

Several anomalies, however, have been identified in terms of a cognitive perspective on learning. Schoenfeld (1999) contended that cognitive perspectives have made headway in explaining how personal knowledge construction occurs, but have made little impact on how identity is constructed and how social interactions influence the individual members of a community. This perspective also does not explain how an individual learns completely new knowledge about which no prior knowledge exists (Solomon 1994). If learning occurs through the reconstruction of prior knowledge, how do children or adults generate completely new understandings? This has been called the 'learning paradox' inferring that you cannot investigate what you don't know, which was first postulated by Plato in his dialogue *Meno* (Prawat 1999). Another anomaly of a cognitive perspective is that it does not explain why some people can perform sophisticated mental functioning in an authentic setting, but not repeat these processes in a classroom setting. Studies involving people conducting calculations in a weight watchers' class (Lave 1988a), selling candy in a market place (Saxe 1988) and learning to iron as apprentice tailors (Lave 1988b) have shown that learning is often context-bound in an authentic situation. These studies promote an alternative unit of analysis that rejects a cognitive perspective on learning as 'in the head'.

A *situated perspective on learning*

In contrast, a situated perspective emphasizes the importance of the situation or context for learning based on the assumption that the thinking of an individual cannot be separated from its context. A sociocultural or socio-historical perspective on learning has been portrayed in various forms, including situated cognition (Brown *et al.* 1989) and situated learning (Lave and Wenger 1991). Putnam and Borko (1997) recently contended that teacher learning also has a social and situated dimension. They suggested that teachers learn a great deal from the social interactions of 'discourse communities' in which they share experiences and also learn in context as they experiment with practice in their own classrooms.

A situated perspective evolved from sociology and anthropology assuming that the unit of analysis or focus for learning is the 'individual-in-social-action' (Minick 1989). What distinguishes this phrase are the hyphens between the words indicating a blurring of individual and context. These suggest that the learning does not take place in different parts of the environment (mind or context), but is shared or 'distributed – stretched over, not divided among – mind, body, activity, and culturally organized settings (which include actors)' (Lave 1988b: 1). Wertsch (1991) described how this unit of analysis is different from a cognitive perspective:

> High mental functioning is inherently situated in social interactional, cultural, institutional, and historical contexts. Such a tenet contrasts with approaches that assume, implicitly or explicitly, that it is possible to examine mental processes such as thinking or memory, independently of the sociocultural setting in which individuals and groups function.
> (Wertsch 1991: 86)

Lave and Wenger (1991) described all learning as situated using the term 'legitimate peripheral participation' to explain how learning in a community is different from a cognitive perspective, as 'we emphasise the significance of shifting the analytical focus from the individual as learner to learning as participation in the social world, and from the concept of cognitive process to the more-encompassing view of social practice' (p. 43). Lave and Wenger's assumptions concerning learning as socially situated in practice have implications for their conceptualization of education. They described five studies of communities, including the apprenticeships of midwives, tailors, naval quartermasters, meat cutters and reformed alcoholics, claiming that 'the important point concerning learning is one of access to practice as a resource for learning, rather than instruction' (p. 85). In these five examples of communities of practice, the emphasis is on learning through participation in an authentic activity, not from direct teaching by an instructor. In this respect, participation in the practice of the community becomes the 'potential curriculum' with the circulation of information among the participants as a 'condition for the effectiveness of learning' (p. 93). A representation of a situated unit of analysis is shown in Figure 3.2 and is similar to a 'blanket' that spreads across a whole context.

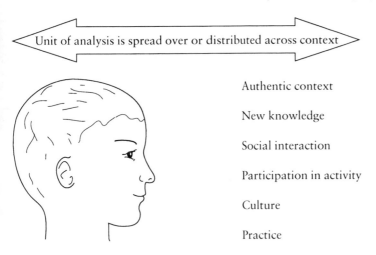

Figure 3.2 A representation of a situated unit of analysis as the 'individual-in-social-action'.

Anderson *et al.* (1996) challenged the key assumptions of a situated perspective by identifying four anomalies:

1 Although some learning is contextual, this is not always the case and there are many studies which show that skills can be taught without being in an authentic setting.
2 Although situated learning claims that knowledge cannot be transferred from one context to another, this is not always the case – different amounts of knowledge can be transferred according to the amount of practice and type of representation.
3 Training does not have to occur in an authentic setting as long as the training is combined with concrete examples.
4 Instruction does not always have to occur in complex, social environments; some training is best taught as component skills and integrated with practice of the whole task within a social setting.

Salomon (1993) also challenged the extreme claims of a situated perspective on learning. He argued that this perspective negates the importance of personal reflection and cannot explain how a community generates its own collective knowledge and extends that knowledge. He contended that the collective knowledge displayed in a community of practice must be related to the knowledge that individuals bring to the group. Moreover, how does this knowledge which is distributed across the community change? Salomon (1993) suggested that the collective knowledge of a community of learners is a '*snapshot frozen in time*' (p. 119; emphasis in original) unless there are a variety of inputs into the community from individuals, new technologies or new settings. Hence, it is likely that the information of a community grows when new members join who hold additional knowledge that is stored in their minds.

Bridging the dichotomy between learning perspectives

Shulman (1988) argued that a dichotomy is sometimes useful for sharpening opposing lines of argument, but the most appropriate view is often a balance between two extremes that considers the virtues of both sides. In support, Schoenfeld (1999) stated that both cognitive and situated perspectives provide valuable insights into learning processes, but both are selective and display tunnel vision. A cognitive perspective highlights the importance of personal conditions for learning, such as prior knowledge, and a situated perspective highlights the importance of social and contexual conditions for learning. But in maintaining their high ground, both perspectives have anomalies that cannot be explained from their exclusive stance and underplay the dynamics of learning when personal, social and contexual conditions interact.

Putnam and Borko (1997) stated that teacher learning can be informed by multiple research perspectives on cognition – the personal nature of knowledge and beliefs, the social nature of cognition, the situated nature of cognition and the distributed nature of cognition. They proposed six conditions for teacher learning that are underpinned by insights from this eclectic approach to different perspectives:

1 teachers should be treated as active learners who construct their own knowledge (from the personal nature of cognition);
2 teachers should be empowered and treated as professionals (from the social nature of cognition);
3 teacher education should be situated in classroom practice (from the situated nature of cognition);
4 teacher educators should treat teachers as they expect teachers to treat students (from the social nature of cognition);
5 teachers need to consider what ideas or content is essential in their learning and gain different expertise (from the distributed nature of cognition); and
6 teachers need to use a range of tools to keep track of the vast information available (from the distributed nature of cognition).

Although Putnam and Borko (1997) drew on different learning perspectives to describe teacher learning, they did not attempt to link them together into a coherent theoretical framework.

Theoretical pragmatism

Some researchers have argued for a pragmatic approach to learning, suggesting that either a cognitive perspective or a situated perspective on learning can be used depending on 'what works'. For example, Cobb (1994) suggested that we should be pragmatic about theories and use whichever one suits a particular purpose or use them in combination with one perspective constituting the 'figure' and the other the 'ground' of the learning process: 'I argue that the sociocultural perspective informs theories of the conditions for the possibility of learning, whereas theories developed from the constructivist perspective focus on what students learn and the processes by which they do so' (Cobb 1994: 13). Sfard (1998) also claimed that we need to use both perspectives. She related a cognitive perspective to an 'acquisition metaphor' and a situated perspective to a 'participation metaphor', suggesting that we need both metaphors to broaden our understandings of the complexity of learning. In agreement, Greeno (1997) defined learning from a situated perspective as 'improved participation in interactive systems' (p. 12), while maintaining that research should use both perspectives.

Some research articles have attempted to find common ground between the two different perspectives. Anderson *et al.* (2000) noted that educational research should be informed by both learning perspectives, but that 'a high priority should be given to research that progresses toward unifying the diverse perspectives within which we currently work' (p. 13). Recently, Cobb and Bowers (1999) argued for an approach to learning that complements both perspectives:

> Regarding units of analysis, the approach we take admits an explicit focus on individual students' reasoning. However, rather than treating that reasoning as solely an internal mental phenomenon, we view it as an act of participating in communal mathematical practices . . . Cast in this way, the relation between individual students' reasoning and communal practices is viewed as reflexive in that students contribute to the evolution of the classroom practices that constitute the immediate social situation of their mathematical development they learn.
>
> (Cobb and Bowers 1999: 9)

Similarly, in the literature for adult learning, Merriam and Caffarella (1999) recently called for learning to be viewed through multiple perspectives, as 'the psychological perspective, which has been used as the major lens through which educators of adults have viewed development, can be widened to include the other lens of biological, sociocultural, and integrated perspectives' (p. 135). Rather than taking a 'what works' approach from either a cognitive or situated perspective and ignoring their anomalies, there is a different way of conceptualizing learning that uses a new lens to draw together the tenets of each perspective into a coherent framework.

A systems unit of analysis for teacher learning

Using two different units of analysis for learning is like looking through different lenses to examine the same event. Both cognitive and situated perspectives are socially constructed for analysing learning processes and both are useful for understanding particular influences, but focus on different aspects. Taking a cognitive perspective is like using a close-up lens to observe the fine detail of an individual's learning, but this zooming in misses out on the surrounding context. Alternatively, taking a situated perspective is like using a wide-angle lens to examine learning in a broad social context, but misses out on individual details. Accordingly, the richness gained from studying the learning generated from the interplay between these two perspectives is not fully appreciated. Instead, what we need is a more flexible lens that takes into account individual processes as well as social and contextual influences.

Salomon (1993) and Salomon and Perkins (1998) believed that both cognitive and distributed (situated) cognitions propose extreme points of view. They contended that learning should not be seen as a dichotomy because 'the issue of where cognitions reside, particularly when discussed in an educational context, cannot be dealt with in an either (in one's head)/or (distributed) fashion' (Salomon and Perkins 1998: 111). They claimed that individual cognition cannot be denied, but it is not the full picture, as individuals think in interaction with their social, cultural and physical surroundings. Therefore, in any context, individual cognition influences the distribution of group knowledge and vice versa:

> The claim that individuals' representations totally account for their intellectual activity is an overstatement as much as is the claim that partnerships with tools or peers totally account for the quality of the process or that the activity itself fully accounts for it. Different factors participate in the process interactively, although their specific influence may vary under different circumstances.
>
> (Salomon 1993: 125)

Hence, there is a relationship between personal, social and contextual elements so that individuals influence each other, the context and vice versa. The example Salomon (1993) provided was that a person can practise basketball by himself or herself at home or in a stadium with a team. Practising alone does not involve as much social interaction as does practising with others, but in both cases social learning influences personal learning but to

different extents. Individual thinking is, therefore, influenced by social participation and vice versa in a reciprocal relationship similar to what Bandura
(1978, 1986) called 'reciprocal determinism':

> By their actions, people play a role in creating the social milieu and
> other circumstances that arise in their daily transactions. This . . .
> psychological functioning involves a continuous reciprocal interaction
> between behavioural, cognitive and environmental influences.
>
> (Bandura 1978: 345)

When individual, social and contextual conditions for learning interact to
enhance each other, it has been called a 'reciprocal spiral relationship'
(Salomon and Perkins 1998: 18), meaning that a synergy is created by their
mutual influence in a 'learning system'.

Focusing on the relationships among elements in a learning system is
consistent with a 'systems thinking' approach to learning. Therefore, in
any context, many elements mutually influence each other, similar to the
interconnections of a spider web. This mindset challenges the traditional
dichotomy between a unit of analysis as 'in the head' (cognitive perspective)
or as the 'individual-in-social-action' (situated perspective). Although Salomon (1993) did not name an alternative unit of analysis, I believe a phrase
such as the 'individual in related action' represents a way of analysing
learning focusing on the relationships between learner and social context.
Learning is therefore distributed *among* influences on learning, rather than
across a social setting (as in a situated perspective) or *within* an individual
(as in a cognitive perspective). This is not a new theory of learning, but a
way of thinking that brings together the key ideas of existing learning perspectives and highlights the interplay between them. A new unit of analysis
such as the 'individual in related action', therefore, is a different way to
look at learning processes and has fewer anomalies than either a cognitive or
a situated perspective, while at the same time encompassing the key tenets
of both.

There are, however, three important differences when using this new unit
of analysis. First, it acknowledges that some cognition does occur 'in the
head', but it does not claim that 'the head' is an exclusive site, as there
are other influences that contribute to an individual's learning and vice
versa. The transfer of learning from one context to another, therefore,
can occur because some of the learning is carried 'in the head', although it
may not represent all the interactions that have occurred. Second, there are
no hyphens between the words as in the unit of analysis from a situated
perspective, since a systems unit of analysis does not represent an 'all or
nothing' response to learning. This means that the learning of an individual
is enhanced if there are other influences related to the prior knowledge of
that individual.

Third, what is important is that relationships, which influence learning, can be different and identified. For instance, a person may be part of a community of practice, but relate to some people more than others. In this respect, an individual can copy or 'steal' required knowledge or skills from particular individuals within a community (Brown and Duguid 1992). This differs from a situated perspective, which considers the whole context as the focus for analysis and fails to distinguish between specific social, cultural, physical and political influences. Using this new unit of analysis as the 'individual in related action' focuses on the *relationships* between different elements and acknowledges that individual learning is influenced by different actions, such as a group discussion, or a practice setting, or by tools. Any context, therefore, can be viewed as a learning system with multiple relationships among people, the setting and artifacts, much like a spider web, but not all need to be operational at one time or to the same extent. In this sense, the meaning of 'action' is anything that provides insights or understanding, such as personal reflection, reading a book, putting ideas into practice, listening to a lecture, watching television, using a computer or public dialogue (Coulter 1999). This notion of action contrasts with an argument from a situated perspective that learning needs to occur in a 'community of practice'. A representation of a systems 'individual in related action' unit of analysis is shown in Figure 3.3. Note that the emphasis is on the relationships between the elements (unbroken lines) that are interconnected like a spider web rather than the elements themselves (broken lines). This unit of analysis, therefore, is not only 'in the head' or distributed across the 'individual-in-social-action', but focuses on relationships between and among elements.

Implications for teacher learning

Different perspectives on learning have been well theorized and present valuable insights into learning processes, but these sometimes tend to be narrow minded. The main implication of using a systems unit of analysis to resolve the dichotomy between cognitive and situated perspectives is that it provides a basis for linking the key ideas from both perspectives. As such, a systems unit of analysis can be the basis for a framework to underpin long-term teacher learning using a combination of personal, social and contextual conditions. Similarly, Putnam and Borko (1997) emphasized that the nature of teacher learning is not unique to one theoretical perspective and a variety is needed to create learning environments that can deal with 'the complexity of teaching and the ill-structured (fuzzy) nature of pedagogical problems' (p. 1263). They contend that long-term teacher learning could have inputs from four perspectives, including personal cognition, the social nature of cognition, the situated nature of cognition and the distributed nature of cognition:

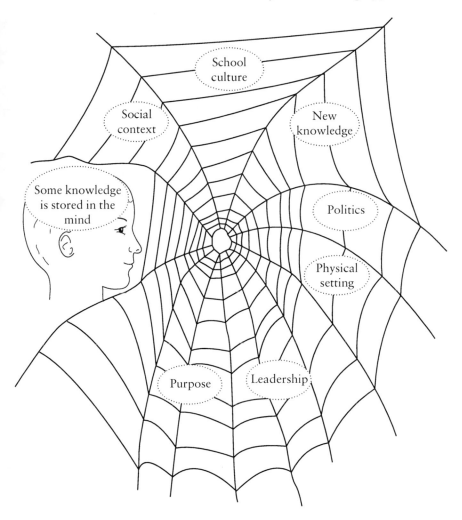

Figure 3.3 A representation of a systems unit of analysis as the 'individual in related action'.

It may be that a variety of contexts holds the best promise for fostering powerful, multidimensional changes in teachers' thinking and practices. Further research is needed to better understand the complex dynamics of these multifaceted approaches to teacher learning.

(Putnam and Borko 2000: 7)

The key, however, for sustainability in teacher learning is the interplay between different conditions that is established by having a connection or relationship between them. There are a variety of conditions for teacher learning that can be derived from different perspectives and integrated into a coherent framework:

Reflection
This derives from a cognitive perspective in which participants rethink their practice to learn from their experiences and helps them to cope with similar situations in the future. Reflection is a process that helps teachers to gain insights into the 'big picture' on the patterns of change resulting from a dynamic, interactive learning system. Fullan (1993, 1999) argued that it is only through reflection at the personal, group and organizational levels that teachers will begin to question their practice and think differently about teaching and learning. This notion of reflection originated in the writings of John Dewey as a way of thinking about a problematic situation that needs to be resolved, as 'the function of reflective thought is, therefore, to transform a situation in which there is experienced obscurity, doubt, conflict, disturbance of some sort, into a situation that is clear, coherent, settled, harmonious' (Dewey 1933: 100–1).

Schön (1983, 1987) saw reflection not only as a way of thinking, but as a hallmark of being a professional. He contended that there was a 'crisis of confidence' in professional knowledge because the workplace is not a static environment. It is inappropriate, therefore, to treat teaching as a craft based on a prescriptive knowledge base to apply in a recipe-type fashion to practice. Instead, professionals need to recognize the 'complexity, uncertainty, instability, uniqueness, and value-conflict' (Schön 1983: 39) of a work setting and have reflective conversations about a situation that is consistent with a conception of teaching as an art or profession. Schön (1983, 1987) identified two types of reflection – reflection-in-action, through which professionals make almost subconscious decisions about the best use of their knowledge built up from previous experiences, and reflection-on-action, which is deliberate reflection after experience. As such, the framing of a problematic situation is a catalyst for reflection and change:

> To achieve change, teachers need to discover that their existing frame for understanding what happens in their classes is only one of several possible ones, and this, according to Schön, is likely to be achieved only when the teachers themselves reflect critically upon what they do and its results.
>
> (Barnes 1992: 17)

Community
The social nature of learning derives from a situated perspective and supports teachers sharing experiences as another important condition for teacher

learning. There are many examples in the education literature of long-term change efforts involving collaboration between teachers and teacher educators who form a community to meet regularly and share ideas about teaching practice (Baird and Mitchell 1987; Cochran-Smith and Lytle 1993; Bell and Gilbert 1994; Darling-Hammond 1994; Mitchell and Erickson 1995; Minnes Brandes and Erickson 1998). When participants share their ideas with colleagues and listen to different perspectives, they gain a deeper understanding of the meaning of their own personal experiences. This social condition for learning was originally highlighted by Dewey (1916), who defined the notion of community as 'sharing in each other's activities and in each other's experiences because they have common ends and purposes' (p. 75). More recently, the notion of sharing ideas in a community has been used in various educational settings, such as school classrooms (Bereiter and Scardamalia 1993), professional development programmes for teachers and teacher educators (Baird and Mitchell 1987; Bell and Gilbert 1994; Cochran-Smith and Lytle 1993) and for teacher training in professional development schools (Darling-Hammond 1994).

Action
This condition evolves from a situated perspective and promotes learning in an authentic context with participants trying out their ideas about their practice, which have been generated in light of personal reflection and community discussions. Learning by doing or experimenting with ideas in practice is also not a new concept. It was one of the main tenets of Dewey's (1938) theory of learning through experience and was later highlighted in Kolb's (1984) experiential learning cycle. The implication is that putting ideas into action gives them more meaning because of knowing the consequences of the action. More recently, the importance of an authentic context for learning was highlighted in views on learning, including situated cognition (Brown *et al.* 1989) and situated learning (Lave and Wenger 1991). Both views emphasize the importance of context in learning and the social aspects of learning.

Conceptual inputs
When teachers reflect on their practice, share ideas as a community and put their ideas into practice, they gain a deeper understanding of what they do. But their thinking is limited to the experiences of the group and the actions within their own setting. To move beyond their experiences, they need new ideas to extend their understanding of their practice. Huberman (1995) called these alternative perspectives 'conceptual inputs' that enrich community discussions by introducing ideas beyond the way the participants usually frame their practice. This input of new ideas helps teachers to 'think outside the square' they teach in. Examples of knowledge sources

that can be used as conceptual inputs include educational research articles or books (Bell and Gilbert 1994; Richardson 1994), the views of teacher educators (Baird *et al.* 1987; Darling-Hammond 1994) and information from professional journals, professional organizations, television programmes or market research (Cusins 1995).

Student feedback

Another key condition for learning is information about the outcomes of a change effort. In an educational sense, it is important for a learning system to have feedback loops to monitor the directions generated by the system (Senge 1990; Capra 1996). This is particularly important when a system has specific educational goals and intends to 'progress' in a particular direction. A major source of feedback for teachers when they try out new ideas is data from their own students. Such information gives teachers a sense of whether what they are trying is working or not and, consequently, this feedback is likely to drive teacher learning. Brookfield (1995) explained that to be a 'critically reflective teacher' means to 'identify and scrutinize the assumptions that undergird how we work' (p. xii). One way to do this is to seek feedback from students by encouraging them to use learning journals, participant learning portfolios, questionnaires and by actively seeking their honest comments.

Independently, these conditions for teacher learning – reflection, community, action, conceptual inputs and student feedback – are not new, but linking them together as a framework increases their potential to underpin long-term professional learning (Hoban 1996). The new unit of analysis proposed in this chapter as the 'individual in related action' provides a theoretical basis for creating such a framework. Importantly, when using this new unit of analysis, different conditions for learning need to relate to each other to enable interplay between them and produce a system for learning. The establishment of such a framework requires that teachers reflect on their own practice *and* share ideas with colleagues *and* experiment with their own teaching *and* look for conceptual inputs to extend their thinking *and* seek feedback from students. Another condition for teacher learning is that it helps if teachers have a *conception of teaching* as an art or profession that provides a motivation or perceived need to have a better understanding of their practice as explained in Chapter 2. Finally, the potential for these conditions to interact and establish a framework for long-term teacher learning is strongly dependent on having *time* for these conditions to operate. This means that time needs to be structured into a school timetable for teachers to reflect and share their insights. In sum, taking a systems thinking approach to teacher learning with the 'individual in related action' as a unit of analysis provides a theoretical basis for linking existing conditions for teacher learning that derive from different perspectives. Part 2 of this book provides examples of how such a theoretical framework to underpin teachers' long-term professional learning may support educational change.

Conclusion

Historically, the field of learning has been fragmented with insights from two main perspectives, with each having a different unit of analysis or focus for learning. A situated perspective, with a unit of analysis as the 'individual-in-social-action', disregards important personal influences such as prior knowledge and motivation to learn. Conversely, a cognitive perspective, with a unit of analysis of 'in the head', disregards important contextual and social influences on learning. Both perspectives provide insights into the learning process, but present extreme views and have anomalies that cannot be explained from their exclusive stance. This fragmentation in learning theory has resulted in the inability to develop a coherent theoretical framework to guide long-term teacher learning and neglects the richness gained from fostering interplay between different learning conditions. The lack of such a framework is one reason why many efforts for educational change have produced disappointing results. Alternatively, a systems unit of analysis as the 'individual in related action' incorporates the central tenets of both perspectives by focusing on the relationships between and among personal, social and contextual conditions for teacher learning. Taking this systems thinking approach creates possibilities for a new theoretical framework to guide long-term teacher learning and increases the likelihood that the complex processes of educational change can be supported.

Part 2

A theoretical framework for a professional learning system

The main argument presented in Part 1 of this book is that different paradigms or world views lead to different understandings about the nature of teaching, how teachers learn and the process of educational change. A mechanistic paradigm discussed in Chapter 1 promotes a conception of teaching as a craft as well as a belief that educational change is a linear process that can be supported by a one-step approach to teacher learning. Consistent with these beliefs, the term 'professional development programme' implies 'training' teachers by providing them with prescriptive knowledge in a workshop to add to their existing knowledge base. It suggests that teacher learning is a linear step-by-step process and assumes that teachers will embrace new content without taking into account other contextual issues, such as how their classroom or school already operates. Learning does occur in a professional development programme because teachers sometimes gain a better understanding of what they already do, but a one-off workshop tends to reinforce existing practices rather than transform them, which is consistent with the notion of 'single-loop learning' (Argyris and Schön 1974).

In contrast, a paradigm for change based on complexity theory as discussed in Chapter 2 promotes a conception of teaching as an art as well as a belief that educational change behaves as a complex system and needs to be supported by a framework to promote long-term teacher learning. This framework is needed because changing classroom practice is a non-linear process that occurs over a long period of time and so needs to be supported by a combination of personal, social and contextual conditions for teacher learning that interrelate as a system. When teachers begin to change their practice, it disturbs the balance of their existing classroom system that is similar to working on 'the edge of chaos' (Waldrop 1992) until equilibrium or order is again established. The learning encouraged is often *transformative*, resulting in a change in teaching practices, and *generative*, with teachers producing new knowledge about, or artefacts for, their own practice. During this process, new ideas are constantly arising, being publicly discussed with colleagues and tested in classrooms with feedback from students. This type of learning generates new ways to rethink and change existing practice and is consistent with the notion of 'double-loop learning' (Argyris and Schön 1994).

This change in mindset from a mechanistic paradigm that emphasizes 'training' and linear learning to a complexity paradigm that is 'educative' involving non-linear learning has implications for the terms used to describe the process. First, the word 'learning' is preferred to 'development' because learning is essentially non-linear, whereas 'development' suggests a linear step-by-step process. Second, the term 'system' is preferred to 'programme' because a system implies a combination of conditions that interrelate to support learning, whereas 'programme' implies a prescriptive plan of events. Therefore, when promoting long-term teacher learning based on a complexity paradigm, the phrase 'professional learning system' (PLS) is preferable to 'professional development programme'. A professional development programme, therefore, is usually a one-off workshop or an isolated professional development day based on limited conditions for teacher learning – the presentation of new *content* over a relatively short *time*. In contrast, the design of a professional learning system is long-term and encapsulates multiple conditions for teacher learning that interrelate as a system. A systems unit of analysis explained in Chapter 3, such as the 'individual in related action', is useful in theorizing about this type of learning because it focuses on the relationships among the conditions as well as the conditions themselves.

A theoretical framework for a professional learning system is based on a combination of the following conditions for teacher learning that need to complement each other to support educational change as a complex system:

- A *conception of teaching* as an art or profession, indicating a dynamic relationship among students, other teachers, school, classroom, curriculum and context. Because of these interactions, there is always uncertainty and ambiguity in changing teaching practice.
- *Reflection* is important, as teachers need to become aware of why they teach the way they do and to focus on understanding the patterns of change resulting from the dynamic relationships in which they are involved.
- Teachers need a *purpose* for learning to foster a desire for change and so content should be negotiated.
- The *time frame* is long-term, as changing teaching means adjusting the balance among many aspects of the existing classroom system.

- A sense of *community* is necessary so that teachers trust each other to share experiences such that topics for inquiry and debate may extend over several months or longer. As a result of this progressive discourse, teachers theorize and discussions are generative so that new ideas are always evolving.
- Teachers need to experiment with their ideas in *action* to test what works or does not work in their classrooms.
- A variety of knowledge sources are needed as *conceptual inputs* to extend the experiences of the participants.
- *Student feedback* is needed in response to the ideas being tried out in the classroom.

On their own, each condition is unlikely to sustain teacher learning, but it is their combination that establishes a framework to encourage long-term teacher learning. Accordingly, opportunities for teacher learning are optimized when the maximum number of conditions for teacher learning are in place and relate to each other as a system to establish interplay among the conditions. This interplay is dynamic and provides a deeper understanding of why we teach the way we do by encouraging the testing out of new ideas in conjunction with staff discussions and student feedback. It is the role of a *facilitator* to help establish conditions for teacher learning as well as ensuring that they complement each other. A representation of the conditions for teacher learning in a professional learning system is shown in Figure P.3.1. Note that the emphasis is on the relationships among the conditions, as indicated by the unbroken lines of the spider web to represent their interconnectedness and synergistic effect.

The next three chapters demonstrate this theoretical framework with case studies of teacher learning projects highlighting some of the conditions identified in Figure P.3.1. Although there are features unique to each project, there are also some common conditions underpinning their designs and these will be explained at the beginning of each chapter. As well as describing how each project works as a system, each chapter will focus on one aspect to gain a deeper understanding of its role in sustaining teacher learning. Chapter 4 describes a professional learning system (PLS) called 'The Oberon project' involving three high school science teachers in Australia that lasted over four years. The chapter focuses on the *non-linear process* of change that results from the dynamic interplay of multiple conditions for teacher learning. Chapter 5 describes 'The Frameworks project', which involved elementary teachers in the USA learning about aspects of literacy, focusing on the role of the *facilitator* in supporting the relationships among the conditions. Chapter 6 describes 'The Christchurch project', which involved elementary teachers in New Zealand learning to use information and communication technologies (ICT), focusing on the importance of *reflection* that helps teachers to make connections and monitor patterns of change in their practice.

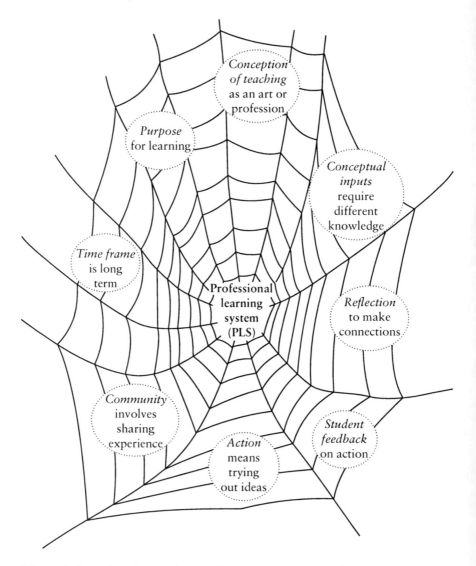

Figure P.3.1　Conditions for teacher learning in a professional learning system (PLS).

four

The dynamics of professional learning: the Oberon High School Science project

Whatever factors, variables, and ambience are
conducive for the growth, development, and
self-regard of a school's staff are precisely those that
are crucial to obtaining the same consequences for
students in a classroom.

(Sarason, 1990: 154)

In this chapter, I demonstrate how using the theoretical framework of a professional learning system (PLS) results in a type of teacher learning that is dynamic and non-linear. For a PLS to function, there needs to be multiple conditions for teacher learning that interrelate to reinforce each other and it is this constant interplay among the conditions that provides dynamism and continuity in the learning process. If the conditions do not interrelate, there is little chance of any interplay and hence of sustained learning occurring. This chapter explains the dynamic nature of professional learning and is exemplified in a case study of a PLS involving three science teachers in a small Australian high school that lasted for four years.

The process of professional learning

In a conventional professional development programme, an innovation is usually presented to teachers in a workshop or a one-off professional development day with the expectation that it is implemented in a linear step-by-step process with little back-up support. However, this implementation process is usually short-lived because of the lack of conditions to support ongoing teacher learning. Often teachers are not reflective, the ideas being presented are not in context with existing classroom practice, there is little collegial support back in the school and there is little time to modify relevant aspects of classroom practice. Because of the absence of conditions for learning, there is little chance of any support being generated to promote educational change.

In contrast, in a PLS, any major change that is introduced to teachers or proposed by them occurs in a learning environment incorporating multiple conditions for teacher learning. These conditions provide support for the change process so that teachers can adjust different elements of their class-room system – such as pedagogy, assessment, classroom resources and timetable arrangements – over time. As all of these are related, changing one aspect of the classroom system often means changing others. Because of this interaction, change usually does not occur in a linear, step-by-step fashion. Instead, the process of educational change is non-linear, involving the adjustment of different aspects of classroom practice in a back and forth iterative way as one change inevitably influences others. And this change process is not easy or short-term and so requires a framework for long-term teacher learning to be established. Fullan (1999) recently described how such a framework for teacher learning can provide an infra-structure to support educational reform:

> When all is said and done, the capacity for transferability in a social system is a function of the quality of the infrastructure. The more the infrastructure builds in continuous learning, generates accountability data, promotes feedback, stimulates innovation and so on, the more the system is capable of large-scale reform. In effect, strong infrastruc-tures access tacit and explicit knowledge on a continuous basis and make it widely available.
>
> (Fullan 1999: 75)

In short, it is the presence of multiple conditions for teacher learning that relate to each other in a PLS that establishes dynamic interactions among them to underpin long-term teacher learning and support the non-linear process of change.

Generating learning cycles

A theoretical framework that incorporates multiple learning conditions can establish a continuous process that sometimes results in cycles of learning. Huberman (1995) identified four cycles that vary according to whether they involve an individual or a group or whether alternative perspectives on teaching practices are included:

1 a closed individual cycle occurs when a teacher learns by himself or herself as they perceive a problem, experiment and assess the result;

2 an open individual cycle occurs when a teacher perceives a problem, seeks the opinion of others, experiments with ideas and assesses the result;
3 a closed collective cycle occurs when a group of teachers meet regularly to share their personal reflections, experiment with ideas and develop new methods of teaching; and
4 an open collective cycle occurs when a group of teachers meet regularly to publicly share personal reflections, experiment with ideas and seek opinions on educational issues from outside the group (conceptual inputs).

The process of learning in an open collective cycle, which may involve action research (Lewin 1946; Carr and Kemmis 1986), is essentially non-linear due to the combination of conditions for learning:

> In effect, the kind of problem solving built into this cycle *assumes* that the process of learning, experimentation, and change will be moderately complex, novel, ambiguous, contradictory, and conflicting. *These are in effect, the ideal conditions for significant learning, be it for adults or children.*
>
> (Huberman 1995: 206; emphasis in original)

Figure 4.1 shows the features of an open learning cycle.

Huberman's open collective cycle is similar to a PLS with a combination of related learning conditions involving personal reflection, sharing ideas with colleagues, making public their personal beliefs, the consideration of conceptual inputs and putting ideas into action. In particular, it is important for a group in this cycle to share ideas *and* have conceptual inputs that interrupt and extend their thinking, which Ross and Regan (1993) called 'sharing with dissonance', whereby the ambiguities and alternative perspectives for teaching are made public.

There are, however, some differences between Huberman's open collective cycle and a PLS. First, the process of professional learning is more dynamic in a PLS because the learning conditions often do not operate one at a time and are not in a sequence within a cycle, as shown in Figure 4.1. A cyclical pattern can occur in a PLS, but the conditions for learning often operate simultaneously and not in a specific order. Second, this dynamic type of professional learning does not happen spontaneously. It needs to be managed, at least initially, until teachers understand how they learn through the process. For this reason, there is a need for a facilitator or a group leader who understands the process of non-linear learning and who can provide conceptual inputs to extend the experiences of the participants. Also, a PLS is not something that all teachers readily engage in or even see a purpose for participation. This is particularly the case when teachers have a conception of teaching as a 'craft' that they have mastered and hence do

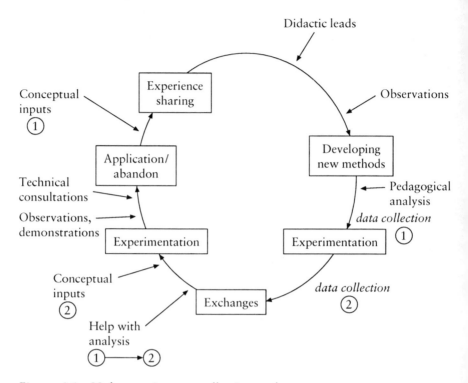

Figure 4.1   Huberman's open collective cycle.

not have a perceived need to learn. Also, the type of learning in a PLS is intensive and time-consuming because it is ongoing and may not suit particular teachers at certain phases in their career (Sikes 1985).

Before teachers are willing to participate in learning cycles, it is helpful if they first develop a conception of teaching as an art or profession. But this is easier said than done when a teacher has a mindset that focuses on the delivery of content using set strategies consistent with a conception of teaching as a craft. Perhaps these teachers first need to reflect on their practice to identify why they teach the way they do and then to share this with others to become aware that there are other ways to think about their practice. Once teachers develop an awareness of the complexity of teaching, they are more likely to become engaged in long-term projects that explore the problematic nature of their work, and it is the confirming or disconfirming of personal beliefs within a collaborative environment that provides insights for personal theory building. But this involvement assumes that the principal has considered how to organize the school so that it is structured to be a learning environment for the teachers.

Creating synergies

What is unique to a PLS and makes this type of learning distinct from a conventional professional development programme is that learning is non-linear because of the dynamic interplay among multiple conditions of teacher learning. A learning environment, therefore, is created from more than just the sum of the conditions; it is the connections between them that is essential. For the conditions to interrelate, there needs to be a 'congruence' or 'fit' between them so that they have a common thread, with each one reinforcing the others. This synergy does not result from the sum of the conditions alone (e.g. reflection + community + action + purpose + time + student feedback + conceptual inputs + a conception of teaching), but rather results from their dynamic interplay, which is more like multiplication (e.g. reflection × community × action × purpose × time × student feedback × conceptual inputs × a conception of teaching). Hence, the interrelationships among the conditions cause a 'multiplier' effect that is greater than the sum of the conditions alone creating a synergistic effect (Lawler 1992). The cause of the multiplier effect comes from the reciprocity among the conditions such that the more reflective a teacher is, the more they contribute to discussions and seek student feedback, which further enhances their reflection resulting in cumulative and continuous learning.

In contrast, there is usually no multiplier effect in a conventional professional development programme when unreflective teachers attend a workshop about an aspect of teaching that is unrelated to their existing practice. Worse still, if teachers think they have mastered their craft, they may not even consider themselves as learners in the first place. Conversely, when reflective teachers regularly share their beliefs with colleagues and seek other opinions to improve their practice, the likely outcome is that they think beyond their 'comfort zone'. In particular, their thinking is challenged when conceptual inputs are introduced in context with the topic of discussion to extend the experiences of the participants and open them to the possibilities for change. This type of professional learning is similar to Argyris and Schön's (1994) notion of 'double-loop learning', which is based on a level of trust and preparedness to take a risk with ideas within a group of learners:

> As individuals come to feel more psychological success and more likelihood of mutual confirmation or disconfirmation, they are more likely to manifest higher self-awareness and acceptance, which leads to offering valid information, which again leads to feelings of psychological success. As groups manifest higher degrees of openness, experimentation, and emphasis on individuality, individuals in them will feel freer to provide valid information that will tend, in turn, to enhance these group characteristics. As individuals feel higher degrees of freedom of

choice, trust and authenticity, they are more likely to test their assumptions publicly, which is, in turn, likely to enable others to feel higher degrees of freedom of choice, trust and authenticity – all of which makes everyone more willing to give valid information that enables individuals to test their assumptions.

(Argyris and Schön 1994: 91–2)

As such, double-loop learning is not 'self-sealing' that confirms existing practice and maintains the *status quo*, but is 'transformative' (Day 1999), facilitating educational change in a non-linear, dynamic process that is similar to the notion of learning on 'the edge of chaos' (Waldrop 1992: 12).

The process of professional learning in a high school science department

A project was initiated in December 1994 in a small rural high school 240 km from Sydney, Australia and ran for four years to December 1998. The study involved three male teachers who constituted the entire science department at the school. At the beginning of the study, one teacher, David, was in his first year of teaching; another teacher, Craig, was in his fifth year of teaching and the head of department, Geoff, had taught for 14 years. The PLS was not designed to be a prescriptive programme, but to create an environment for the teachers to learn about their own practice and to assist them with any changes that they decided upon. A feature of the system was to introduce conceptual inputs in the form of interviews with grade 9 students in their school providing comments about teaching and learning across different subjects. This involved me interviewing the teachers' students and collating the data onto audio-tapes for the teachers to listen to during their meetings. As a teacher educator working at a rural university 50 km from the school, my main role was to negotiate the design of the PLS with the teachers and interview their students as conceptual inputs for their group discussions.

At the beginning of the study, 10 students were interviewed from each teacher's grade 9 class to gather their views about their learning experiences in high school. In total, 30 students were interviewed and were asked to describe their positive and negative learning experiences in science as well as positive learning experiences in other subjects across the school. The focus of the interview was to ascertain 'ways that help you to learn and ways that do not help you to learn' in classes (see Table 4.1 for interview schedule). Data from the interviews were then transcribed and analysed to identify aspects of teaching and learning using Cambourne's conditions for learning as categories (Cambourne 1988). One condition refers to the

Table 4.1   Student interview schedule

Questions

1 *Rapport question*: Can you tell me about yourself, your interests, your hobbies?

2 *Science context questions*: Can you think of a concept or topic in science that you have been taught in the last year that you understood well so that you can clearly remember it? Please tell me about it and can you think of anything that helped you to learn it?

3 *Alternative context questions*: What subject do you believe that you learn best in? What is special about that subject? Can you tell me what happens in the subject that helps you to learn?

4 *Hypothetical questions*: Can you think of a topic in science that you understand well? I want you to pretend that you are a science teacher and you are trying to teach some children about this new topic. How would you go about teaching this to the students keeping in mind the strategies that help you to learn?

5 *Open question*: Do you have any other general comments about anything else in school or at home which helps you to learn?

6 *Hermeneutic/dialectic question*: I am going to tell you some of the things that other students have told me which help them to learn in school. Could you give me your opinion on them?

---

context (immersion), three refer to the role of the teacher (demonstration, expectation and response) and four refer to the role of the learner (engagement, responsibility, use and approximation). As the questions in the interview referred to strategies that help students to learn, a good deal of data collected referred to the social interactions between teachers and students that support learning. Any data that did not fit into these eight categories were placed into other categories as they emerged, as Cambourne's conditions do not include prior knowledge/experiences or reflection.

The student comments about a particular category (positive and negative comments were interspersed) were collated by re-recording them onto 16 separate audio-tapes that provided 10 hours of student comments relating to different conditions for learning. The themes of the audio-tapes were as follows: prior knowledge, reflection, relationships, modelling, expectations, responsibility, practice, trial and error, feedback, interest, discussion, science labs, writing, reading, best science teaching and best subjects for learning. For example, the tape on prior knowledge had 12 student anecdotes with students describing how their previous knowledge helped them to understand particular concepts. The purpose of this collation was to present the student data in a coherent manner to the teachers and it was anticipated that mixing up the comments would maintain student confidentiality. If a student comment related to more than one condition (e.g. trial and error and science labs), then they were recorded onto both tapes. During the month that the student interviews were conducted and collated, the teachers were asked to reflect on their practice by writing in a journal based on the question: 'Why do you teach the way you do?' The teachers wrote in their journal for a week but then gave up because they did not have time.

Listening to the student tapes (conceptual inputs)

At the beginning of 1995, we held our first meeting on a professional day and listened to three of the student tapes as a trigger for teacher reflection and discussion. During this time the teachers stopped the tapes at whatever place they selected and discussed the issue raised. An after-school meeting was held the next day to discuss some action plans in light of discussions about the student tapes. The teachers then decided on ideas to try in their teaching, which was followed up several weeks later by another meeting to listen to another tape. These meetings continued over four years on a monthly basis and in all there were six full-day meetings and about 40 after-school or lunchtime meetings to discuss ideas about teaching and learning. As the facilitator, I participated in the meetings with the teachers for the first six months before going overseas for two years to undertake doctoral studies. The teachers continued the project voluntarily in my absence.

After participating in the professional learning system for two years, the three teachers held two meetings (several weeks apart), which were audio-taped, to explain their view of the process of professional learning that they had experienced. At the end of the first meeting, the teachers sketched a model that represented the process of their own learning (see Figure 4.2).

Several features are evident about the teachers' perceptions of their own learning processes in Figure 4.2. First, the figure shows that change (in the centre) is influenced by multiple conditions for learning that the teachers labelled as prior knowledge (input), time to discuss ideas (out of school), practice, time for preparation, discussion for collegiality, teacher reflection (further tapes and discussion), student tapes (central), teacher interviews (central), outside agent (Gary with big picture) and programming (visible output). Second, the process is *non-linear*, as shown by the criss-cross array of arrows in the diagram, and *dynamic*, meaning back and forth with most conditions having multiple arrows, which is similar to Waldrop's (1992) notion of learning 'on the edge of chaos' (p. 12). Interestingly, the teachers wrote across the bottom of their diagram in large writing, 'This is the group 1. Does it make sense? – it is a complex relationship'.

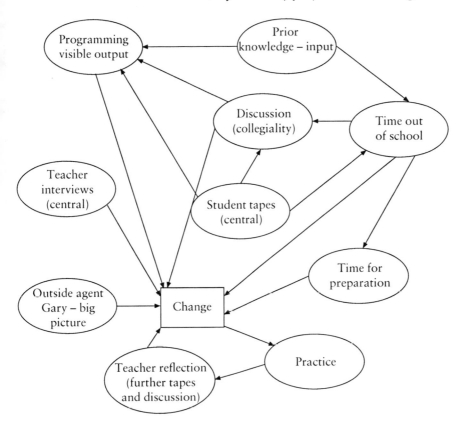

Figure 4.2 Teachers' model of their own learning process.

At their second meeting about the model, which was audio-taped, the teachers described how it worked, outlining the process of their learning and how the conditions related. They stated that what started the process was reflecting on their own practice in light of listening to the student tapes, which allowed them to compare their ideas about teaching and learning to those of their own students. During the recorded meeting, Geoff, the department head stated:

> The thing that starts you off is the combination of listening to the student tapes and having the opportunity to reflect on your own performance and to put down what you think about teaching onto tape in our interviews. Now, all of that was really important because it's like a starting point, it uses something to base what you're doing on.

As the teachers continued to reflect, listened to the student tapes and shared experiences with colleagues, they generated ideas to try in their practice. However, this was not a one-off event because the personal reflection and discussions with colleagues continued as they developed into a *community*, sharing experiences and ideas for the common purpose of improving their teaching. Geoff described the model in their second meeting:

> The important thing was that it continued over time and all the time we were coming back to these, the reflection, discussion, the tapes, and we kept going back to these inputs that came in. And then other things came in from the side, your input, your views, things like that, all taken on board. The collegiality, talking to the others, working towards a common purpose that encourages you because you tend to lose the plot of it in the day-to-day hurly-burly.

Having reflected on their teaching, listened to the student tapes and shared experiences with their colleagues, the teachers started to think about change. They tried out ideas in their classrooms and monitored the student feedback, which they discussed in subsequent meetings. Geoff stated:

> What happens then is you start to think about change and then what happens is you look at change and then you get the feedback . . . from the students, how you feel it's going, from the collegiality again, from your colleagues talking it over.

What the teachers emphasized in their meeting was that the process of their learning was based on a combination of conditions that acted together like a cycle:

> The basis of it is that skeleton, that starting point – the student tapes and your own opportunities for reflection, and then the change, feedback, more reflection, change, feedback, that cycle all the time bringing in ideas from outside, from other inputs, from your colleagues, from you and so on. And I think if any of these factors had been missing, then it wouldn't have worked.

The teachers described the professional learning process as a 'cycle of change' because their learning was linked to a framework that was different to conventional professional development programmes that present ideas in isolation to their practice. Geoff summarized this framework for the group:

> So the whole thing becomes a cycle of change where you start with the student tapes and you start to reflect on the various aspects that you practise and you bring in all these external influences and you bring them together in your head and try to work out what you're going to do yourself in a classroom. And the important thing about it is that, and this is where it is different to other forms of professional development

and this is why it's caused change, is that it is continually reinforced because it is ongoing and because it has this framework that we keep coming back to, we feel as though we're part of a project and part of a process that's ongoing and not short-term. It's not a stick a finger in the dyke here, stick another finger in the dyke there, learn about literacy here, learn about assessment there – it's a whole integrated package.

In sum, it was the combination of the conditions for teacher learning – personal reflection, group discussion, student tapes, action, time, purpose and student feedback – that acted together as a system, resulting in the teachers being continually engaged in learning about their own practice. And the key for change was that the conditions were complementary, focusing on the teachers' own practice as they reflected upon it, shared experiences about their own teaching and listened to student interviews about their teaching. Importantly, the process for change was non-linear, created by the dynamic interactions among the multiple conditions for teacher learning that is similar to learning 'on the edge of chaos' (Waldrop 1992). The next section provides examples of teacher change followed by examples of changes in science department policies.

Examples of teacher change

David: changing from a 'structured teacher' to a 'flexible teacher'

At the beginning of the project in 1993, David was 23 years old and was completing his first year as a secondary science teacher. His professional qualifications included a Bachelor of Applied Science and a postgraduate Diploma of Education. His duties at the school focused on the teaching of science to grades 7, 8 and 9, grade 11 Science for Life (a general science course) and grade 12 Biology. He was also the grade 7 patron, which involved providing pastoral care to students in their first year of high school. His expectations for his involvement in the professional learning project were to 'gain a better understanding of the ways in which students at the school learn best, to gain a better understanding of my own beliefs about teaching, and to improve my teaching' (Survey 1, December 1994, Q. 11).

David's beliefs as a 'structured teacher'

At the beginning of the project, David described himself as a 'structured' teacher because his lessons were tightly organized to provide students of the same ability with the same knowledge. He categorized the science knowledge that he taught into two types – 'working knowledge' for less able students and 'in-depth knowledge' that more able students should learn as well:

> Well basically I feel that my job here, my role as a teacher, is to give the kids a working knowledge that they can take away with them. I like them to get something concrete every lesson that they can pick up, something new that perhaps they didn't understand or didn't know before. I feel that if the kids don't do that, then sometimes maybe I am wasting my time. At the same time I like to filter out material that's inappropriate for certain classes and certain kids . . . I think I have a fairly structured style as I said earlier.
>
> (Interview 1, December 1994, TU 13–27)

David explained that his beliefs about being a 'structured' teacher were based on his assumption that his own students would learn science in the same way as he did at high school. Furthermore, his structured way of teaching matched his ordered approach to life as well:

> I think that a certain amount goes back to my schooling when, in par-ticular in science, I had it very straightforward. If ever we did an experi-ment it was aim, method, results, conclusion. It was always straight down the line and a lot of it was theory and library work and stuff like that, which I like I guess. I get sick of it sometimes, but I do like it that way or I used to when I was at school. Why else? I guess well maybe every-thing I do in life is structured too. I sort of always think about it and by doing this I do that step, then that step, then that step and that step.
>
> (Interview 2, December 1994, TU 23)

Accordingly, he adapted the level of content he taught to the perceived ability levels of students in his classes. For example, when David taught the topic of 'Plants' to grade 9 students, he presented 'working knowledge' to all students, such as general descriptions of plants, types of roots and how plants survive, and more detailed 'in-depth knowledge' to more advanced students, such as plant classification using botanical names. In both cases, he planned lessons to present science knowledge to students in a step-by-step sequence progressing from simple to more complex concepts such that 'I think in my own mind I see doing little units of work that fit into a bigger unit' (Interview 1, December 1994).

David's beliefs as a flexible teacher

In May 1995, five months after the project started, David was beginning to have doubts about being a structured teacher as – 'I'm not convinced that what we are teaching at the moment is what we should be teaching' – and was contemplating 'a pretty big shake-up'. Having listened to some of the student tapes in group meetings, he began to think more about 'how the kids are going to learn it'. This was a change from his previous beliefs because he realized from listening to the tapes that students did not learn very well when he presented knowledge in 'small blocks'. He described his change of 'mind-frame' in an interview in May 1995 and how the project influenced him to be 'a lot more flexible' than he was before as a 'structured' teacher:

> The thing that has affected me the most is when I'm thinking of what I'm doing, I try to think of how the kids are going to learn and how they're going to learn it best and I don't think I ever had that mind-frame before. I never thought of it in that way before . . . The way I teach, that has changed. I think by focusing more on looking at the ways the kids learn, I think I've become, as I tried to describe earlier, a lot more flexible. I'm trying to do different types of things with kids that I wouldn't have thought of before.
>
> (Interview 3, May 1995, TU 77–82)

A developing characteristic of David as a flexible teacher was that he now did not expect all students to learn the same knowledge in class and was prepared to change his teaching during a lesson depending on how the students were responding. For example, when he taught the topic of 'Astronomy', he used a jigsaw technique and allowed students to choose among 15 different options on the topic. At the end of the topic, students gave presentations on their research to the whole class. Another characteristic of David was that he now tried to get an understanding of his teaching from his students' perspective by putting himself in their place during a lesson and imagining what they were thinking of his teaching. If he thought that the students were not responding to a particular teaching strategy, he would change this at the time rather than adhere to his predetermined plan.

In summary, at the beginning of the professional learning project, David described himself as a 'structured' teacher whose practice was primarily based on the way that he learned science at school. Accordingly, he organized lessons in a specific 'step-by-step' sequence based on blocks or chunks of content so that students acquired the 'working knowledge' or 'in-depth knowledge' that they needed for future schooling. Six months into the project he described himself as a 'flexible' teacher who would change his lessons to suit the way the students were responding and his understanding of student learning. He explained that listening to the student tapes challenged his assumption that students learn best in the structured way that he learned at school and that discussions with other teachers provided him with different ideas to try. Hence, as he understood more about how students learn, he changed his teaching to accommodate their different ways of learning.

Craig: changing from a 'fun teacher' to a 'problem-solving teacher'

At the beginning of the project in December 1994, Craig had been teaching science for 5 years and was at his second high school. His professional qualifications included a Bachelor of Science (major in Chemistry and Geology) and a postgraduate Diploma of Education. He taught general science to classes in grades 7, 9 and 10 as well as grade 11 Chemistry and 4-unit science to grade 12 and was patron for grade 8. His expectations for his involvement in the professional learning project were to get 'something useful, to get more out of teacher–teacher interchange rather than academics coming in and giving a professional development seminar' (Survey 1, December 1994, Q. 11).

Craig's beliefs as a fun teacher

At the beginning of the project, Craig stated that his teaching had not changed much in five years and he described himself as a 'fun' teacher whose role was to 'give the students a good understanding about why/how things are or happen in our environment, also to give them good skill levels in useful skills' (Survey 1, December 1994, Q. 9). His five years of teaching experience had taught him that students often do not retain information provided to them, as 'most of them will forget 90 percent of what you tell them anyway when they leave school; most of them probably forget 90 percent of what you tell them when they leave the classroom' (Interview 1, December 1994, TU 18).

Craig's beliefs about being a fun teacher were based on the assumption that his own students would learn science in the same way as he did at high school by conducting short experiments that demonstrated science concepts. This was the way that he was taught science in grades 9 and 10 by his favourite science teacher. Craig believed, therefore, that students learnt science most effectively by doing experiments, so 'three-quarters of what I do is lab work and 25 percent is theory. It is a bit hard to work out a percentage, it depends on a topic. If I have six or so lessons in a week, probably in four we would do some kind of lab' (Interview 2, December 1994, TU 15). Hence, Craig taught science by presenting a sequence of science concepts, which were supplemented by experiments:

> Basically I just sit down, write down everything that comes to mind I've done in the past in a topic and then one of the things I think about is labs. And I think about what I can do on the topic and think about the labs that relate to them depending on what we've got. A couple of the experiments I remembered from what I did at school, some were from university but most of them I suppose I got from another teacher when I first started teaching.
>
> (Interview 1, December 1994, TU 75–7)

For example, when he taught 'Magnetism', he provided students with magnets so that they could try to work out what materials in the classroom were attracted to magnets, followed by activities to demonstrate the concepts of attraction and repulsion. This was followed by a sequence of concepts to explain electromagnetism and then electric motors.

Craig's beliefs as a problem-solving teacher

Although Craig still believed that experiments were the best way for students to learn, there were some major changes in the way he organized them as a result of listening to the student tapes and sharing experiences with his colleagues. By May 1995, he had realized that his view of organizing experiments differed from the views of his students and this initiated a change: 'it became clear from the tapes and stuff, like I always wanted to make the stuff fun for the kids, but it became clear that my idea of what was fun and their idea of what was fun were slightly different. They're sort of the same along the same lines, but the way I did it possibly wasn't right' (Interview 3, May 1995, TU 3). Accordingly, he changed the way he organized experiments from being short and prescriptive that he directed 'bit by bit' to being longer, more open-ended and with less definite endpoints so that students could investigate their own ideas. His labs now involved 'more problem solving rather than instructional activities' to enable students to explore their own ideas, which resulted in much longer experiments. He described how the students on the tapes preferred to learn in science:

> The majority of kids, not all, but the majority of kids said they like doing things hands-on, so that's all this practical stuff. They like the fact that they have some trial and error, if they muck it up they can start again. But on the other hand with those problem solving type things, they like a little bit of direction and a little bit of prior knowledge always helps. They like to do things by themselves but they like to know where they're going. They like to know what the endpoint is going to be without getting the answer and they want to know what way they're going to go, but they want to hop along the line by themselves. And the fact that they like that means they can own what they're doing and if they make a mistake they have got to fix it up, so they are doing it in their way but with some direction.
>
> (Interview 3, May 1995, TU 61)

A characteristic of being a 'problem-solving' teacher was a change in the way Craig expected students to record their experimental results. Instead of insisting that students follow a traditional 'problem, method, results, conclusion' format, he encouraged students to write about their science experiments in a less structured way using their own words: 'it's messy in some cases but I get a much better understanding of what is in the student's mind. Therefore I can evaluate the success of the activity better and also it has allowed for stages/speed of learning to be more individual' (Survey 2, December 1995, Q. 3). He also introduced more flexibility into his teaching, allowing the students to cover 50 percent of a topic with the class, then choosing an elective to concentrate on for the remaining 50 percent. In November 1995, Craig stated that he thought that students should be researching topics that interested them rather than him teaching the whole class the same concept at once as he did in his first five years of teaching.

In summary, at the beginning of the professional learning project in December 1994, Craig described himself as a teacher who tried to make science 'fun' for his students, assuming that they would learn science in the same way as he did at high school. Consequently, when he thought of content to teach in a topic, he thought 'about the experiments that relate to them' and taught them in a prescriptive way. By May 1995, however, from listening to the student tapes, he realized that the students' ideas about fun and his ideas were different, so he decided to change the way he organized his experiments. As a result, he encouraged students to 'own what they are doing' in experiments and to explore their ideas, rather than simply following his instructions.

Geoff: changing from a 'reflective teacher' to a 'much more reflective teacher'

At the beginning of the project in December 1994, Geoff had been teaching science for 14 years and was at his third secondary school. His professional qualifications included a Bachelor of Science and a postgraduate Diploma of Education. This was his first appointment as the head of a science department and he taught general science to classes in grades 8 and 10 and Physics to grades 11 and 12. His expectations for his involvement in the professional learning project were to 'improve and clarify teaching methods and to look at teaching in relation to student learning' (Survey 1, December 1994, Q. 11).

Geoff's beliefs as a reflective teacher

At the beginning of the study, Geoff described himself as a conventional teacher in his first 10 years of teaching who organized lessons so that all students covered the same content that he presented in a linear sequence:

> When I taught astronomy, I set out a deliberate sequence and the sequence came from me. And what I did I had in my own mind that the sequence would start from the history of astronomy and from the

earth and then build out from the solar system into the universe and try and show a structure. Now, for most parts, the way we would have done it, we would have had some individual assignments and things like that, but mostly we would have gone from one part to the other and I would give them notes from the board and overheads, that sort of thing. At the end of the six weeks, we would have a test, and every one of the kids in the class would have had exactly the same experience.

(Interview 1, December 1994)

He described himself as a 'reflective' teacher because, over the previous few years, he had begun to question not only the content of his teaching but also his teaching methods: 'I have started to question and reflect on how I teach it as well as what I teach'. This reflection was stimulated when he started to think about why some students failed in science and coincided with several professional development courses that he took about learning styles and constructivist views on learning. However, he found himself in a state of flux when trying to change his method of teaching from teacher-centred to being more student-centred by giving students more responsibility to conduct their own work, rather than him instructing the whole class together.

He found his attempt to change 'very uncomfortable' and experienced dilemmas as he experimented with his teaching. Perhaps this was because he was working in isolation from other teachers and was trying to change the balance of his classroom system. For example, he stated that he had taught 'The Human Body' in a conventional way three times every year for 13 years by presenting the content in a linear sequence to the whole class at once so that all students studied one body system at a time. He changed his approach when he organized it differently with his 8A science class by using a 'jigsaw' method. He gave each of the students a system to study to become expert enough so that they could conduct their own research and then teach it to the class. Surprisingly, he found that the students' assessment results were the best that they had ever achieved. This was a mystery to Geoff and a concern, because he had less control over the process than before. In addition, he experienced some dilemmas when he taught in this manner because he had less control over what the students were learning. In fact, he sometimes felt like going back to his conventional teacher-centred methods because he sometimes felt that he needed to regain more control over what the students were learning.

Geoff's beliefs as a 'much more reflective teacher'

Twelve months after the project started, Geoff described himself as a 'much more reflective' teacher, stating that he had done more reflection in those

12 months than he had done in his whole teaching career. Consequently, the project provided him with a foundation for change as he had a better understanding of his own practice. In December 1995, when he filled out his second survey, he wrote:

> This project [PLS] has crystallized my ideas about what is good science teaching. It has confirmed some aspects (e.g. students learn by doing), but it has extended my knowledge of why I am doing things. I am much more reflective now about how successful my teaching is and also more aware of real learning by the students.
>
> (Survey 2, December 1995, Q. 1)

As a result of listening to the student tapes and sharing experiences with colleagues, Geoff had developed a 'knowledge base about how the kids are learning and what they understand by their learning . . . then it all adds up to a real base for your teaching' (Interview 3, May 1995, TU 47), which increased his understanding of the relationship between teaching and learning.

Geoff gave an example of how his teaching had changed by providing students with more opportunities to explore their own ideas based on his insights into learning from listening to data on the student tapes. For example, when he now taught 'Astronomy', the first half of the topic addressed a common core of outcomes, while in the second half of the topic students chose various electives to investigate based on their interests:

> One of the ways that this [PLS] has affected us is we've actually looked at our programmes and we've made our programmes centre about a core of outcomes which are actually knowledge outcomes, not nearly as many so the core is much smaller than I would have expected students to learn in the past. So the students have the same core experiences in our topics in grade 7, that core of knowledge is centred around the earth. So the way I've done it now is that each of the students specializes in one area. Some of them did eclipses, some of them did tides, some of them did the phases of the moon, some of them did the seasons, the lower-ability kids did day and night. They each had to present a little play where they themselves became a part, became a planet or so on, and then they presented that to the rest of the class. And the rest of the class had to ask questions about it and then I questioned them. And the other thing that the rest of the class had to do was they had to make up little diagrams and notes for themselves about what the students learned.
>
> (Interview 4, November 1995)

This type of programming was typical of the way the teachers reorganized all the science topics in the year 7–10 curriculum as a consequence of participating in the professional learning system.

In summary, at the beginning of the project Geoff described himself as a 'reflective teacher' who had been attempting to change his own instruction over the previous few years but was in a 'state of flux' because he was unsure whether these changes were beneficial for his students. As a result of the professional learning system, he described himself as a 'much more reflective' teacher as the student tapes confirmed and extended his beliefs about teaching and student learning, which he had generated himself before he started listening to them. At the end of the project, he stated that he thought he was a reflective teacher before the project started, but his reflections were based solely on his own experiences and understanding of teaching and learning. He now realized that alternative perspectives on his practice were needed to enhance his reflections and these were provided by discussions with his colleagues in light of listening to the student tapes.

Examples of educational change in science department policies

Over a period of four years, there were several new policies developed in the science department and this highlights the non-linear process of change as one influenced another. During the first two years of the PLS, the teachers changed their understanding of their practice and, as a consequence, redesigned all of their grade 7–10 science programmes from focusing on teaching prescriptive knowledge to emphasizing student outcomes. After the teachers spent two years reviewing their teaching programmes, they realized that their assessment schemes were still designed for the old knowledge-based programmes. They then spent the third year of the project developing a scheme for profile reporting to suit their new outcomes-based teaching programme. They were the only subject department in the school to develop their own assessment scheme and reporting procedure. Another innovation introduced by the science department was that they were very aware that secondary students spend a good deal of time copying notes from the board or from books. The teachers wanted to encourage students to write about their own ideas and so they introduced a new writing policy that 'allowed students to express themselves using their own writing and language'. This policy encouraged students to document their science experiments in their own words much like a reflective journal.

The student tapes that were made at the beginning of the PLS were listened to during the teacher meetings over a period of two years. After this time, the teachers had listened to all the tapes and then decided that they wanted more current student data about their classroom experiences. The teachers consequently decided to design their own procedure for the students to give them regular feedback on their teaching. They initially asked students to fill in learning logs for each lesson to give them feedback. After trying this for a year, the teachers came to the conclusion that this was not successful, as the students did not have a 'language' to identify features of teaching practice. To address this issue, the teachers designed a teaching profile that listed particular strategies that the students could select to identify what teaching strategies 'worked' for them to support their learning. The students used these during the fourth year of the project. At the end of that year, each of the three teachers won a prestigious New South Wales Minister of Education Award for Teaching Excellence. Within two years, the three teachers were successful in gaining promotion positions to other schools and the PLS ceased at that point.

Discussion

As a result of their involvement in the professional learning system, each of the three teachers changed their beliefs about teaching and learning. David's change was the most dramatic, which is not surprising, considering that he was in his first year of teaching at the beginning of the project. He began his career as a very 'structured' teacher whose pedagogy was mainly based on a view of teaching as transmission of knowledge (Barnes 1992). He believed that his role was to deliver prescriptive knowledge to students in a deliberate step-by-step sequence from simple to more complex. His understanding of student learning was simplistic, as he assumed that all students learned science in the same structured way as he had at school. As he developed a deeper understanding of student learning, he changed into a 'flexible' teacher and began to adjust his teaching to accommodate different ways of student learning. Craig also showed substantial change in his beliefs about teaching that had remained relatively stable during the first five years of his career. His views about teaching were also based on the assumption that his students would learn science in the same way as he had at school by doing science labs to demonstrate a particular concept.

Geoff, however, did not change his beliefs about teaching and learning as much as the other two teachers. He had many more years of teaching experience than the other two and was already a reflective teacher before the professional learning system started. Nonetheless, the project had a major influence on him, as it confirmed many of the ideas that he had been trying out in his teaching, but was unsure as to the benefit of these changes for students. The student tapes reinforced many of his ideas and encouraged him to continue experimenting with his teaching and to seek ways of improving his practice. In particular, the student tapes gave him a knowledge source about student learning upon which to base his teaching.

The type of teacher learning explained in this chapter was different to what the teachers had previously experienced in conventional professional development programmes in two main ways. First, there were multiple conditions in operation to sustain the teachers' professional learning over a period of four years. This included a combination of personal reflection, sharing experiences as a community, action and scheduled time for discussions. Second, there were conceptual inputs in the form of recorded interviews with grade 9 students describing their learning experiences across different subjects. Importantly, the student tapes were conceptual inputs that were in context with each teacher's practice and so assisted in establishing a relationship among the different conditions for learning. For both David and Craig, listening to the student tapes in their meetings challenged their 'apprenticeship of observation' (Lortie 1975) that their students learned science in the same way as they had at school. In effect, challenging their assumptions caused some dissonance in their beliefs about teaching and acted as a catalyst for reflection on their practice (Hoban 2000a). Listening to the student tapes initiated a need for David and Craig to change and encouraged them to engage in conversations about improving practice with their colleagues. For both Craig and David, involvement in the PLS encouraged them to change the balance of their classroom system from one that emphasized teacher control to deliver 'chunks of knowledge' to one that emphasized student learning.

Conversely, for Geoff, listening to the student tapes confirmed many of his beliefs about his practice that he had been exploring to improve his teaching based on his 'gut instincts'. Furthermore, the student data gave the teachers directions for change as they identified effective teaching practice across other subjects within the school. This was a valuable resource for teaching ideas because it is the students, not teachers, who are exposed to a wide range of teaching approaches across different subjects on a daily basis. And teachers in high schools rarely compare their ideas across subject departments. Also, there were other benefits from listening to the tapes, as David began to 'think like a student' in class and Craig considered many of the suggestions made by students about good teaching practice and reorganized the way he conducted science experiments.

The professional learning system was long-term because it was driven by multiple conditions for teacher learning that interrelated as a system. Each of these conditions – reflection, community, purpose action, student tapes, time and student feedback – are not new in terms of teacher learning, but what this professional learning system did is link them on a recurring basis. The heart of a PLS is the dynamic interplay among the conditions – teachers reflected on their practice *and* listened to data from students on their teaching *and* shared their ideas as a community *and* experimented with their practice *and* gained student feedback on subsequent efforts for change.

Furthermore, these conditions interrelated because they had a common purpose – to improve each teacher's own practice. This means that the professional learning system had a personal touch focusing on improving the existing practice of the teachers.

When the conditions for learning dynamically interact like a system, a synergy is created because each one enhances the other so that the influence of the whole professional learning process is greater than the sum of each of the conditions alone. If a teacher reflects on his or her practice and does not share this with others, the teacher's thinking is confined by his or her own experiences and interpretive frames. But when teachers share their reflections with others, the discussion confirms or disconfirms their thinking and hence leads to a deeper understanding of their instruction. This is further enhanced if the ideas are tried out in practice and the outcomes of this experimentation are then reflected upon and discussed again at subsequent meetings. The consequence of this dynamic process was that change in teaching occurred that was non-linear, resulting in the teachers adjusting the balance of their classroom system. Hence, a PLS is a framework that encourages dynamic interplay among the conditions so that they relate to each other to drive the professional learning system like the blades of a propeller. However, there is a fundamental condition that is essential for this interaction to occur – *time* to engage in reflection, share experiences as a community, put ideas into action and seek feedback. The teachers in this project documented 'time out of school' and 'time for preparation' in Figure 4.2 as a fundamental condition for their learning.

Conclusion

This chapter shows that a professional learning system provides a framework to support teachers in developing a deeper understanding of the relationship between how they teach and their students' learning. In particular, designing a PLS provides a learning environment for teachers to share what they value most – their own experiences, the experiences of other teachers and the experiences of their own students. This sharing helps make explicit the similarities and differences between these different perspectives on classroom practice and provides a context for learning from others. Also, this learning may lead to educational change, but not in a step-by-step linear way. In this project, the teachers learned about their own practice and then decided to change their teaching programmes, which had unexpected consequences for other aspects of science teaching in their classrooms.

But where is the time in a school week for the reflective discussions that are fundamental to a PLS? Schools, and secondary schools in particular, are often not designed to be learning environments for their teachers. Weekly meetings are common in secondary schools, but their purpose is usually to disseminate administrative details or new programmes. Rarely are meetings dedicated to enable teachers to share what they teach, how they teach or for making explicit their assumptions about why they teach in a particular way. The consequence is that a secondary teacher's pedagogy is often dominated by his or her knowledge of subject matter rather than ideas about student learning or different aspects of pedagogy. Perhaps administrative details normally discussed in staff meetings could be put on a weekly bulletin to make time in meetings for sharing ideas about aspects of teaching and learning.

This chapter highlights how three secondary teachers within a subject department worked together on their own professional learning for four years. One challenge resulting from this project concerns how to engage other subject departments in the school to function also as small professional learning communities. If this is not feasible, then perhaps interested teachers across subject departments could meet regularly to share ideas about their pedagogy so that how students learn in different subjects could be at the heart of discussions. The science department at Oberon High School was also fortunate in having a department head who was already a reflective teacher before the project started. Clearly, with time and guidance, other teachers can learn to reflect on their practice and many are usually keen to exchange experiences with other teachers. But such conditions for teacher learning need to be structured into the organization of a school. Central to this framework is an understanding of how a combination of conditions for teacher learning in a PLS is needed to dynamically interrelate to promote the non-linear process that results in educational change.

five

The role of a facilitator in a professional learning system: the Frameworks project

Jan Turbill

The dilemma of agenda-setting relates to the dual and sometimes conflicting goals of introducing participants to a particular content, and creating an empowering and emancipatory environment that requires that the participants own the content and process.

(Richardson 1992: 287)

In my many years as a professional learning facilitator in language arts, many principals have asked me, 'How can the culture of my school be changed?' For me, this question becomes, 'How can I support a learning culture in a school?' To generate such an environment requires a long-term plan, so that exploring new ways of teacher learning becomes part of the everyday discourse of teachers. In this chapter, I explain a professional learning system called 'Frameworks' that was designed to support the teaching of literacy in grades 3–8 (Turbill *et al.* 1991, 1993). The first section of the chapter explains the teacher learning model that underpinned 'Frameworks', together with an explanation of the role of a facilitator in a professional learning system (PLS). This is followed by an example of teacher learning from the project.

'Frameworks' is the name given to a PLS that focuses on language and literacy learning for elementary teachers. The name was chosen deliberately as its authors believed that teachers need to have professional learning experiences that will lead them to construct a strong personal theoretical framework around which they can build their personal theories of language and literacy learning. Frameworks began as a long-term site-based language and literacy project in response to the needs of staff developers in

New York state. This state had brought ELIC (the Early Literacy Inservice Course) into their districts in the late 1980s. This course, originally written by the South Australian Department of Education for K-2 teachers, was licensed through Rigby Education US and first run in 1988. Over 60 ELIC tutors were trained and moved out into school districts to run the 10-week sessions at the school level across New York state. In late 1989, the Wayne Finger Lakes Board of Co-operative Services (BOCES), located in upstate New York, invited myself, Andrea Bulter and Brian Cambourne to create a similar project for teachers of grades 3–8. In 1990, an eight-week project was trialled in Rochester, NY with 36 facilitators being trained. The unique partnership between the University of Wollongong in Australia and the Wayne Finger Lakes BOCES in the USA continued for 10 years.

Facilitators were initially tutored by the authors over five days. The training took the prospective facilitators through the eight sessions so that they could experience the content but, more importantly, the conditions that they would be asking their participants to go through. A third of each day was spent on facilitation skills. As time went by, 20 trained facilitators moved on to become 'trainers of facilitators'. Within the week there was a strong emphasis on creating a community of learners among the group. The success of these communities was evident in the final session of the week when groups came together to present a representation of 'what Frameworks means to me'. In many cases, the relationships developed within these communities continued long after the project was finished in the form of networking and support for themselves as they ran the project within their own schools. Several research reports have been produced that evaluated the various courses within the Frameworks project (henceforth simply called Frameworks) from the perspective of those who participated in it (Heckenberg *et al.* 1994). From such reports we can assume that Frameworks 'worked', in that it changed teachers' beliefs and practices in positive ways with respect to the teaching of literacy. However, it is why and how it worked that is the focus of this chapter.

'Frameworks' as a professional learning system

Frameworks has the potential for changing the learning culture of schools in ways that empower teachers (Swain 1994; Turbill 1994). One of the key features of this project is that teachers who experience the sessions begin to view themselves as thinkers and learners rather than simply as 'doers' or practitioners of someone else's thinking. Instead, they begin to view themselves as perpetual learners who accept that they are change agents in a classroom, while being in a constant state of change themselves. This, in turn, has the potential to lead to empowered students (Duffy 1990).

The professional learning model that underpins Frameworks can be viewed as one that views school cultures as 'social open systems' (Betts 1992; Asayesh 1993; Turbill 1994; Capra 1996). They are seen as 'open' systems because energy or ideas are able to be imported and exported, as opposed to a 'closed' system that does not have external input and needs to be self-sufficient. To function as an effective social open system, Banathy (1991) stated that schools have to:

- interact with their constantly changing environment;
- cope with constant change and accept uncertainty and ambiguity by continually adapting;
- seek new purposes with self-direction, self-correction and self-renewal; and
- increase the involvement of all staff and improve the distribution of information throughout a school.

In this section, I review the conditions for teacher learning underpinning 'Frameworks'; this is followed by a section on my role as a facilitator. I argue that a facilitator is crucial to enhance the relationships between the conditions to help establish a system for long-term teacher learning. The model of teacher learning that underpins 'Frameworks' is shown in Figure 5.1.

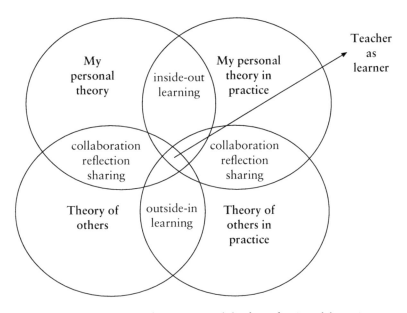

Figure 5.1 'Frameworks' as a model of professional learning.

Why does a system of professional learning such as Frameworks produce such positive results? The model assumes that four basic knowledge domains are necessary to provide different perspectives on the teaching of literacy, as shown by the four circles in the model. Teachers can learn from each knowledge domain, but it is when the four interrelate as a system that we create the possibility for sustained, long-term learning. And such learning is needed to change teaching practices. When teachers have a sense of their own needs *and* the opportunities to access information ('inside-out learning'), they are placed in a position to interact with and engage in 'new knowledge' ('outside-in learning') *and* to take from it that which they need. This process of transforming new knowledge with old knowledge through the use of the interrelated learning conditions of reflection, sharing and collaboration allows teachers to make the knowledge their own. It is the synergy created through the interplay of these conditions that underpins sustained professional learning. In short, these learning conditions on their own may or may not create change, but together as a system they generate a critical mass for continuous learning and the professional learning system takes on a life of its own. In this process, teachers are constantly comparing their personal knowledge about literacy teaching with the knowledge of others and testing it in the context of their classrooms. The teachers thus become confident 'owners' of the knowledge as it applies to their particular contexts and needs. They become selective, critical analysts (even cynical) of what others say and are no longer simply prepared to accept the information at face value. They become able to adapt the practices of others to suit the needs of their students in their contexts and so become personally empowered. There are two dimensions to this model.

The personal dimension: inside-out learning

My personal theory

The intersection of the top two circles in bold in Figure 5.1, 'My personal theory' and 'My Personal Theory in practice', is what I call 'inside-out learning'. The importance of professionals being able to gain insights into their own thinking, beliefs and values so that they become aware of what drives their practices has long been recognized (Schön 1983; Cambourne 1991). All teachers have what I call a 'personal theory' of that which they teach; however, for many it is in an embryonic form and often subconscious or 'tacit' (Polanyi 1966). Many teachers find trying to identify why they do what they do in their classrooms not only a difficult task, but also quite anxiety producing.

Reflecting on one's own beliefs about teaching and learning in any curriculum area is important. It is also important for teachers to reflect on and make conscious the strategies and conditions they use as a learner in that curriculum area. Since Frameworks is a professional learning system concerned with the teaching of language and literacy, a major aim of the project is to help teachers gain insights into the language and literacy strategies and practices that they themselves use when engaging in literate behaviours. The reason why there is such an emphasis on participants analysing how they themselves learn is that we suspect this metacognitive awareness will have implications for how they teach. This means addressing the following questions:

- What is learning and how do I learn? What strategies do I use as a learner? How do I feel when I am successful or not so successful? What does this mean for my teaching?
- What is language? How do I learn language? For what purposes do I use language? What does this mean for my teaching?
- What is reading (writing, spelling)? How do I read (write, spell)? What skills and knowledge do I need to read (write, spell)? What does this mean for my teaching?

Working through these questions helps teachers to make explicit their tacit knowledge. Often this knowledge does not 'sit right' with what they currently do in the name of teaching literacy. A sense of uncertainty or 'intellectual unrest' is an inevitable consequence of being challenged and is usually accompanied by confusion, uncertainty, anxiety and stress. More importantly, such intellectual unrest is a necessary precursor to successful learning and thus, while often uncomfortable, plays a vital element in maintaining the level of energy within the social system.

My personal theory in practice

The other knowledge domain in the personal dimension is 'My Personal Theory in Practice' in my classroom. Many professional learning activities, or what I call 'structures', ask teachers to examine what they do in their classrooms. However, asking them to reflect on why they do it is quite another issue and for most very difficult. My research supports the assertion that this difficulty can be diminished through skilful use of the teacher learning conditions of reflection, collaboration and sharing. When these language learning conditions are judiciously brought into play through a skilful mix of various structures, teachers begin to examine their own beliefs and values, their own personal learning strategies, their classroom practices, the needs of their students and the amount of (or lack of) congruence between what constitutes their own personal theory and their classroom practices. Because it involves the process of bringing tacit know-ledge to conscious awareness, I call this kind of learning 'inside-out learning'.

Such inside-out learning has significant implications for teachers' class-room practice. When a learning experience is personalized for the teachers, they begin to 'see and experience' learning and language learning from the inside and, metaphorically, 'live' in the shoes of their students. Many see for the first time why some of their classroom practices are either useful or meaningless exercises. Because this 'inside-out learning' helps teachers appreciate the importance of knowing and understanding the purpose for engaging in sessions or other learning activities with respect to their own professional learning, they also begin to appreciate how vital this is for their students. They begin to gain a sense of the role that language plays in their learning and thus what role it must also play in their students' learning. This is another way of stating that, because of inside-out learn-ing, teachers become metacognitively aware; that is, they become aware of their own learning strategies and are therefore consciously able to mon-itor their own learning experiences. This awareness, too, begins to spill over to their classroom practice and will be highlighted in a case study towards the end of this chapter.

This personal dimension is vital for effective teacher learning. By giving teachers the opportunities to focus on their own beliefs and practices, recog-nition is given to that which is already known. The 'intellectual unrest' that stems from the tensions created when teachers begin to make explicit their tacit knowledge about why they do what they do in their classrooms forces them not only to identify their own personal needs as learners, but ultimately to take responsibility for meeting them. Furthermore, as teachers begin to understand the implications for their own learning, they more readily empathize with their students and understand the teaching implica-tions for their students' learning. But there's more to teacher learning than a personal, inside-out dimension. In a social system, learners need to interact with others, which is what I call the 'external dimension'.

The external dimension: outside-in-learning

This dimension is the intersection of the 'Theory of Others' and the 'Theory of Others in Practice' in Figure 5.1. When these two domains of knowledge interact they produce what I call 'outside-in-learning'. This is the opposite of inside-out learning because it originates outside the teacher-learner. It is this form of learning that has dominated conventional professional develop-ment programmes. As well as inside-out learning, teachers also need to have opportunities to hear and see the theory and practices of others; that is, the current research and thinking of others, including the views of their peers. Like its counterpart, 'outside-in-learning' also raises intellectual unrest, especially if teachers hear, read and see 'things' that are different from that which they currently know, believe and do. 'Intellectual unrest' thus appears to be a function of the interplay between and among all four domains of knowledge within the personal and external dimensions of the model. However, the necessary interplay between personal 'inside-out learning' and the social influence of 'outside-in learning' often does not occur spontaneously and that is why a facilitator who understands the processes of teacher learning is needed.

The facilitator's role in a professional learning system

In the first section of this chapter, I described the model that underpins Frameworks (Turbill 1994) as an interactive and integrative system for professional learning. In such a system, the facilitator plays a pivotal role. This is not an 'outfront' role, rather one that 'leads from behind'. Also, the role is an integral part of the system and no more important than any other part or person in that system.

However, I didn't always think this way about the role of a facilitator. My views as a 'facilitator' in the professional learning of teachers over the past 20 years have evolved and passed through many phases. These can be best summed up in Table 5.1, which shows three roles of the facilitator that differ according to a particular model of teacher learning. When teacher learning is perceived to be all about practising good teaching ideas, then the role of the facilitator is to provide novices with tips on 'how to teach'. Conversely, if teacher learning is perceived to be about understanding and implementing theory, then the facilitator's role changes to being a 'knower' and disseminator of theory. However, if beliefs about teacher learning involve helping teachers become aware of why they teach the way they do as well as introducing theory to extend those beliefs, then a facilitator's role becomes much more complex. The tricky part is knowing when and how to introduce theory or 'conceptual inputs' to extend the beliefs of teachers. Choosing the right time and type of conceptual input for teachers requires professional judgement on behalf of the facilitator about the school context and the type of conceptual inputs teachers value and understand. This decision is similar to the notion of the 'agenda-setting dilemma' (Richardson 1992) that facilitators experience when deciding upon the content of conceptual inputs, while being conscious of issues about sharing power with teachers in the project.

The key role of a facilitator in a PLS is to help develop the relationships among the conditions for teacher learning, such as collaboration, reflection and sharing. One way is to provide structures to encourage interplay between the knowledge domains shown in Figure 5.1, as sustained

Table 5.1　Beliefs about teacher learning and the role of a facilitator

Teacher learning model	Beliefs about teacher learning	Role of the facilitator
(practice)	• Focus on practice • Teachers perceived as 'do-ers'	• Facilitator seen as an expert who provides the novice with 'great tips and recipes'
(theory) —into→ (practice)	• Theory drives practice • Teacher's role is to put theory into practice	• Facilitator's role is to understand and interpret the theory for teachers
(theory) → (beliefs) —matches→ (practice)	• Theory drives practice • Theory needs to guide teachers' beliefs • Teachers' beliefs need to match their practices	• Facilitator to help teachers recognize their beliefs and how these are reflected in their practice through conditions for learning

teacher learning lies at the intersection of all these conditions and knowledge domains. When these conditions and knowledge domains interrelate in certain ways, a learning culture is created in which teachers begin to identify and articulate a personal theory of practice. Sometimes this personal theory is supported by or challenged by the 'theory of others' and how this theory looks in practice. Whether challenged or supported, the conditions of collaboration, reflection and sharing inevitably lead to new teacher learning, which ripples across classroom practice and ultimately impacts on student learning.

The key conditions of reflection, collaboration and sharing are not new to professional learning (Schön 1983; Brody 1994; Hannay 1994; Saban *et al.* 1994; Cole and Knowles 2000). However, for the most part it seems they tend to be used as activities in their own right. Therein lies a problem, because these conditions are activated by certain activities or structures and thus should be viewed as a collective and not as independent learning processes. According to Fullan (1992: 110):

It is not just being good at co-operative learning but mastering an array of instructional models; it is not just being involved in a reflective practice project but being a reflective practitioner; it is not participating in an action research investigation but conducting constant inquiry; it is not being part of a peer coaching project, but being collaborative as a way of working. In short, teachers must come to internalize these ways of being to the point where it becomes second nature to be a perpetual learner.

In spite of such wise advice, I would argue that the major purpose of many professional development programmes is still to give information *to* teachers through a top-down process. If we are to take Fullan's advice seriously, we must create learning cultures for our teachers in which the conditions exist that allow for active learning to occur. Sarason (1990) sums up the facilitator's challenge when he argues that schools need to be learning cultures for all who participate in them, 'because teachers cannot create and sustain the conditions for productive development of children if those conditions do not exist for teachers' (p. xiv).

Ways to support interplay between knowledge domains

A professional learning system has the potential for providing the blueprint to create such conditions and thus optimal learning cultures at the school level in which teachers can become perpetual learners. The challenge is in getting the right 'mix' of professional learning structures and conditions in place so that optimal learning conditions not only exist, but are operationalized in such a way that they become synergistic. My research identified four key features that need to be considered so that all four knowledge domains shown in Figure 5.1 are dynamically interacting. These are called *structures, conditions, language-in-use* and *relationships* and are interconnected yet interdependent. They create the energy force (Capra 1996) within a systems model of professional learning.

Structures

Components in the culture that are set up to facilitate the learning process are called *structures*. They are the 'things' that the teacher or facilitator in that setting has some control over. These include activities and workshops, input sessions, readings, videos of classroom practice, keeping a learning journal and identifying specific questions to respond to in that journal. The purpose of each structure must be made explicit so that the learners not only know what is expected of them, but also why participation in that structure is worthwhile for their learning. The structures incorporated into any learning setting need to allow for learners not only to access new knowledge (i.e. the theory of others), but also to motivate participants to begin the process of 'looking inside themselves' so that they begin to make explicit their own inner thinking; their tacit knowledge, beliefs and strategies (i.e. develop their own personal theory).

Examples

1 Structures need to be chosen so that there are opportunities for learners to:
   - gain access to new knowledge in the form of current research and thinking and practices of others in the field. Knowledge sources may include video input, readings, audio input and short lectures;
   - have opportunities to reflect on and share this information with others. These may include small group interaction using question starters, writing in journals and collaborating on a given problem to put theory into practice;
   - have opportunities to see demonstrations of the theory being put into practice;
   - have opportunities to trial the new practice in their own classrooms;
   - be involved in sessions and activities that encourage learners to reflect on their own learning conditions and strategies, their own beliefs about learning and that which they are learning, their own practices.
2 Structures need to operate for sustained periods of time so that learners have time to try things, read, reflect, share both during periods when the learners come together as well as between these periods.
3 Structures need to allow for teachers to carry out action research activities over a period of time.

Conditions

The structures incorporated into a learning culture operationalize certain *conditions*. These conditions facilitate the transformation of new knowledge with what the learners already know as well as digging deeper into what they already know, think and believe, so that this tacit knowledge becomes propositional knowledge. These conditions broadly are reflection, sharing and collaboration and are operationalized by the structures that are put in place. For example, participants may be asked to use a learning journal (a structure) in which they write reflective responses to a reading (condition) that they were asked to think about in reading time (structure). Before writing in their journal as an individual structure, participants might be asked to work in groups of three (structure) to share (condition) their views about the reading and collaborate (condition) to identify three key points that they all agree upon. These are written on a chart and put on the wall for the whole group to read (structure) and share (condition).

In Frameworks, the structures were quite deliberately chosen and organized into the activities so that the learning conditions would be optimized. Whenever there seemed to be a problem or what we called 'inhibiting factors', we returned to the model to guide us in our choice of a particular structure or its timing or placement in the project. For example, after each session, participants were asked to read an article that was especially written to support or 'scaffold' the concepts highlighted in the session they had just experienced. Participants were expected to read this article and come prepared to discuss key points in the first 20 minutes of the next session. In the main, the fact that participants knew that they would form small groups to discuss certain questions that were used as discussion starters, and that the facilitator would move around and 'listen in' on their discussion, meant that there was strong motivation for reading the particular article. By the third session (the second day in the facilitator training and usually the third week when carried out at the school level), the research found that participants began to enjoy the interaction that followed these readings. This, in turn, led them to realize that they learned a great deal from each other during these sharing sessions. They also realized that the consequences of not having read the article that week left them 'in the dark' and they were not able to participate in their group. The structures and conditions were at work and hence scaffolded teacher learning.

However, there was one occasion when we found that these structures did not 'work'; that the participants were not reading and thus the sharing sessions were not working either. It happened during a time when we were running the project for Kindergarten-Year 2 teachers in the Broken Bay Catholic School Diocese, Sydney, Australia. At the beginning of each school year for three years, we ran three projects with some 30 teachers in each group (some 250 teachers overall). The teachers were released from class for intensive days. While the teachers were also trained as future facilitators, there was no expectation for them to actually go back to their schools and run the project with their peers. Thus, their perception of the project was more for their own professional learning and they were very interested in the practical aspects of the project. During our first course, we soon realized that the teachers were not reading the articles each night for 'homework'. It became clear that their expectations from the course were different from the past groups we had worked with. This group could see no reason to 'do the readings'. They were more interested in the practical activities they were asked to do.

After two days it was evident that because this 'structure' was not operating, participants were not gaining the in-depth understandings that were needed for the discussions and for the future sessions. What should I do?

First, I discussed the problem with the group. I explained my reasons for them doing the readings. They explained their reason for not doing them. I listened and I wondered how I could get them to read. On day four, I reorganized the daily schedule. I shortened the delivery of the session so that there was time at the end of the session (before lunch) for them to have 20 minutes for 'reading time'. On the third day, we tried this new 'structure'. Given time to read, they read the article that followed the session. After lunch when we began the next session, the participants moved into their groups for discussion on their reading. The discussion was great – on-task and very animated. Just what was needed after lunch! With the success of 'reading time' before lunch we decided also to build 'reading time' into the morning before we began the first session of the day. Again great discussion followed. Participants began to bring greater understanding to the next sessions because of their reading and discussion of the key concepts that underpinned the project. And many began to re-read the articles at home that night! In the next week's training with the new group of participants, reading time was built into the daily schedule twice a day. Reading time enabled the participants to read, showed them the value of professional reading and that they were not just having to read 'theory' but that they could begin to 'turn' what they had perceived to be 'boring theory' into their own classroom practice. This is just one example of how the system works. The constant interplay between the structures and conditions means that the facilitator has a great deal of flexibility in 'adjusting' the project to suit the needs of a particular group.

A major outcome of the interaction between the structures and conditions is the development of a shared meaning and a shared language among those in the learning setting. This move towards a shared meaning forges new and often lasting professional relationships among members of the group; relationships that involve trust, caring, understanding and an appreciation of each other's perspective and opinions. Another important outcome is the realization that there is no right or wrong answer. The conditions of sharing and collaborating with peers highlight that there are several perspectives and understandings of certain concepts. Working their way through confusions and uncertainties places members of the group in risk-taking situations, as they reflect on and share their opinions in front of peers. These conditions give learners insights into their own learning and thinking, which, in turn, reflect on how they will deal with other learners, and so it goes on.

The conditions also are the active ingredients in the transformation process of making connections between what the learners know and what they are learning. The process of bringing to conscious awareness the process itself leads learners to become meta-aware of their learning and learning conditions. These conditions in action lead learners to experience what Barth (1990) referred to as a 'community of learners'. Once experienced, there is a deeper understanding of what this concept itself means and teachers are more able to begin to set up similar 'communities' in their classrooms.

Examples

1 If the structures suggested are put in place, the conditions discussed must also operate implicitly; however, staff developers need to recognize and understand explicitly the conditions involved and how they interact.
2 Staff developers need to make explicit not only the 'how' of the conditions but, more importantly, the 'why' of these conditions. For instance, why is the process that learners go through in collaborative learning useful to them as learners?
3 Learners need many opportunities to reflect on and articulate the conditions they go through as learners.
4 Thus staff developers need to demonstrate explicitly the value of the conditions that the learners are being asked to go through, as well as to demonstrate the value of each individual's conditions.

Language in use

The *language in use* as the structures and conditions are put into place is both an outcome of these in action as well as the integrating force for operationalizing them. Learners need language for learning. Language carries the meanings and concepts of that which is to be learned. It is also the tool that can be used for clarifying meanings and concepts. Language is used to make explicit the conditions that each goes through as each goes about the task of learning. Language is used to make connections; as a tool for transforming new knowledge into already existing knowledge. At another level, the overall ethos of the learning community is created through language. The relationships that learners establish with each other within that community is a manifestation of the tenor embedded in the language used.

Having a language (or 'patterns of discourse') to describe the concepts and patterns of language which is to be learned is vital if learners are to transform the information into their own. Understanding the terms used to label various concepts and ideas is an important part of this process. However, making this discourse part of their own language can only occur if learners are given the opportunity to be immersed in that discourse through both the oral and written modes; equally important is the opportunity to attempt to use the discourse in supportive, non-threatening settings. The conditions of sharing, collaborating and reflecting are all crucial language learning tools; they allow for the learning of language, the learning through language and the learning about language simultaneously as the language is being used.

Examples
1 Staff developers need to understand the functions that language plays in society generally and in learning in particular.
2 Structures need to be chosen that will maximize the use of language for learning.
3 The role of language in learning needs to be made explicit to learners so that they develop a knowledge of the role that language plays in their learning and learning generally; so that they achieve metalinguistic awareness of the language tools they have for learning and functioning in society.
4 Facilitators need to use language in such a way that they demonstrate through their language that they value the expertise that each member of the learning setting brings to the learning enterprise; that they encourage risk taking; that they support each learner.
5 Facilitators need to create a community of learners.

Personal relationships

The *relationships* created in a learning culture play an important role in that setting. They impact on the learner in many ways. I argue that the facilitators play a vital role in taking the responsibility for initiating, maintaining and monitoring the structures and conditions within the setting. A facilitator needs to be someone whom the group trusts; who does not need to have all the answers but is willing to facilitate the process of solving them; who is available to provide the support that each individual needs at the appropriate time; and who is known to have the support of the administration.

Teachers' students are also important people in their learning. If what teachers are learning does not have some perceived or actual positive impact on, or response from, the students in their care, then teachers will begin to question the worth of what it is they are trying to implement. Teachers' classrooms thus become vital learning settings in their own right and the relationships developed with their students can either enable or hinder further learning. Relationships beyond the immediate context of the school also impact on the learning culture. Much of what teachers do spills over into their personal lives. It becomes more difficult for teachers' learning if there is no perceived support outside the classroom, be it at the district level, from the parents of the students or from the people they live with. Thus it is important for all these relationships to be taken into consideration when setting up a learning culture.

Examples

1 A facilitator is a person whose role and responsibility it is to orchestrate the structures and conditions within the learning enterprise. This person may be a fellow teacher, the principal or an outsider (it may be more than one person). What is important is that the person does not perceive herself or himself as an 'expert' who has all the answers, but as someone who has the skills to facilitate the process of establishing a caring and trusting setting for the learners.

2 It is important that the teachers know that what they are learning is not only understood by the administration but is strongly supported both philosophically and financially (if necessary). It is also important that teacher learners understand what is expected from them by the administration as a result of making a commitment to take part in the learning enterprise.

3 Structures need to be in place that inform and, where necessary, allow for negotiations with the parents of the students. The teacher learners should not feel that this is initially their responsibility, although ultimately it should become so.

4 Facilitators need to be cognisant of other pressures placed on teachers in their personal lives and, where necessary, take these into account. For instance, it may become necessary to set up structures (with comfortable space and food) for those teachers who need some quiet time at school before or after the students have left. It would be even better if some time was allocated within the school day for teachers to read, reflect and share if and when it becomes too difficult and stressful for this to be carried out at home.

5 Teachers need to be made aware that their learning does not stop at the end of a session or a school day; that it will be necessary for them to find some time to try things in their classrooms as well as find some quiet time to reflect on what happened, what worked and what did not and why; to read and reflect on what they are learning, and so on.

6 Teachers need to become aware that their classrooms are key learning settings not only for their students but also for themselves.

7 Teachers should not feel they are being 'coerced' into the learning enterprise by others, or that such involvement is required because they 'need' it (i.e. remedial professional learning).

8 Time, money and people need to be allocated for opportunities of 'follow up' for teacher learners.

The final section of this chapter highlights a feature of the Frameworks project that encourages teachers to become aware of how they learn and how these personal insights can transfer to influence their own classroom practice.

Jim: a case study of teacher learning

Just how the model of teacher learning shown in Figure 5.1 worked is best demonstrated by sharing a case study report of one of the participants in the research I carried out. This research examined how the model of teacher learning helped teachers by providing them with insights about how they become aware of how they learn. I knew it worked as I had seen many successes; however, I was not sure just how and why it worked in the way it did. Jim was one of 10 teachers that I interviewed each week after each of the eight sessions that comprised the project.

Background

Jim was a teacher of many years' experience in a small rural elementary school in upstate New York. He volunteered to be interviewed as one of four case study people in his school's group. His reasons for volunteering were 'you need a male's perspective' and 'I have seen new literacy programmes come and go so I am not easily convinced'. Whatever his reasons, Jim was always willing to speak openly and as he put it 'from the hip'. Jim was 'browned off with teaching' as he felt that children no longer wanted to learn, 'especially by Grade 5', and the children and their parents no longer respected teachers and what teachers did for their students.

Jim therefore came into the project with a rather negative view of the teaching profession, students and the overall school support for teachers. He admitted he did not give his teaching a great deal of thought any more, 'as I have been doing it for so long, it just comes naturally'. When asked what philosophy 'drove' his teaching, he was unsure but added, 'I am fairly traditional I guess. I provide kids with information to read, words to spell, and we work through their grammar textbook. I grade them by giving them unit tests at the end of each unit we do to see how much they have learned'. Jim took the project seriously and read the set readings each week as well as trying out the classroom practices that were part of each week. He noted things that he learned in his learning journal and came ready to discuss what he had learned in the group reflection session that occurred at the beginning of each class.

Jim's view of learning

The first evidence that Jim was beginning to explore his own beliefs occurred when he experienced the 'learning session'. In this part he examined how we went about learning something new. The group's responses were synthesized into one integrated 'learning theory'. This was labelled 'a natural learning model' (Cambourne 1988) because it related to how learning occurs in everyday settings. Jim readily made the connection that the view of 'natural learning' proposed in the project was in conflict with what drove his classroom practice; however, it was very much the view of learning that drove his teaching (coaching) of wrestling, which he did outside school. This was similar to a view of everyday learning whereby new ideas are initially demonstrated, but to personalize them Jim had to put them into practice, undertake multiple efforts with trial-and-error and seek feedback from others. This learning is not just an individual process, but involves social interaction and experimenting with ideas in practice. Jim could relate his view of learning to various learning contexts outside his classroom, including learning in his own home, and the conditions that operated in that setting, such as when his own children were learning to speak and now learning to read and write. Natural learning, he believed, made 'so much sense'. However, he was having trouble showing how this related to his classroom practice. He wrote in his journal, 'How can anything so natural be so difficult to understand?' This connection created intellectual unrest for him, as he could not see a clear way as to how he could put natural learning into operation in his classroom. He was becoming increasingly aware that there was another view of learning being put forward called 'whole language': 'I kind of see it is as, there it is over there and I can see it. I know what it is but I'm not sure how to get there. I've got to build something so I can get over there. That's the way I'm seeing it right now. That's a start for me'.

As he proceeded through the project, he continued to identify how he himself learned best. The sessions he participated in were set up so that those participants would experience a variety of ways to work collaboratively, to reflect and share. At the end of sessions, participants were asked to reflect on the structure of the session and how those structures impacted on their learning. These opportunities for inside-out learning to occur gave Jim further insights into how his students might learn. He indicated that the project suited him because he knew he took responsibility for what he learned from the sessions. He could try things out at his own pace, he could adapt the activities to suit himself and his class, and he could revisit the readings in his own time. He also became aware that the seeking of guidance and opinions from others did not necessarily mean that he had to accept them. He was making a great deal of 'tacit knowledge' visible to himself and viewing himself as learning from an inside-out view. This, in turn, created a great deal of intellectual unrest for Jim, yet he was willing to continue to explore the issues as he was hearing his peers struggling with the same dilemmas. He was raising many questions for himself that he needed to be answered. He couldn't just dismiss them as 'someone else's theory'. This was coming from him.

Implications for Jim's teaching

During the eight-week project, Jim began to move towards a more child-centred teaching approach, reflecting the beginnings of a paradigm shift in his thinking about the nature of language and learning. Because he was asked to try practical activities each week with his students and reflect on what had happened and why, he took time to reflect on his teaching and students in ways that he had not done before. He became aware that he was focusing more on what students can do rather than making the assumption 'that all fifth-grade students are the same'. He was surprised that they often knew more than he expected and many of them could also articulate how they went about their learning. This connection led to the understanding that he, the teacher, was not responsible for all the learning that his students did; that the teaching process was not a simple 'transmission of information' for students to take on board and be able to reproduce on call at a given level. 'I finally have come to realize that when I teach a "friendly letter" this one way (the way the English textbook outlines) . . . my students are going to write a different friendly letter to me and to each other, and there is nothing wrong with that'.

In Jim's shift from a teacher-centred approach to a child-centred approach, he became not only aware of, but accepted the fact that, his role in the classroom had changed and that his ability to teach this way, 'to guide student learning', would improve over time. 'I accept that as a wrestling coach, so why haven't I been doing it as a teacher?' Another connection he made in his shift to child-centred teaching was that students already might have a great deal of knowledge about that which he was trying to teach:

> The way I see it, because you take students who know how to do it and you see that they have that knowledge and maybe pick up a few more during the lesson, then you also find out (what they need to know). So it's no-one's fault if they can't do it on the spot. It's not my fault and now I have something to go with [for future teaching].

Jim was becoming aware that the teaching/learning responsibility was a joint one between himself and his students. He could 'guide' their learning, only if he learned from them to facilitate this learning. It would seem from his comments and his journal entries that he was beginning to understand the concept of 'a community' with shared responsibilities for a common purpose.

Jim's classroom environment

In trialling the many strategies and activities as part of his involvement in the project, Jim began to change his classroom practice. He was more consciously trying to establish an ethos that he saw other teachers doing in the videos he watched and from what he heard his peers sharing in groups. In addition, he was attempting to transfer insights about how he learned to how his children should learn in his class. He introduced more group work and more collaborative work 'because I find it works for me and my learning so it should work for my kids'. In the first instance, he and his students found this change difficult as he was not sure what he was doing or what the expected outcomes were. The students were equally unsure.

He also found that he did not know how to formulate the questions he needed to ask to implement his new practice: 'the new activities were very difficult for me to explain. I found I didn't have the words to describe them at first'. He did, however, feel that this issue would improve over time, as 'I need to be more specific with directions. I will get better at guiding things. When I guide sometimes (now) I feel like I've supplied everything but the last syllable of the word I wanted them to say and I don't want this'. He admitted that he began to look forward to coming to the next session so he could hear how his peers went with the activities and he could ask them questions. He also admitted that writing in his learning journal was valuable: 'at first I thought it was just a new fangled idea – but now I realize that I learn from writing in it and I realize how much I am learning about my kids'.

The facilitator and other support structures

Jim spoke often of the support provided by the facilitator of the project: 'I've known Gail for about 15 years. We travel to and from school together. In all those years we talked about a lot of school stuff but now we talk about kids and learning and good literacy activities. It's scary!' Jim acknowledged that the facilitator's role was not an easy one and he developed a great deal of respect for the way his colleague handled the role: 'I think we all work so hard because we see how hard she is working for us. That's good to have in a school like this where we have all been here for a long time'. Jim also regarded his students as support in his learning. He was surprised that his students were so willing to help him:

> Gail told us to let the kids in on what we were doing, so I did. I told them that I was learning new things and would be trying them out with them and that I needed their help. Some were stupid but most were great and I think we have developed a different sort of relationship.

Jim's attitude to the change process

Jim stated clearly that he didn't like being involved in change for change sake: 'I hate to keep making changes, to invest the time and effort into making the change that might be just a waste of time and energy'. He further indicated that he became impatient with the time that it took to implement new innovations. He was anxious to get everything in place as quickly as possible. He further stated that it had been this attitude to change that kept him from having changed his literacy education practice in previous years.

With respect to the project, Jim said he initially felt confused and quite nervous about the concepts and practices he was being asked to consider. Although this sense of confusion was clarified for him as he moved through the sessions, he stated that he often felt overwhelmed by the amount of information that was coming his way. However, in spite of these feelings, he also felt challenged by the project and indicated that he enjoyed it. Jim stated that he found it difficult 'to look inside' himself and reflect on his own learning and language use. He also found it difficult to articulate his personal beliefs and understandings of language and learning. He valued highly, however, the opportunity to be able to do this and the fact that he was given the responsibility of making the decision as to what he would take on board and what he would change in his classroom. He indicated that now he had begun to do this, he knew he would continue the practice: 'I feel much more confident about my views now. I don't think I really knew them before'.

Insights into the process of teacher change

As Jim began to gain some insights into the change process, his attitude towards it appeared to change during his involvement in the Frameworks project. He began to realize that there was no right or wrong way to implement the innovation, and that he would 'get better at doing it the more he used it'. This notion was supported by the fact that he became aware that he could try the strategy (adopt it), adapt it and then was expected to create ways of teaching from it to suit the needs of his students and his beliefs; that it was expected that his practice would change as he became clearer about his own beliefs about language teaching.

Although Jim indicated that he hated changing for the sake of change and that he wanted to change everything at once, he began to accept that change takes time and that he was not expected to change everything and, in fact, that it was his choice as to what he changed and why. He did not see the end of the project as a point in time where he had to know it all. He acknowledged that it was his responsibility to develop a clear plan for his future professional development. He commented at the completion of the project:

> I think it's time to step back and really sharpen and to find my beliefs, establish a project that may take a few years to develop. I'll probably

always be changing and I guess I am having a hard time realizing it's never going to be one set thing. I really feel that I have the knowledge now to put something together but it's going to take some time.

The interaction between inside-out learning and outside-in learning was clearly a challenge for Jim. However, this in itself was a learning experience for him. He came into the project as a willing yet negative participant, not really expecting to learn anything new: 'I really didn't think there were new things for me to learn', he indicated in his final interview. 'Yet what I learned was about myself as a teacher as much as anything. I learned how I can begin to do what I do better. And I learned that my kids will never show me respect unless I show them respect. It's a mutual thing'.

Conclusion

Structures, conditions, language-in-use and personal relationships are all central to support the dynamic interaction between the knowledge domains in a professional learning system. All have the potential to become *enablers*, and thus facilitate learning, or *inhibitors*, and thus act as barriers to learning. At various points in time, one or all of the above could have the potential to inhibit learning. The key to success is having sufficient enablers in place so that any barriers or inhibitors have only a temporary life span. Inhibitors need to be recognized by both the individual and the group for what they are, so that something can then be done about them. Fullan (1993) supports this when he says, 'Problems are our friends; but only if we do something about them' (p. 28). It is knowing what can be done, or at least where to start, which needs to be in place.

The model of professional learning known as 'Frameworks' discussed in this chapter has the potential of creating a learning culture in which there are sufficient enabling factors to support learners. No structure alone is sufficient and no one structure is more important than another, but together they can operate synergistically as a system so that any potential inhibiting factor in the learning culture will have only a temporary life span as learners work through that which they want to know. It is my belief that the model has the potential to permeate the learning culture and school organization overall. Fundamental to creating this culture is a self-awareness in teachers about how they learn in a professional learning system so that insights into the dynamic nature of learning can be encouraged in their own students in a classroom setting. It begins to lead to 'real learning [that] gets to the heart of what it means to be human' (Senge 1990: 14). Such learning, Senge argues, is the basic meaning of a learning organization – an organization that is continually expanding its capacity to create its future.

six

A reflective cycle for teacher learning: the Christchurch ICT Cluster project

Rob Walker

The primary reason technology has failed to live up to its promise is that it has been viewed as an answer to the wrong question. Decisions about purchases and uses of technology are typically driven by the question of how to improve the effectiveness of what schools are already doing – not how to transform what schools do.

(David 1994: 169)

This chapter focuses on one of the most widespread efforts for educational change in the last 10 years – the introduction of computers into classrooms. But have these attempts for change resulted in new pedagogies or reinforced traditional beliefs and practices? Salomon (2000) argues that technology has not changed educational traditions, but in many cases has been 'domesticated to be totally subservient to the ongoing practices' (p. 6). He contends that a stronger educational rationale is needed as a vision for change, rather than adapting new technologies to accommodate and reinforce existing ways. Perhaps the reason why new technologies have not changed current practice has to do with how they were introduced to teachers. This chapter describes a three-year professional learning system (PLS) to promote the teaching of ICT (information and communication technologies) in elementary classrooms in Christchurch, New Zealand. The first section highlights the importance of ICT for educational change. The second section explains a PLS specifically designed to support teachers in implementing these technologies. The third section focuses on the importance of a reflective cycle in helping teachers to make connections about their learning as a result of their involvement in the PLS.

If technology is to act as a catalyst to support change in a teacher's pedagogy, there needs to be a change in the relationship between teaching and learning in a classroom. This means restructuring pedagogy by changing the roles of teachers and students. With new technologies, the teacher need not be the sole source of knowledge, but instead a facilitator or guide to support student learning. Students in their new role become empowered as creators of things they couldn't create before, or as researchers with technology providing access to information from all over the world. It introduces students to a real-world inquiry approach, rather than relying solely on textbooks and the teacher for information to learn. This new way of thinking about learning requires many changes. For example, it involves challenging teachers' thinking about how technology is used and needs technical support, appropriate hardware, software, continual skill development, new policies, new assessment procedures, school planning for networking and enough resources for class use. To accommodate all these changes, teachers need a framework to support their professional learning as well as time to readjust many aspects of their classroom practices.

However, changing classroom pedagogy from one based on traditional beliefs and practices to one based on students having more responsibility for their own learning is an extremely difficult challenge. It means changing the nature of the curriculum from one based on fragmented knowledge to one based on real-life problem solving. But even with all the educational reform efforts over the last 10 years, this has proved to be a near impossible task. Means and Olson (1994) believe that the key to educational change is technology, but not by sporadically delivering computers and software to classrooms, which often reinforces existing practices, but by using technology as a vehicle for a new educational vision:

> Technology by itself is not the answer to this nation's educational problems. We believe that the power of technology will come from its combination with serious educational reform. Schools must first rethink their mission and structure, starting with the needs of students and a set of instructional principles, before they can understand the ways in which technology can help them. When technology is integrated into a broad effort for school reform, and is considered not as the instigator of reform or a cure-all, but as a set of tools to support specific kinds of instruction and intellectual inquiry, then educators, students, parents, and communities have a powerful combination that may indeed, bring necessary, positive change to this nation's schools.
>
> (Means and Olson 1994: 220–1)

Educational administrators, therefore, have to move beyond promoting the traditional one-shot workshop model of disseminating knowledge or presentations by experts if educational change is to be enhanced by technology.

Moreover, there is a sense of urgency. Educators can no longer sit back and ignore the enormous changes in technology that are increasingly affecting our lives. It is a reality now that is unavoidable. Negroponte (1998), a world leading thinker in the area of technology and its influence on society states, 'Like air and drinking water, being digital will be noticed only by its absence, not its presence' (p. 288). Sadly, though, professional learning in ICT for educators has rarely catered fully for their needs in a holistic way. Old professional development models with the expert computer-user being the source of all knowledge and skill does not necessarily work in schools. For teachers and administrators to engage in effective, sustainable and long-lasting change, old paradigms for teacher learning must be broken down and replaced with a new mindset. It is now of utmost importance to introduce new technologies in conjunction with quality professional learning so that schools can link with an increasingly technologically oriented world to support the effective integration of ICT into classroom learning.

Means and Olson (1994) identified eight guidelines for implementing technology in schools:

1 authentic, challenging tasks are best supported with flexible technology applications rather than canned instructional programmes;
2 schools should have project-based, cooperative teaching and learning skills in place;
3 technology implementation can be a safe context that allows teachers to become learners again and share ideas about curriculum and method;
4 teachers need time to develop their own technological skills;
5 easy access to technical assistance is critical, especially in the early years;
6 technological innovations are more effective when teachers feel ownership;
7 schools need permission and support for innovations from the district, state and federal levels of the education system; and
8 outside funding and support may be required to provide teachers with the level of technical assistance and professional development they need to implement technology-supported education reform.

Many of these considerations are consistent with the design of a professional learning system that began in 1998 in Christchurch, New Zealand. This three-year project was designed to support elementary teachers in using new tools for ICT in four schools in Christchurch, New Zealand. A feature of the ICT project was the employment of a full-time facilitator to support teachers (the author of this chapter). The centrepiece of the project was the use of a reflective cycle as one of the key conditions to help teachers make connections about their learning. The next part of the chapter describes the professional learning system, which will be followed by a focus on the cycle established within the project to support teacher reflection.

A professional learning system to promote the implementation of ICT

October 1998 was to be a turning point in the development and integration of ICT in New Zealand schools, as the Ministry of Education had just launched its 'Interactive Education – An Information and Communication Strategy' for schools. This strategy was designed to help schools integrate ICT into the learning process and improve schools' use of ICT for administrative purposes. A key initiative in the strategy was the establishment of ICT professional development schools, whereby up to 23 lead schools around the country were to be contracted for up to three years to provide professional learning to a cluster of other schools.

The schools

The Christchurch ICT Cluster is a group of four schools committed to creating learning environments and school cultures that embrace ICT to support and enhance teaching and learning. Each school was invited to join the cluster because the principal and the staff had the potential to create real improvement in how they use and understand the use of ICT. Represented within this group are low and high socioeconomic areas, rural and central city areas, various sizes of school, as well as a wide range of student and parent populations. Together, these four schools represent a diverse range of people working towards a common goal.

Fendalton Open Air School was the lead school of the cluster and is an elementary school in Christchurch, New Zealand. It is an urban school with a roll of approximately 540 students with grades K-6. For the last few years, Fendalton has been a leader in the area of ICT and the support and professional learning it offers its staff. Late in 1998, Fendalton was successful in winning one of the 23 lead school contracts from the Ministry of Education. The other three schools in this cluster are Roydvale School, Richmond School and Ashley School. Roydvale School is a K-6 school with approximately 220 students. Eight teachers are employed at this school, two of whom are in a job-sharing position. It is a middle-class school located in urban Christchurch. Richmond School has approximately 220 students from K-6 and it has eight teaching staff. Richmond School draws its students from a lower socioeconomic area in central Christchurch, which results in a more transient and multicultural student population. Ashley School is a middle-class country school situated 35 km north of Christchurch with six teaching staff. It has approximately 140 students with grades K-8 and Ashley draws its students from a predominantly rural area. The Christchurch ICT Cluster was founded on the belief that teachers are the dream makers and hold the key to improving education and how it embraces ICT. It is teachers who make the difference to education and learning for children. Making learning even more exciting and powerful through effective use of ICT was a major goal. The expectation was that teachers from the Christchurch ICT Cluster would become leaders in this area and provide exemplary models for others in education in the future.

Design of the professional learning system

This project rejected the conventional professional development programme approach of introducing new technologies to teachers followed by a 'one-off' workshop to support implementation into class programmes. Instead, a professional learning system was designed to provide teachers with a school-based learning environment to support the complex nature of educational change. A rich environment for teacher learning was established with six main components or subsystems that contributed to the design of this professional learning system. These six subsystems are: the practicum subsystem; the lead teacher subsystem; the principal subsystem; the leading with ICT subsystem; other supports subsystem; and the kids as coaches subsystem. An overview of the main elements or subsystems of this professional learning system is provided in Figure 6.1.

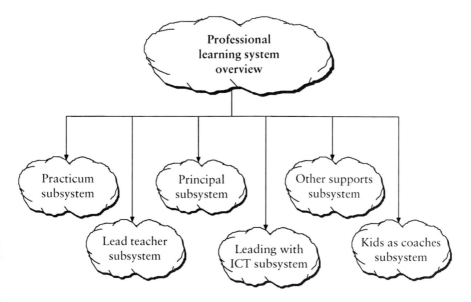

Figure 6.1 Overview of professional learning system.

Aspects of each subsystem were negotiated with the participants, and the role of reflection and team-building contributed to the influence this had on learning for staff, principals and students alike. The kids as coaches subsystem started in the second year of the project, the leading with ICT subsystem started in the third year of the project, while the other three subsystems were part of the project since its inception. Each of these subsystems will be described in turn, starting with the practicum subsystem.

Practicum subsystem
The practicum was our key strategy for supporting teacher change. The practicum was an intensive six-month course, whereby 10 staff from the four schools came together on nine occasions to work with the facilitator. The project had as its focus the development of school cultures where staff develop a sense of community and their need to use ICT to improve teaching and learning. During each practicum day, staff worked on a range of things:

- sharing what they are doing in their classrooms;
- learning new skills and looking at how these can be integrated into the classroom;
- examining professional readings and looking at how these fit with ICT;
- reflecting on their experiences and thinking; and
- visiting other classrooms where good teaching and learning with ICT is being modelled.

The practicum provided the structure and process for reflection in and on experience. During the three-year project, every staff member in each school participated in the practicum. This gave continuity and built a 'critical mass' of staff who became increasingly reflective in their practice and sought further learning with ICT. These elements interacted together to provide a culture that supported teacher learning and school change, as shown in Figure 6.2. As can be seen, a wide range of strategies was used to provide a combination of conditions for teacher learning. These strategies operated in a dynamic way and changed to meet emerging needs of staff in the practicum. Central to this process was a reflective cycle, which helped teachers to connect with many elements of the model and underpinned teacher learning. The cycle for reflection and how it interacted within the professional learning system will be described after the other subsystems have been explained.

Lead teacher subsystem
The lead teacher subsystem focused on supporting a teacher in each school towards becoming a leader in ICT and education, and helping them to encourage the process of change. The lead teacher's roles were to: support teachers as they worked to make ICT an integral part of their classroom

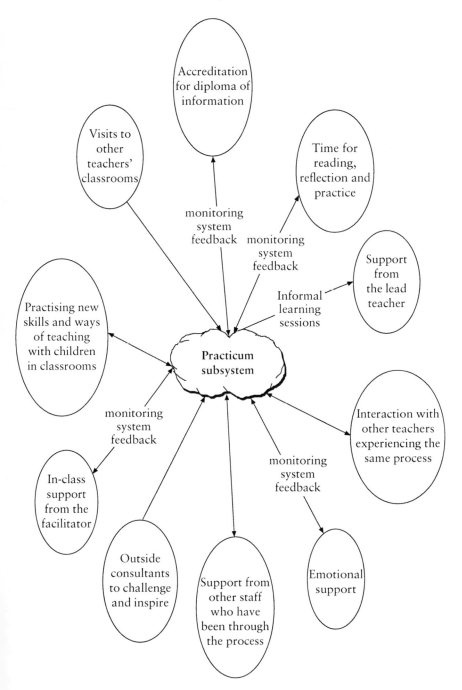

Figure 6.2   Elements of the practicum subsystem.

programmes; help with the organization and management of the contract in each school; and work towards the further development of their own personal teaching to integrate the ideas presented in the contract. Elements of the lead teacher subsystem included conference attendance, bus trips to other schools that were making effective use of ICT, and a series of meetings each semester to look at a range of aspects. Examples of such aspects included: higher end skills development; looking at models that helped to develop an understanding of teacher professional learning; looking at the nature of change; discussing practicum staff progress and looking at how best to support them; visiting industry sites to see ICT in other settings; presenting to other educators at workshops and conferences; sharing successes and challenges from their classrooms; and looking at systems that supported change in their schools.

Principal subsystem
The principal subsystem focused on the personal skill development of each principal, as well as wider issues pertaining to ICT and education. Their role was to oversee the development of ICT in their schools and lead by example. The elements of their programme included: looking at research; visiting industry sites to see ICT in other settings; regular meetings to share, discuss and debate issues relating to ICT in their schools and in education; and conference attendance at certain times during the year. The lead teacher and principal subsystems complemented the support provided for teachers and encouraged the process of change.

Leading with ICT subsystem
The leading with ICT subsystem began in the third year of the project. It was designed in response to the need to build the next layer down from the lead teachers and to continue the learning of staff who had stretched themselves as a result of the practicum. This would strengthen school ICT leadership depth and facilitate ongoing learning with ICT should any of the lead teachers move on. This subsystem focused on the following: increasing the depth and breadth of teachers' skills; further exploration of and research on the learning model; strengthening teachers' reflective practice; establishing model classrooms; strengthening teachers' leadership skills; and keeping up to date with new research and best practice.

Other supports subsystems
Throughout the project, the lead teacher, principal, kids as coaches, leading with ICT and practicum subsystems provided a range of opportunities to staff. These included conferences, weekly workshops, informal 'just-in-time' sessions, seminars and workshops with educational experts who had a long-term relationship with the cluster and 'techie brekkies'. Staff were

encouraged to attend conferences that focused on thinking as well as ICT. These provided inspiration, challenge and a wide range of skill-learning opportunities. The project subsidized attendance at these events. Because different conferences provided different types of learning opportunities, we were able to target these specifically to different groups of staff. Weekly workshops were made available to staff within the four schools, so that they could spend two hours learning new skills to improve their personal skill. These workshops were open to anyone in the four schools and were run by our business partner, Infovision Technology. Skill-learning opportunities included those for basic skills (e.g. basic desktop and file management, spreadsheeting, database, graphics, multimedia, Internet, email, digital image capture, etc.) and high-end skills (e.g. image editing and manipulation using Adobe Photoshop, web site construction, collaboration software, networking, etc.). In addition, each school's lead teacher organized just-in-time support sessions to meet an immediate need for staff. This type of support was crucial because staff could have skills-based learning opportunities *as and when* they needed them, which emphasized learning new things 'just-in-time', rather than 'just-in-case'. A key element in this type of support was the use of 'techie brekkies', flexible sessions that occurred at different times and could include breakfast. This type of support usually focused just on skills, while at other times it focused on the integration of skills into the curriculum.

Kids as coaches subsystem
The kids as coaches subsystem began in the third year of the project and was aimed at bringing children from each of the four schools together regularly, so they could develop their skills and look at how they could support other children and staff when they were back in their own school. This was an exciting innovation which aimed to: explore what kids could do when given powerful new tools; allow kids the opportunity to direct ICT in their schools; and helpkids explore learning with ICT and develop skills that would be taught to peers in their respective schools. The next section focuses on the role of reflection in the PLS, with emphasis on the practicum subsystem, as this was our key strategy for supporting teacher change.

The role of a reflective cycle in the professional learning system

When moving from a linear 'professional development programme' approach to a non-linear 'professional learning system' approach, teachers need to understand how to make connections between various inputs to enhance their learning. Central to the design of a professional learning system is a reflective cycle to assist in this process. Consistent with a complexity world view, learning complicated tasks such as new technologies is a non-linear process requiring multiple conditions to sustain teacher learning during the change. To monitor the patterns of change, it is essential that teachers reflect on their experiences to make their own connections about their learning. This type of reflection is a key condition for success in a changing technological world. Caine and Caine (1997) believe that reflection-on-action is a key to being able to change one's behaviour as a learner:

> One part of everyday self-reference is reflection-on-action . . . reflection-on-action means that after a person acts (whether an athlete or architect), feedback is supplied, usually by an external source, and can then be used by the person to self-monitor and improve.
>
> (Caine and Caine 1997: 134)

They describe reflection-in-action as the person's ability to observe their performance while it is going on, 'to assess what is happening, and to make changes midstream' (Caine and Caine 1997: 135).

There were four requirements for the practicum. These areas tied in directly with the process for reflection and encompass the criteria that staff worked towards:

1 to reflect critically on each of the readings;
2 to produce examples of quality learning from the students in their class;
3 to increase personal skills and show evidence of this; and
4 to continue this learning for a further six months.

Teachers in the practicum reflected on new knowledge, current thinking, new skills, strategies for using ICT in their classroom and their ongoing professional goals. This helped the teachers to see themselves as learners and become what Diltz (1996) terms increasingly 'open to doubt'. This is a process that takes time, is challenging and presents difficulties that need to be overcome. How the system responds to these challenges and difficulties is crucial and feedback is a central element in the system's ability to support change. Figure 6.3 shows how this reflection is a key condition in this professional learning system; it also demonstrates how multiple conditions for teacher learning acted collectively to create and support change. Through this cycle, teachers made connections from the influences on their learning and became aware of the overall patterns of change.

As can be seen in Figure 6.3, teachers recorded their reflections based on five dimensions or trigger questions. These questions were chosen to support the reflective cycle by helping teachers to dig deeper into their thinking and broaden the scope of their reflection. Teachers needed to reflect on what they were thinking, what they were doing and new knowledge as it came to light. The use of the five questions in an ongoing way helped to

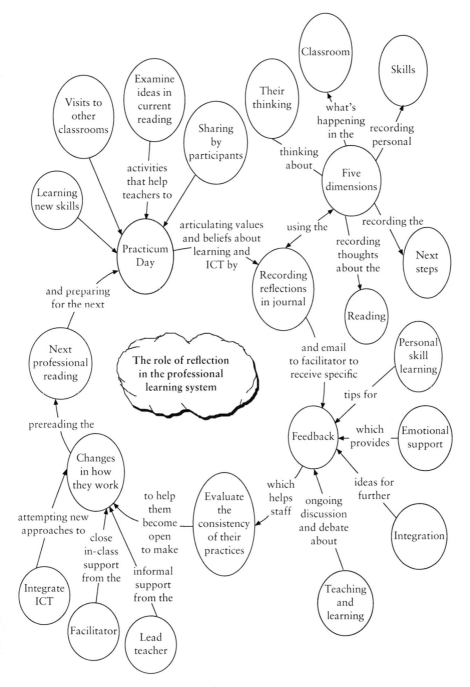

Figure 6.3   A reflective cycle in the professional learning system.

Table 6.1   Questions to guide reflection in the reflective cycle

Trigger questions for reflection	Relevance to the reflective cycle
1 What do teachers think about the reading?	New knowledge provides a stimulus for thinking about new things as well as current knowledge
2 What do teachers think about how their thinking is changing?	Metacognition provides self-evaluation and information for emotional support
3 What are teachers doing in the classroom that relate to the project and ICT?	Links to the classroom give a grounding in practice
4 What are teachers learning in terms of their personal skills?	Personal skill learning gives task information about what the teachers are learning
5 What are teachers intending to do next?	Goal setting provides a link to action and what teachers intend doing next

establish a 'reflective cycle', which, in turn, supported teachers in inquiring into their process for change and continuous improvement. Indeed, some staff likened the practicum to an 'inquiry into my own teaching'. This cycle of reflection here paints a comprehensive picture of change over time. The questions are summarized in Table 6.1.

The questions listed in Table 6.1 interrelate to provide a pattern and a map of an individual teacher's journey as they learned to integrate ICT into their classroom, as well as the patterns of challenge and success along the way. These five questions will be described in turn, showing how they provided a platform for inquiry into teacher thinking and behaviour.

What do teachers think about the reading?
Through the use of a series of professional readings, teachers were taken through a process of relating what they currently knew to a range of theories about teaching and learning. Some of the ideas in these readings may have been new to some staff, while others may have been familiar with them. First, staff examined the content of each reading in a general sense; they then related this to their use of ICT. These readings ranged from specific classroom strategies, such as good questioning techniques, to examining global issues such as quality in education. This provided a range of ideas that acted as a stimulus to help ease teachers into the idea of the value of ongoing professional reading and dialogue about this.

Teachers were required to keep a reflective journal and one aspect of this was to comment on the following professional readings, which comprised the core content of the practicum and formed the basis of the first part of the criteria:

Atkin, J. (1999) *Understanding How We Learn*, ICT Cluster seminar notes, 12 April.

Caine, R. and Caine, G. (1997) *Education on the Edge of Possibility*. Alexandria, VA: ASCD.

Knapp, C. (1992) *Lasting Lessons: A Teacher's Guide to Reflecting on Experience*. Charlestown, WV: Eric Clearinghouse on Rural Education and Small Schools.

Lazear, D. (1994) *Seven Ways of Teaching – The Artistry of Teaching with Multiple Intelligences*. Melbourne: Hawker Brownlow Education.

McKenzie, J. (1997) The question is the answer – creating research programs for an age of information, *Now On web site*, October 1997 (available online at: http://emifyes.iserver.net/fromnow/oct97/question.html).

Tapscott, D. (1999) Educating the net generation, *Educational Leadership*, 56(5): 6–11 (available online at: http://www.ascd.org/readingroom/edlead/abstracts/feb99.html).

What do teachers think about how their thinking is changing?

This supports the metacognitive aspect of reflection that teachers should encourage within their classrooms. ICT can be a challenge for teachers who are either hesitant or may have little or no experience in this area. Because of this, it was important here that teachers were given a means to express how they were feeling. Emotional support was found to be vital in the area of professional learning for teachers in ICT. This aspect of the reflective journal was extremely important. Information shared allowed the facilitator and lead teachers to adapt how they supported individual staff. This might have meant a 'shoulder to cry on', or for someone to visit and ask how their teaching is going. Emotional support was dependent on the relationships among individual staff, a lead teacher in each school and the facilitator. Information shared gave the facilitator useful insights into teachers' attitudes and how comfortable teachers were within the process of change.

What are teachers doing in the classroom that relate to the project and ICT?

We found that teachers didn't always naturally jump straight in and try new things. It was more likely that a teacher would try to change something if they were thinking about it already in relation to what they were reading and thinking about at that time. The focus on one particular reading or theory of learning at different times helped teachers to focus on specific aspects of their beliefs about learning or aspects of their class programme.

The underpinning belief was that any professional learning must be set within a practical context for it to be authentic and long-lasting. This element to the reflective process encouraged ownership and accountability within staff and built the need within a supportive climate.

What are teachers learning in terms of their personal skills?
We always strived to encourage staff to learn new skills when those skills would be useful to them personally or in the classroom. In this way, teachers learned new things 'just-in-time' as opposed to 'just-in-case'. If teachers learned new skills as they needed them and attempted to integrate them into their class programmes, they naturally became facilitators of learning, as they didn't always know the answers and were having to learn alongside their students. As time progressed, staff developed their hunger for new skills. This was a natural way to help teachers change their role within the classroom. This invariably caused challenge and sometimes stress for the teacher, as they were no longer 'in control', which tied in with the emotional support component and the reflection and feedback process. We called this 'teacher ICT literacy development'. Teacher ICT literacy development created increased need within schools as staff became excited about their new discoveries, as the world of possibilities opened up to them.

What are teachers intending to do next?
These teachers were constantly made to 'look into the future' and think about what they were going to do next by recording what they planned. This created a link to intended action in their classrooms. This type of goal-setting built ownership for staff as they had to be continually upskilling, while thinking about how they would integrate these skills into their classrooms. Our aim here was to strengthen ownership of personal learning and a positive attitude to discovery, exploration and continual skill development in teachers.

These five questions, when used together, provided triggers for reflection, thereby providing an excellent platform for inquiry, challenge, change and improvement. This created a long-term belief in the value of a strong reflective process and ownership of their learning.

Using a database for reflection and feedback in the reflective cycle

An important feature of the reflective cycle was the provision of feedback to each teacher by the facilitator in an ongoing way. This was a vital element in the reflective cycle and a database system was designed to help the facilitator to monitor the reflective journal and the in-class work of each staff member. This database provided comprehensive feedback for teachers while they were on their practicum. Teachers received feedback on both their personal reflections using the five trigger questions and on their progress as they attempted to integrate ICT in their classroom. The process for reflection involved each practicum staff member emailing their reflections to the facilitator, the facilitator recording these in the database, the facilitator recording his feedback and then emailing this back to the teacher. The process for in-class support feedback involved the facilitator working alongside teachers in the practicum and recording feedback, then emailing this to the teachers. This happened throughout the practicum and was a key element in the reflective cycle. It provided another type of feedback on what the teacher was attempting to do in terms of classroom integration. It supported teachers as they learned new skills in the classroom and increased teacher ownership of skill learning by providing specific feedback as part of the reflective cycle. The next section provides excerpts from a teacher's journal as recorded in the database, supplemented by in-class support feedback comments, to illustrate how multiple ways of reflection and feedback facilitated the process of change.

Colleen: using the reflective cycle to support teacher change

This section contains excerpts from a teacher's electronic journal that illustrated the process of change during the first six months of her practicum. Colleen taught a class of year 2 students (6- and 7-year-olds) and she had been teaching for approximately 20 years. Before joining the practicum, Colleen had not used ICT in her classroom except for word processing and drawing pictures. I will use the five trigger questions for reflection to illustrate the close relationship between the changes that were happening in the teacher's classroom and the multiple conditions for teacher learning as shown in Figure 6.3. Together with this, I will supplement the reflective journal statements with feedback based upon in-class support visits. These face-to-face visits supported the practicum teachers in changes that they wanted to initiate in terms of how they used ICT in the classroom similar to 'just-in-time' support. These excerpts demonstrate the inter-related nature of reflection in the professional learning system and how this develops over time. The structure of this journal shows the teacher's reflection with regard to each trigger question, together with feedback from the facilitator. Reflections and feedback are indented. After each reflection and accompanying feedback, a brief explanation shows how this fits into the professional learning system. These excerpts show that change was not a linear process and efforts to use ICT were initially not as successful as intended.

Q. 1. Thinking about the readings

Colleen's reflections, 2 August 2000

I agree with many of the statements, e.g. 'the most potent force
for change is the students themselves'. However, there are many
statements, mainly in the Eight Shifts of Interactive Learning, that
do not apply only to learning through technology. Learner-centred
education begins with an evaluation of abilities, learning values,
social contexts and other important factors that affect the student
(a class description?). OK, ICT may help these teaching strategies
along, but aren't they what we have been talking about and using
(in part or whole) for years? The last paragraph about the challenges
financially and personally has long been a stumbling block, or excuse
for keeping the *status quo*. Hopefully the cluster will help us to be
part of the change.

Facilitator's feedback, 13 August 2000

I agree with you partly in that I think 'Yes', we have been talking
about these sorts of things you mention; I wonder if we really
practise them however? How do you see ICT fitting into this? Can
it inhibit or help these things? What are the things that influence
this? I, too, hope the cluster may be able to help us deal with the
financial realities we face. We do have very limited access, but the
flip side of that is that we have very innovative teachers who can
make the most of what we have got – I think you are one of these!

This part of Colleen's first reflection demonstrates that her notions about
the role of the teacher were being challenged, through statements such as,
'OK, ICT may help these teaching strategies along, but aren't they what we
have been talking about and using (in part or whole) for years'. At this
stage in the practicum, Colleen didn't really use ICT with her class, but she
was keen to do so. Note the emotionally supportive statement in the last
paragraph of the facilitator's feedback, which turns a negative into a positive. This shows a key aspect of the professional learning system – the role
of emotional support. This is important, as it would help Colleen continue
to open up further during the process. Colleen mentions the financial realities
of lack of equipment as well as the fact that this is an excuse for not making
progress for many students. Note here that the facilitator's feedback turns
this around, stating that teachers can be innovative in their use of ICT,
rather than letting a lack of resource act as a barrier to trying new things in
the classroom. This reading invariably challenged the role of teachers, which,
as mentioned earlier, 'opens them up to doubt'. I believe this is an important

aspect of the process of change. This reflection shows us that she was open to the practicum and to her own professional learning.

Q. 2. Teacher thinking

Colleen's reflections, 2 August 2000

As I have been working with young children for so long, the 'Chew and Spew' method has never been part of my teaching strategies. Children need to relate the new information to their previous knowledge, use it and make some sort of meaning out of it that fits into their schema. I do often model an activity, but expect the children to be using that model in their activities to help them construct meaning. Interaction is a key feature of learning – between the child and teacher and between child and child. My aim is to get children thinking and acting with autonomy. My most frequently asked question must be, 'What do you think it might be?' Their guess is often right and to have that confirmed is more powerful than for me just to tell them an answer. Of course I need to know the children's abilities and needs, to plan and prepare activities appropriate to their level and according to the National Curriculum.

My thinking about ICT . . . it is part of the children's future and should be part of their present. I can see huge value in programs like Kid Pix developing problem-solving and thinking skills. Most of my children are not good enough readers to use the Net. I can guide this and model it as shared reading – I haven't yet! I don't need to be convinced to use ICT, but I need some strategies for making it easy to use in the classroom.

Facilitator's feedback, 13 August 2000

You have touched on something that Stephen Heppell mentioned a couple of times in his keynote at the conference – the need for a mentor of some sort. Your idea of using the net as a shared reading experience is best; that will also give you opportunities to help them develop a reading conscience when they move to more independent work using the web. It's great that you don't need convincing of the need/value of ICT – your journey will be much more easy in this case!!!! Strategies – let's have a look at your planning and also do some planning next practicum day to help this. Have you seen www.sunshine.co.nz?

These comments show that the teacher was relating the ideas in the reading to those she held already, that of 'schema'. This is important for creating a change paradigm, as we believe that teachers need to relate their current knowledge to new knowledge to aid the process of reflection. In the second paragraph, Colleen notes that she used an existing teaching strategy, that of shared reading, to teach her class how to use ICT. Note the clue in the facilitator's feedback on examining her planning to help her find useful strategies for integrating ICT into the classroom, which would help her to break tasks down into manageable steps as she attempted to integrate ICT more and more. The facilitator has also suggested a web site for her class, which has age-appropriate reading material on it. While Colleen was preparing for the next practicum day (see Figure 6.3), she was attempting to use the Internet with her class, which, in turn, helped her to examine how she worked.

Q. 3. Classroom action

Colleen's reflections, 2 August 2000

I am not very organized. Other things seem to take over even when I have planned and made charts to follow. The children have all written stories and had a go at Kid Pix. Otherwise, it is Maths programmes at Maths time and Language programmes at Reading time. We have used the digital camera (teacher dominated!) and video camera – the kids did get a go. I have been waiting to be on the practicum to really get a good programme going.

Facilitator's feedback, 13 August 2000

Being 'not very organized' is OK. Integrating ICT will actually create a bit of 'disorganization' at first, then you will figure out systems with the class that make life easier for all. This takes time, so my advice is 'jump in and get wet'. The more exploration you do the better placed you will be to think through systems, procedures and little strategies that help you. Your flexibility in timetabling will be challenged by this, which will be fun.

The emotional support element in the process for reflection was acting here, whereby the teacher was feeling disorganized and the facilitator was validating this as a natural part of the process of change. The fact that she felt disorganized shows that she was attempting things in her classroom that she hadn't before. Analysis of the in-class support sheet dated 16 August shows that Colleen was learning to use the popular children's programme Kid Pix with her class. She was focusing on recording the children's voices to help them explain their project. This is consistent with a change in her classroom, as she had given all the children in the class the opportunity to create a picture using Kid Pix. As part of this, Colleen was trying to teach her class how to save these pictures correctly. She was also starting to learn about the use of databases to help manage her administration.

Colleen had already made some changes in how she worked with ICT; for example, by creating charts to provide support and scaffolding to help develop independence in her class. Other changes included attempting to use different forms of ICT (i.e. the digital camera) and also evaluating how effective she was with this. She wasn't evaluating how well she used ICT before the practicum. She mentions that her use of ICT at this stage was teacher dominated, and in 'subject specific' areas where she was most comfortable. This was accepted by the facilitator as a natural part of moving through the process of change. Colleen would in time move from the known to the unknown, as she attempted less teacher-dominated ways of using ICT with her class.

Q. 4. Personal skill development

Colleen's reflections, 2 August 2000

Following up from the Computer Conference workshops – practising making Kid Pix slide shows and using the Mac at school to word process on, instead of doing it at home on my PC. I've had a look at Guru Net, which gives hints and shortcuts for the Internet.

Facilitator's feedback, 13 August 2000

Good for you – that's great to hear. What is the URL for Guru Net?

Here Colleen can be seen doing things that she hadn't before the practicum. She had attended a local conference to help further upskill herself, which was giving her more impetus to make more attempts to integrate ICT. She was using her computer at school, rather than just the one she has at home. She was also starting to use a different form of ICT, the Internet, at school as well. The skills she had learned during this conference, as well as her use of the Internet and Kid Pix in the classroom, were being reinforced during in-class support visits from the facilitator during this time.

Q. 5. What am I doing next?

Colleen's reflections, 2 August 2000

Write a cooperative story with the children and get children to each make a page of the continuing story. Take photos of children and put them onto a desktop picture when they are class leader. Use topic pictures for the other computer desktop. (Can I make a photo a screen saver?)

Facilitator's feedback, 13 August 2000

Keep up the good work.

Colleen was starting to make this transition from learning to use the technology to using the technology to make learning better. She was attempting new approaches to integrate ICT, as shown in Figure 6.3. She was making connections between what was shared during the practicum day and her classroom. Colleen was taking on board some of the ideas shared during the practicum day, where one of the activities was to write a continuing story with other teachers. This shows the importance of connecting the personal reflection with activities on the practicum day – through sharing with participants and other teachers whose classrooms practicum staff may visit. Most ICT use at this stage was still teacher dominated, but Colleen was starting to explore a wider variety of ICT activities. This would translate in time to her being able to modify and improve the strategies she attempted in the classroom as children became more skilled and, as a class, everyone became more aware of better ways to both learn to use the technology and to use the technology to help their learning. Colleen was starting to ask questions about how to do things that she didn't know, which is another sign of the change process having an effect on the teacher and how she saw herself as a learner.

Q. 1. Thinking about the readings

Colleen's reflections, 12 September 2000

I tried to look at each of the 12 findings presented by Caine and Caine and relate them to my experiences. The brain processes create parts and wholes simultaneously. One part of the brain reduces the information into parts and the other perceives it as a whole. Global ideas should be given from the beginning – I agree with this very much. I get so frustrated when someone tries to teach me in small steps, before knowing the whole picture.

Facilitator's feedback, 20 September 2000

I'm interested in your thoughts about 'Global ideas should be given from the beginning. I agree with this very much. I get so frustrated when someone tries to teach me in small steps, before knowing the whole picture'. How do you apply this knowledge of how you like to learn to situations when you are learning new things to do with ICT?

The facilitator encouraged Colleen to look at herself as a learner in relation to one of the principles described in the reading in an attempt to help her become more aware of herself as a learner. The aspect of the reading that the facilitator was reinforcing was the idea of introducing global ideas to learners first, rather than the steps involved. I have found that this is something that doesn't happen much in teacher professional development in ICT – people tend to focus just on the small steps first.

Q. 2. Teacher thinking

Colleen's reflections, 12 September 2000

The Caine and Caine reading made me reflect on my ideas about learning. Their theories fit into my thinking. Some ideas expanded on my thoughts and others voiced them. I still keep in mind, how does ICT enhance children's learning (for the extra time, expense and hassles, it has to be doing a lot)? I have highlighted the headings above where I think that ICT would have more effect on learning. Multiple intelligences – The ideas from 'Seven Ways at Once' are great – thanks. Quality – my Quality World workbook looks interesting – I'd still need to know more to use it.

Facilitator's feedback, 20 September 2000

Yes, the headings you have highlighted are not really focused on enough in teacher PD in ICT. This reminds me of a conversation I had with Geoffrey and Renate Caine, where we were talking about 'humanizing the ICT/PD experience for educators', and how if we get this right then our model will be awesome.

Colleen was making connections in her thinking to ideas in the readings, by highlighting areas where she thought ICT could help more than others. This shows that Colleen was becoming increasingly reflective as she recorded these changes in her thinking.

Q. 3. Classroom action

Colleen's reflections, 12 September 2000

I'm in a muddle – I seem to have tried a bit of this and a bit of that and have not done anything thoroughly. I want to try everything! I don't seem to be producing examples of quality learning. Management needs some fine-tuning. Half the class took a digital photo of a friend – one photo is on the desktop. I'd like to get all the class's mug-shots on file. A few children have been involved in making graphs. Whole class graphs, with all the names, are too big to read easily off the screen. We'll try group graphs and stating a preference from a short list (e.g. cat, dog, horse, mouse, bird – pets). I videoed some dancing with Rooms 4 and 5, but got completely carried away with Art on Friday and forgot to get the camera out. Haven't got to the editing yet.

Facilitator feedback, 20 September 2000

It's OK to be in a muddle sometimes – remind me to get you a really good quote about muddling. It talks about how we should muddle, muddle and muddle some more to learn effectively. I guess the key is to not 'stress out' too easily – especially with ICT!!!!

There are three indicators that Colleen was starting to make changes in her classroom teaching. The first is that Colleen was evaluating the consistency of her approaches. This is shown through Colleen thinking about the quality of work her students were doing, as she was concerned that her students were trying too many things at once and not completing them. Changes in this area were reflected through different types of discussions in the classroom and through the use of tools such as rubrics and self-evaluation techniques with children. Quality was a topic for the professional reading and the practicum day at this time.

The second indicator of change was that Colleen was attempting to integrate ICT in a wider variety of ways, which was, initially, causing her frustration. Stretching out and trying too many things at once is a characteristic of teachers who are trying to push themselves into the world of new possibilities. In-class support feedback dated 12 September 2000 indicates that Colleen was attempting a wider variety of things in her classroom: creating graphs with her students; sending emails to other classes in other places; setting the desktop picture (or wallpaper) for her computer; using Inspiration to help brainstorm for her topics; ClarisWorks drawing; as well as modelling to the class. This particular part of her feedback also was letting Colleen know that she needed to get her computer fixed in her classroom so that she could send and receive emails and that this was a priority. I noted that the teacher needed to access the system by getting the lead teacher in her school to organize this and that it was a priority for her continuing development. This shows that the professional learning system was supporting Colleen and that the facilitator was checking on the effectiveness of the system (from this, part of my follow-up would be with the lead teacher).

The third indicator of change was that Colleen was making more use of groups rather than using ICT with the whole class. This was a shift from teaching the whole class together at once to working more with groups; again, this is characteristic of a teacher working within a strong reflective cycle. Colleen was attempting things in her classroom that she had owner-ship of and this was allowing her to try new ways of grouping children when they were using ICT.

Q. 4. Personal skill development

Colleen's reflections, 12 September 2000

With guidance, I got a photo onto the desktop. With practice and help from Rob and Thomas I have come to grips with spreadsheets and graphs – well enough to take the class through it. I put the practicum members' email addresses into my address book at home – there doesn't seem to be a connection for our classroom to be on the Internet and it is too cold and lonely to be playing on the school (crappy) computer in my spare time. I am doing more hunting around and discovering, rather than having to ask for help so much.

Facilitator feedback, 20 September 2000

Great, you did it. One of the wonderful things about ICT is its ability to use visual images – that is why I set one of the practicum prerequisites as being able to bring digital photos into the computer. There are many other things you can do with images once they are in the computer. Permit me to ask you a question: 'Is it important to take the whole class through something?' Why or why not? When?

Good for you, your ability to solve your own problems with ICT is improving. This is REALLY important, as you need to be as self-sufficient as possible. Plus it feels really good to be able to solve problems for oneself!

Another sign of change was that Colleen was transferring skills into other situations such as her home. Her confidence was increasing, as was her ability to figure out problems for herself. This shows development in independence. The facilitator was helping her to make connections about her use of groups and the use of ICT by asking questions about her view of 'whether it is important to teach the whole class the same thing at the same time'. This reflects the ongoing debate about teaching and learning in relation to the feedback aspect of the professional learning system. Analysis of in-class support feedback sheets shows that she was attempting more complicated ICT activities with her class and a wider variety of ICT tasks. She was beginning to use children in her class to help her solve ICT prob-lems, which had not been the case before the practicum. The aspect of the teacher's role that was being challenged by the facilitator here was the notion of teaching the same thing to the whole class at once.

Q. 5. What am I doing next?

Colleen's reflections, 12 September 2000

Strategies to make life easier with ICT – study this and use it.
Clocking in – Helen's work with the fizzy drink impressed me and I
think my kids would love to do it.

Facilitator's feedback, 20 September 2000

Great, these strategies have been developed from many teachers.
They will help you. Some might seem quite obvious, but are worth
exploring! Yes, Helen's work with the drawing strategy is really
working in her classroom. She is making loads of progress because
her kids are developing many basic skills as a result of this simple,
easy-to-manage strategy. Keep up the great work!

Finding easy-to-use ideas that work in the classroom is possibly one of
the biggest challenges for teachers who are learning to integrate ICT. Here
you can see the uptake of an idea from a teacher who has been through an
earlier practicum. This shows how a classroom visit during a practicum day
helped Colleen make this change in her classroom. Classroom visits by the
facilitator were commented on by almost all practicum staff as being one of
the most beneficial aspects of the project and were a key aspect of the
reflective cycle.

Q. 3. Classroom action

Colleen's reflections, 6 November 2000

The Space topic lends itself very well to using ICT and I had heaps
of ideas, but I have not used them all and some have backfired.
Ideas used: Inspiration for brainstorming 'What we know about
Space' and for recording thinking skills ideas from buzz groups on
topics such as 'Questions to ask an astronaut in an interview' and
'What if the Earth had no gravity?' My first attempt was a disaster
and I ended up writing it and putting it on Inspiration after school
– but never say die, I tried it again the next day and it worked well.
The Inspiration experts have been gradually tutoring others – in a
topic 'What I like to do'. Hyperstudio for drawing a planet and
making a moon or spacecraft move around it and CDs for
information.
Ideas yet to be used include: use of the Internet for information
and to download pictures for slideshows, using a database for

space contract questions. We are using email and are currently corresponding with a class in Ohio.

During one of the practicum days and facilitator in-class support visits, peer tutoring was discussed and modelled, which shows how sharing by other practicum staff during the practicum days and how in-class support aspects of the reflective cycle helped to encourage change. Children were coaching each other rather than the teacher being responsible for the coaching, which demonstrates a major change in how Colleen was operating with ICT.

Summary of Colleen's change

During the six months of Colleen's practicum, she experienced many successes, challenges and frustrations. These are all natural parts of a reflective cycle that supports a teacher working in this professional learning system. Many of the changes proposed were necessary to push Colleen out of her comfort zone before they could happen in practice and to make her reflect upon how she was using ICT with her students. Colleen was able to see herself as a learner alongside her class, which further reinforced her to attempt to integrate ICT into her class programme in a wide variety of ways. Colleen sent an email to the facilitator six months after the practicum finished that shows that her integration of ICT into her regular planning for teaching has been sustained:

A final email reflection from Colleen, 20 May 2001

The main thing I have learned from the project is that I try to keep in mind that what I do in the class is to help children to learn. So as they are on their learning journey, how can ICT help them? I always consider how I might use ICT when doing a unit or weekly planning – if I write it in, then I get myself organized to do it and it happens. Having a place for ICT on the planning sheets is important.

I feel comfortable and confident about using ICT and I can now think of new ways of doing things and taking new ideas on board readily. We have been fortunate to have huge amounts of support and expertise in our cluster and I feel empowered computerwise. I think a huge plus in using computers is that children love to use them, so are motivated to be fully involved in the learning. Something I have learned is that children are great at teaching each other and they just need the system set up so they can go for it.

I have also found value at letting them have a go in an unstructured way once they have learned a skill such as making a

Kidpix slideshow. Several children have puddled around and 'done their own thing' with a slideshow.

I see the Junior school as building a platform for use of ICT in education – we can only do so much when their reading and writing skills are limited. As in all junior teaching, modelling is vital. The children are currently using a variety of programs, such as Kidpix, Inspiration, Appleworks and Email.

Interestingly, as Colleen learned about ICT, she was able to make changes to the way she set up the conditions for student learning in her class, as 'they just need the system set up so they can go for it'. Through ongoing reflection using the five trigger questions to guide her, she became more critical of how she was using ICT, as well as what she used ICT for. This change showed a teacher who is now more willing to integrate ICT into her class: 'I always consider how I might use ICT when doing a unit or weekly planning'. This has now transferred to the children she teaches, who are able to solve their own problems independently and also choose appropriate tools for the job at hand. Empowerment of the teacher has led to empowerment of the students in her class.

Conclusion

Many of the teachers who were involved in the three-year project were initially not confident in using ICT in their classroom. Through their involvement in the professional learning system (PLS), teachers gained this confidence, especially as a result of the practicum. For example, there were improvements in technical skills, pedagogical shifts and changes in how teachers actually saw their role in the classroom. The teachers also developed higher-order thinking skills. This was evident in the ways they used ICT and also in how they were increasingly able to solve problems. They were more comfortable when they did not know the answer, and there was a developing attitude of open-minded problem solving among more staff than existed before the project started. An aspect of the PLS that contributed to this was the ongoing discussion about how to solve technical problems. The lead teachers were now developing into educational leaders in their own right. This professional learning system had encouraged them, through a variety of inputs and opportunities, to develop both their skills in using ICT and also in how they could lead other teachers to become ICT literate.

The various elements of this PLS contributed to a rich learning environment for the teachers. We created a multi-layered, multi-faceted system with many conditions to support teacher learning, which resulted in educational change. The aspects of this environment were constantly evolving, refining and redefining themselves to best meet the needs of the individual and the organization. It is helpful to view this PLS as an 'organic system' that is both complex and dynamic, which produces both generative and transformative change for teachers and students. Such a system must evolve continuously and adapt to meet the needs of the learners it exists for – the teachers.

Teachers have become more reflective in how they think about what they teach and how they teach. Notably, staff room conversations have changed to include more thoughtful discussion about both teaching and learning and also about how ICT can be used. This is evidence of a cyclical ongoing dialogue about teaching and learning with a heightened awareness of the power of ICT to enhance both. Because teachers were talking and sharing instructional ideas and strategies more, they were attempting new ways of grouping children and using time in the classroom, as they learned that children can do things with ICT without their help. This came about due to the intensive nature of the support, the feedback and the various inputs from supporting teachers. Teachers are more comfortable in sharing their expertise with others and providing a helping hand when someone is stuck with a particular skill. The aspects of the PLS that contribute to this are the in-class visits during practicum days and the sharing that occurs in other situations such as cluster celebrations of learning, not to mention the informal 'coffee break' type sharing. This shift to teachers supporting one another more than they were before the project is evidence of a growing attitude of 'teachers as active learners'.

If we are to get long-lasting change in how teachers think about teaching and learning with ICT and what they actually do in the classroom, we need to have a strong reflective cycle in place. Change is non-linear and happens over time, so staff need space and energy to reflect in a continuous way, which has common elements that are recursive. These repetitions create cycles that build upon one another and strengthen the overall process, allowing teachers to delve deeper into their thinking about teaching and learning with ICT. This strong reflective process must be grounded in practice and must validate, as well as challenge, currently held beliefs about teaching and learning. A strong reflective process must be infused into the multiple layers or conditions to support teachers' professional learning. Reflection in and on action is vital to the success of this project. Our five specific trigger questions or dimensions supported this type of reflection. Because they were embedded within the various aspects of the professional learning system, they built on and reinforced the change we sought. This type of reflection, sharing and challenge creates what Caine and Caine (1997) refer to as an environment of 'high challenge–low threat'. Thus, openly supportive relationships are essential to this process of change and continuous improvement.

A reflective process that is monitored on a continuous basis will encourage and support the process of change as it unfolds, because it will serve to increase individual accountability in teachers and therefore help develop ownership – feedback is also vital to the reflective process. This feedback must also be infused into the multiple conditions for teacher learning, both informally (e.g. other teachers, lead teachers, the facilitator, self-feedback) and formally (e.g. written feedback on formal reflections). This strong reflective cycle, together with the close monitoring and feedback, helps to draw out of people a deeper understanding of themselves as learners through the processes of continual debate, challenge and analysis. It allows teachers to make the paradigm shift towards them being learners alongside their students.

Teacher change is the key to educational change and the way children's learning will happen in the future. Without creating a positive learning environment for teachers, we cannot hope to create educational change on a wider scale. The Christchurch cluster project was very successful in supporting ICT, but it was also very resource dependent. So the future of the Christchurch ICT Cluster is uncertain. We are currently faced with three challenges: (1) further developing the four schools as a learning community; (2) ensuring sustainability of the cluster; and (3) researching our effectiveness and our impact on teacher and student learning. How we manage to respond to these challenges will determine how long the cluster of four schools will continue to work beyond the initial funding from the Ministry of Education in New Zealand.

A fundamental belief that I bring to teacher professional learning, which affects how well we can achieve change, is that educators must be able to apply what they know and believe about learning to themselves as learners. If they cannot do this, then educators will not be able to move towards becoming technologically literate and will be educators of the past, not of the present. Part of helping teachers to see themselves as learners with ICT is helping them make connections between their current beliefs and practices and how they learn themselves with ICT. This is a challenge for both teachers and people designing and implementing professional learning for teachers. In particular, this project shows that opportunities for student learning are related to opportunities for teacher learning.

Acknowledgement

The 'Christchurch ICT Cluster project' was funded by the New Zealand Ministry of Education. The project was expanded in 2001 with the addition of another 28 clusters.

Part 3

Extending the possibilities of professional learning

The main argument presented in this book is that a paradigm based on complexity theory provides us with a more useful way of making sense of the nature of teaching, teacher learning and educational change than does a mechanistic paradigm. Accordingly, educational change is not an event or a linear step-by-step process, but behaves as a complex system with an inertia to resist change or with an in-built dynamism to encourage change. And the approach of systems thinking is a mindset that helps us to understand how complexity works by focusing on the interrelationships among combinations of elements that interact dynamically to create possibilities for change.

When viewed in this way, the chances for managing educational change are increased if efforts are supported by a framework based on a combination of conditions for teacher learning that helps teachers to cope with the non-linear process of change. Such a framework requires teachers to be *reflective* about their practice, to engage in change efforts with a *purpose*, to participate in regular conversations with their peers as a *community*, to seek alternative perspectives in the form of *conceptual inputs*, to try out ideas in *action* and to seek *feedback* from their students. Importantly, school organization needs to be restructured to include *time* for teachers to share their classroom experiences. This framework is enhanced if participants also have a *conception of teaching* as an art or profession that makes them aware of the complex nature of their practice and provides a perceived need to learn more about teaching. It is the interplay among these conditions that establishes continuity in the teacher learning process and provides a critical mass to support teachers through the dilemmas of changing classroom practice. I think it is important for all members of the educational community – teachers, administrators, policy makers and researchers – to understand how a framework such as a professional learning system works, as this gives them a basis to design a learning environment for teachers that increases the likelihood that change will occur. To sustain change, a professional learning system needs as many conditions for teacher learning as possible to be in place so that they enhance each other to create a synergy.

Although a professional learning system (PLS) is a powerful framework for long-term teacher learning, it is not an easy environment to establish. Even if teachers understand how to generate the multifaceted framework, it requires sacrifices in time, a commitment and a plan to change and, in some cases, expense to establish the conditions and sustain the relationships between them as exemplified in the three chapters of Part 2. The Oberon Project highlighted in Chapter 4 was very successful in bringing about change in the teaching of high school science, but it only involved three teachers who already collaborated in a small department. The Frameworks Project described in Chapter 5 involved after-school meetings once a week, and continued in some situations where a learning culture was established in a school as a result of the project. And the Christchurch Project explained in Chapter 6 was very effective, but was costly in terms of hiring a full-time facilitator to work in four schools and needed many relief days for teachers. It is often the expense of these projects that limits opportunities for involvement to a small number of schools. So this type of continuous learning promoted by a PLS is rare and is challenging to sustain in terms of the number of interacting conditions that need to be in place.

What makes it especially difficult to establish a PLS is the other influences beyond establishing a framework for learning that make change even more complex. These were mentioned briefly in Chapter 2 and are represented in Figure 2.1. I will not dwell on these, as they have been well explained by others, but include influences from school politics (Ball 1997; Blase 1998), gender politics (Acker 1983; Datnow 2000), teachers' professional lives (Goodson and Hargreaves 1996), career phases (Sikes 1985), school culture (Fullan 1993; Hargreaves 1994; Fink 2000), leadership (Leithwood, 1992; Leithwood *et al.* 1999) and context (Bascia and Hargreaves 2000). This is not to say that educational change is impossible to achieve, but it is a difficult process and the chances for change are decreased unless a framework for teacher learning previously outlined is in place. The key challenge for administrators, facilitators, policy makers and school leaders in encouraging educational change, is to establish a learning environment for teachers in schools by addressing the conditions for learning and ensuring that they relate to each other for *continuity* in the process. Without this support framework in place, it is difficult for teachers to manage the dilemmas and tensions of educational change. But continuity in teacher learning is difficult to achieve because many of the conditions to support it may be missing, not connected, or there is a lack of time or a place for regular meetings.

In this final part of the book, I summarize the important considerations for designing a professional learning system and explain how new technologies such as the Internet can address some of the difficulties in establishing and maintaining such a framework. In Chapter 7, I explain how Internet technologies help to connect conditions for teacher learning by breaking down the traditional barriers of time, distance and location that often impede continuity in the learning process. Furthermore, the Internet has the potential to create new possibilities for learning as technologies become more sophisticated. These include creating online communities that are scalable to involve more teachers and using the Internet as a vehicle to promote scholarship in teaching. In Chapter 8, I draw together many of the ideas presented in the book with a final discussion of key questions that need to be considered when attempting to design a professional learning system.

seven

Using online technologies for continuity, community and scholarship in teacher learning

The principle of continuity of experience means that every experience both takes up something from those which have gone before and modifies in some way the quality of those which come after.

(Dewey 1938: 35)

Three key aspects are helpful to sustain teacher learning over long periods of time – *continuity* in the learning process, establishing a sense of *community* among teachers and viewing teaching as a form of *scholarship*. Continuity is important, as it is the dynamic interplay among the conditions for teacher learning, such as teachers reflecting on their practice, experimenting with their ideas and sharing experiences with colleagues, that gives momentum to the learning process. Unfortunately, the busy schedule of teachers in schools, especially in high schools, causes many interruptions to their learning and often puts change in the 'too hard basket'. Also, the notion of building community is important, as it helps to generate a commitment to change and a trust that engenders a willingness to share ideas with colleagues. This sense of community is enhanced if teachers view their work as scholarship involving ongoing inquiry to improve practice and accepting that ideas about teaching should be made public and scrutinized.

This chapter explains how online technologies such as the World Wide Web (WWW) can support teacher learning by providing flexibility to establish continuity in the teacher learning process, helping teachers to share ideas through the notion of an online community and making ideas public to encourage scholarship in teaching. Examples of two different online communities are provided, together with explanations of their benefits. The chapter concludes with a discussion about the strengths and limitations of using online technologies in the design of a professional learning system (PLS).

Using the Internet for continuity in teacher learning

Continuity in teacher learning means sustaining the relationships between the conditions that underpin the design of a PLS. This is vital for the change process, because altering classroom practices means rethinking many aspects of teaching and learning. This is especially the case if teachers are attempting to alter the balance of how the different elements of their classroom system interact. According to Day (1999), 'the greatest problems for teachers in engaging in the kinds of sustained interactivity necessary for meeting the learning and achievement needs of individual students continue to be time, disposition and support' (p. 202). Even if a new curriculum is accompanied by a framework for teacher learning, it often means irregular meetings, perhaps once a week or once a month, rather than continuous interaction during implementation. And in the meantime, teachers are preoccupied with planning multiple lessons, conducting assessment tasks, marking children's books, implementing policies and attending meetings that are mostly to do with school organization. In short, there are myriads of interruptions in a school that impede teachers focusing on efforts for change. Even if teachers do have time for regular reflection on teaching approaches, this type of learning is limited to personal interpretation unless there is also time for the sharing of these ideas, for trying them out in practice and for seeking conceptual inputs to extend their understandings and challenge their beliefs.

So the chances of a PLS being established are enhanced if there are designated times and places for teachers to meet regularly to encourage interplay between different learning conditions. For instance, the 'Oberon Project' discussed in Chapter 4 highlighted how teachers reflected on their practice *and* shared ideas with colleagues *and* listened to interviews about student learning *and* put ideas into action by testing them out in their classrooms. However, opportunities for interplay between these conditions are bounded by time and location; for example, teachers need to nominate and coordinate specific places and times to share their reflections. Also, this sharing needs to occur on a regular basis to build a sense of community and trust, but such regularity is difficult to organize in a busy work schedule. This is one of the limitations for developing a learning community, as it takes a great deal of time, commitment and trust to create a workplace culture that encourages teachers to want to share ideas with colleagues. Using the Internet, however, provides flexibility for when and how this can occur and so increases the opportunities for interaction.

The proliferation of Internet technologies over the last 10 years is creating flexibility for teacher learning in four ways. First, learning can occur at *any time* and is not restricted to a particular hour or day of the week. Second, learning can occur *anywhere* with access to a computer and the

Internet. It does not have to occur in real settings such as in a classroom or in a school. Third, learning can occur with *anyone*, so if a particular school environment does not support teacher reflection, an individual can link with other reflective teachers in different contexts and countries. Fourth, new online learning tools provide a *diversity* of approaches for knowledge construction. For instance, when contributing to an asynchronous discussion forum, its structure enables participants to reflect on previous comments and share ideas with others at different times so that interactions are like a 'slow motion conversation'. Alternatively, a person can download and read information from the Internet such as teaching programmes, seek new information about instruction from all over the world, or have a live chat with teachers in other countries in a synchronous discussion space. Also, for some people, the Internet provides a comfortable medium for expressing their ideas, as they may prefer to be anonymous in disclosing their experiences for sharing rather than talking about them face-to-face. A consideration for using the Internet, however, is that no more time is created in the regular hours of work at school, and there may be a growing expectation that teachers will use their home computers and Internet access to participate in online communities in their own time. In sum, using the Internet to communicate *anywhere, any time* and with *anyone* is breaking the boundaries that limit conventional learning. It is this flexibility that provides new ways to share and to establish continuity in the teacher learning process.

Theoretically, possibilities for online learning are blurring the boundaries between personal, social and contextual influences on learning. Tools such as email, chat spaces, bulletin boards and Internet browsers break down the conventional barriers that restrict learning experiences to particular times, places and people. Online tools, therefore, allow cognition to be *distributed* over a context and enhance the cognition or intelligence shared as the 'resources that shape and enable activity are distributed in configuration across people, environments and situations. In other words, intelligence is accomplished rather than possessed' (Pea 1993: 50). As such, online technologies distribute learning more seamlessly across a context by breaking down the conventional barriers that divide personal, social and contextual conditions for learning. For example, when participating in an asynchronous discussion, the user is reflecting upon a topic (a personal condition), is sharing with others (a social condition) and can use the tool in an authentic context as they document their insights from a real-world problem-solving situation (a contextual condition). As discussed in Chapter 4, it is the regular interplay among these conditions that has the potential to sustain learning for the support of educational change. Using the Internet, therefore, can address some of the difficulties of establishing conditions for teacher learning by providing flexibility for when and how learning occurs, and it can also create new possibilities for sharing experiences with teachers in different contexts.

Using the Internet to establish an online community

John Dewey originally used the term 'community' to describe an ideal learning environment for a classroom, as it creates a social spirit centring on 'sharing in each other's activities and each other's experiences because they have common ends and purposes' (Dewey 1916: 75). He suggested that a classroom curriculum should be focused on group activities with teachers working together with students as they share ideas about everyday activities such as farming, cooking and building. Through these interactions, personal experiences are scaffolded or extended by social interactions with others (Vygotsky 1978).

More recently, the term 'community' has been used in a variety of phrases in the literature for teachers' professional learning. These include 'community of practice' (Lave and Wenger 1991; Lieberman 1996; Moore and Shaw 2000), 'learning community' (Sergiovanni 1994), 'teacher community' (Grossman and Wineburg 2000), 'community of learners' (Brown and Campione 1994), 'discourse community' (Putnam and Borko 1997) and 'action learning community' (Hoban *et al.* 1997; Hoban 1999). Although these terms have slightly different meanings, what is common between them is an emphasis on interactions in a group for the purpose of sharing ideas and practices. It is the social interactions and commitment to a common purpose that is the 'glue' of the community and what makes it different from a crowd or a group that meet to simply exchange opinions. Bellah *et al.* (1985) highlight this special type of social interaction in their definition of community as 'a group of people who are socially interdependent, who participate in discussion and decision making, and who share certain practices that both define the community and are nurtured by it' (p. 333). Communities are important for professional learning, as they highlight the sharing of information, encourage commitment to change and enable participants to 'steal' knowledge from each other (Brown and Duguid 1992). For teachers, it is sharing ideas with other teachers that they value most of all in professional learning, as this enables them to resonate with each other's experiences to develop a deeper understanding of their own practices (Berry and Loughran 2000; Moore and Shaw 2000). Munby and Russell (1994) theorized the deep-seated value of personal experience in their term the 'authority of experience'.

Over the last 10 years, the rapid development of Internet technologies has led to the term 'online community' when using the Internet to keep teachers connected with each other and to the workplace: 'in our vision of communities of understanding, digital technologies are used to interweave schools, homes, workplaces, libraries, museums, and social sciences, to reintegrate education into the fabric of the community' (Kozma and Schank 1998: 19). Schwier (1999) preferred to use the term 'growing' community rather than 'building' or 'constructing' community, as it is based on the development of relationships with the people in it that may change over time. He identified four conditions for an online community to grow:

- each community needs a *leader* to provide a vision or purpose for the community;
- various technologies need to be transparent for ease of use, so that the participants can easily use the tools for different purposes;
- a safe and open atmosphere is needed to promote the sharing of ideas; and
- liberal use of narrative is useful so that participants can tell their stories in their own words.

Once an online community is established, other features have been identified that help to sustain it (Ackerman and Palen 1996; Kollock and Smith 1996):

- shared purpose, social norms and multiple roles;
- ongoing activity, critical mass of users with persistent identities;
- public venue and recognition of performance;
- archive of prior interactions and contributions; and
- support for peripheral participation or lurking.

When an online community does exist, it takes on a life of its own and is a dynamic entity that grows and declines with the interest and participation of its members (Schwier 1999). The heart of an online community is the willingness of members to share personal ideas and experiences with others. Although some people like to share ideas in face-to-face meetings, others prefer to use an online medium and perhaps are more prepared to disclose their experiences to people who do not work in their immediate school environment, as they feel this to be less threatening.

Online tools to support community interaction

Different types of Internet technologies have been emerging rapidly over the last 10 years to support the development of online communities. Initially, email was the main tool but others have evolved over time. According to Zalles (2001), web-based tools can be used for the following purposes:

- the posting of teacher resources such as lesson plans, assessment items, articles and artefacts such as children's work;

- transmission of content for professional development;
- communication via synchronous and asynchronous discussions with email, whiteboards, chat spaces, list servs, video-conferences and file sharing systems;
- access to databases for posting information, links to records and metatag; and
- layering of information over digital library resources so that members can exchange.

For the establishment of an online community, however, consideration must be given to the educational purpose of the community so that appropriate online tools are selected to address that intention. A range of online tools that can be used to contribute to features of community are summarized in Table 7.1. Although many online communities have been attempted over the last five years, many have fallen into decline and few have extended beyond several years.

'TAPPED IN' as an online community of practice

'TAPPED IN' (http://www.tappedin.org/info/) started in 1997 in the USA and stands for the Teacher Professional Development Institute. It is supported by SRI International and the National Science Foundation (Grant no. REC 9725528). Currently, TAPPED IN has about 11,000 members, of whom about half are K-12 teachers; the rest are librarians, researchers, university faculty and graduate students. TAPPED IN is a growing and successful online community of practice because it is underpinned by a strong educational philosophy of encouraging teachers to share their ideas and practices.

Schlager *et al.* (2002) have stated that many online communities have produced disappointing results because their designs do not address what is needed to encourage informal collaboration by teachers:

> Many TPD [Teachers Professional Development] projects view on-line CoP [Community of Practice] as an outcome or by-product of their own efforts, rather than as a larger entity in which their efforts can take root, bloom, and propagate. This *project-centric* view of CoP (the project *is* the community) lacks (and in some cases conflicts with) essential elements stressed in both the CoP and education reform literatures . . . missing are the informal back channels of communication, information sharing, and trust building that are central to cooperation and the spread of innovation within a CoP.
>
> (emphasis in original)

Table 7.1 Online tools and how they contribute to a community

Clear focus driven by the members
- Think tanks
- Online tutorials
- Online meetings

- Resource upload/ download
- Quick Starter pages
- Links to professional associations

- Publication area
- Member project proposals
- Feedback and suggestion forms

Employ appropriate technologies and styles of communication
- Resource database
- FAQs
- Listservs
- Threaded discussions

- Chat topic and guests
- Links
- Browser-based publishing
- Archives

- Project activities
- Template and PDF files
- Ideas forums
- Functions and events

Members feel part of a social network where their expertise, leadership, content and contributions are valued
- Groups (K-6, 7–10)
- Leadership and mentor programme
- Buddy activities (novice/expert)
- Collaborative project development

- Member moderated/ lead discussion
- Expert online program
- Rewards and accreditation for member activity
- Promotion of local activity

- Student publishing online
- Schools link-up for local and international project partners
- Publicizing and encouraging member workshops and publications

Provides ongoing discussion, sharing of, and collaboration on, commonly valued artefacts
- Syllabus forums
- Links
- Celebration of student works and achievements
- Teaching programmes

- Database to support sharing units of work
- Classroom practice forums
- Member moderated/ lead discussion

- Tutorials
- Student research forum
- Calls for participation in member-developed projects
- Workshops and conferences

Source: Stuckey and Hedberg (2000).

TAPPED IN has been designed specifically to provide a variety of ways to encourage informal conversations to promote information sharing and hopefully lead to trust building. Taking this into consideration, the goal of TAPPED IN 'is to help the education practitioner community understand the affordances of emerging Internet technologies and to rethink their current TPD [Teacher Professional Development] approaches to include innovative on-line community services and activities' (Schlager *et al.* 2002).

The design of TAPPED IN is based upon the notion of a community of practice (CoP), which assumes that learning is fundamentally a social activity centring on informal conversations about professional experiences (Lave and Wenger 1991; Wenger 1998). In particular, TAPPED IN supports teachers in establishing social networks by promoting informal conversations about work practices that teachers value (Lieberman 1996). Moore and Shaw (2000) claim that it is the sharing of professional experiences that teachers value most in their learning, as 'teachers craft knowledge and practical understandings concerning their students' learning and their own classroom practice is an underrated and under-used resource for teachers' professional learning and building school capacity for change' (p. 3). The four corner-stones or operating principles that shape the design of TAPPED IN as an online learning environment (Schlager *et al.* 1998) are to:

1 support the same ebb and flow of communication and information shar-ing that face-to-face work teams engage in over time;
2 be scalable and sustainable such that the teachers' community of prac-tice requires the participants of several organizations with a variety of approaches and perspectives;
3 be flexible so that a community can grow in the spaces between tenant organizations; and
4 foster teacher professional development as a lifelong process that occurs in the context of daily practice.

Together, these four cornerstones guide the design of the online commu-nity to encourage the informal sharing of ideas. An important feature of how this works is the involvement of educators with different backgrounds to provide different perspectives:

> A CoP can be an effective *hothouse* in which new ideas germinate, new methods and tools are developed, and new communities are rooted . . . CoPs that cross organizational boundaries can grow and evolve over time as groups form and disband, projects begin and end, and indi-vidual members participate actively for a period of time, go dormant, and then find new opportunities to participate. Through organic growth, an on-line education CoP can achieve the economies of scale, diversity and informal communication channels needed to spread innovation and become an ever-widening source of expertise.
>
> (Schlager *et al.* 2002)

The interface of the TAPPED IN web site has been designed to resemble a 'conference centre' to promote the kind of participation and professional interaction of a social network as shown in Figure 7.1. As soon as you log onto the site, a help dialogue box appears that is serviced live by volunteers from 8 am to 8 pm.

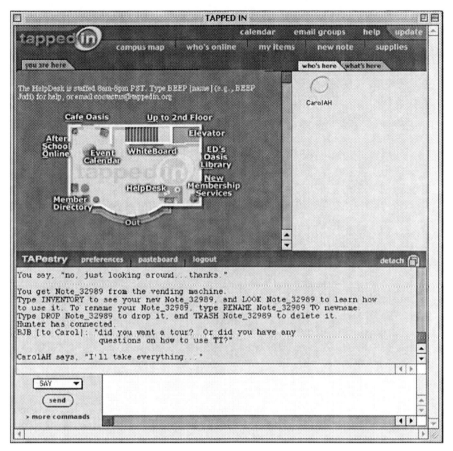

Figure 7.1 Interface on the TAPPPED IN online community.

Structures to support the informal conversations of a community

TAPPED IN is not a professional development provider of prescriptive courses or a portal to market a range of resources. Instead, it focuses on supporting 'scalable and sustainable' teacher learning at all levels by encouraging teachers to take ownership and to share their experiences in mutually supportive groups. There are four floors of virtual meeting rooms that have been designed to cater for different purposes to suit a variety of conversations and audiences. Within these rooms there are structures for four different types of forums. These include working sessions for two to five people to address a specific task, lecture sessions with a guest speaker, structured sessions with three to twenty participants following a particular threaded conversation and expression sessions for three or more people engaged in unstructured conversations. Communication can occur synchronously (live chat rooms) or asychronously (email) in different ways (speaking, whispering or note taking) using a variety of support tools (virtual whiteboards, one-to-one chat areas or web page projection). As such, there are a variety of special structures in TAPPED IN to encourage teachers to share ideas:

- *Community help desk.* As soon as a participant logs on to the online discussion area, there is an immediate opportunity for help to guide new users through the site with some live online help. Another reason why TAPPPED IN is attractive to teachers is that this help desk is often maintained by the participants of the community.
- *After-school online.* This is one of the most successful features of TAPPED IN, which has up to 36 real-time discussions each month that target a particular group of teachers, hot topic or technologies. Participants can log on from anywhere in the world and the web site provides a designated time for all of the major world time zones for each discussion.
- *Newsletter and mailing list.* To keep members informed about different events, there is an electronic newsletter called *On the Tapis* and a calendar of events that gets sent out once a month. This is also a good way to put out requests for help from other teachers.
- *University classes and teacher workshops.* Transcripts are available of past conversations from special meetings or workshops.
- *Personal offices.* Participants can attain a personal workspace in the shape of a personal office. This will be on one of the many floors of a virtual office block. An office can have a personal whiteboard for leaving messages as well as opportunities for personal online conversations.

Clearly, the feature of TAPPED IN that makes it so successful as an online community is that is has a range of facilities to help teachers share informal conversations about teaching and learning. This feature is an expression of the educational philosophy that underpins TAPPED IN, which clearly values teachers' practical knowledge and experiences as the centrepiece for teachers' professional learning. However, the Internet can be used in other ways that also contribute to a sense of community.

Using the Internet for promoting scholarship in teaching

Traditionally, teaching is not a profession that is characterized by the public sharing of ideas, the celebration of successes or the display of personal practices for the purpose of seeking critique (Brookfield 1995). Instead, many school cultures promote teaching as a private act performed by individuals within the confines of their classrooms and is rarely evaluated by peers. The result is that there is often little progressive discourse in schools whereby teachers share ideas and build on the work of others. It is no wonder that Wilson and Daviss (1995) stated that 'the teaching profession is marked by a series of missing links – separations between areas within the profession that, if joined, could create the technical culture necessary to sustain progressive innovation in education' (p. 92). They argued that teaching should be more like industry, which makes new ideas public, with links between researchers and practitioners to establish a progressive discourse. And there is no better medium to make ideas public than putting them on the World Wide Web, where they can be accessed anywhere in the world at any time as long there is a computer, a modem and an Internet connection. Providing a medium for teachers to make their ideas public not only enables them to share the products of their work, but also encourages them to make explicit the formal and practical knowledge that underpins their practice. Also, from the receiver's perspective, enabling teachers to access ideas about classroom practice from teachers who they do not even know may also encourage them to share their ideas with others. There are also organizations that purposely promote the sharing of ideas and artefacts about teaching.

The Carnegie Foundation for the Advancement of Teaching was founded in 1905 by Andrew Carnegie 'to do all things necessary to encourage, uphold and dignify the profession of teaching'. This foundation attempts to highlight and celebrate teaching as a form of *scholarship* as was initially discussed in *Scholarship Reconsidered* by Ernest Boyer (1990). According to Lee Shulman, current President of the Foundation, for teaching to be considered scholarship 'it should manifest at least three key characteristics: It should be made *public*, be susceptible to *critical review and evaluation*, and be accessible for *exchange and use* by other members of one's scholarly community' (Shulman 1998: 5; emphasis added). Scholarship in teaching, therefore, involves the creation of new knowledge through a process of making teaching practices *public*, seeking *critique* and *using* other teachers' ideas. Hutchings and Shulman (1999) recently added a fourth attribute for scholarship in teaching – to seek inquiry and address issues about student learning. Importantly, they emphasize that scholarship in teaching is not necessarily about demonstrating excellent practice, but is about acknowledging the problematic nature of teaching and investigating issues by making their practice public and inviting scrutiny to bring a sense of rigour to the inquiry.

Knowledge Media Laboratory: the gallery of scholarship for teaching and learning

One specific initiative of the Carnegie Foundation that aims to make teaching practices public is the 'Knowledge Media Laboratory' (KML). This is an effort to assist teachers to document their practice, publicize it and seek feedback using the affordances of the Internet. Currently, the KML provides workspaces for over 100 participants in the Carnegie Academy for the Scholarship of Teaching (CASTL) programme. Each scholar develops some teaching-related work and shares this publicly by placing it on the World Wide Web in a way that is similar to a modern museum. At the website (http://www.carnegiefoundation.org/kml) one can find examples of teachers' work that have been made public for review and feedback. Examples include 'Learning from Cases' (Hammerness, Darling-Hammond and Shulman), 'American Literature Course Portfolio' (Bass), 'Learning to Think Mathematically' (Cerbin) and 'Cooperative Learning in General Chemistry' (Jacobs).

One example that is particularly interesting for high school teachers is a web site (http://kml2.carnegiefoundation.org/gallery/kaustin) designed by Esther Wojciki (Palo Alto High School) and Kim Austin (the Carnegie Foundation). It demonstrates how Esther established a high school course to teach journalism based on a community of learners who produce a high school newspaper. The students produce a real newspaper called *The Campanile* and there are programmes offered at the sophomore, junior and senior years with varying degrees of difficulty. Figure 7.2 shows the

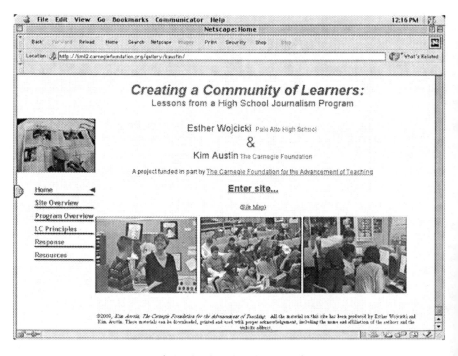

Figure 7.2   Homepage of the high school journalism project.

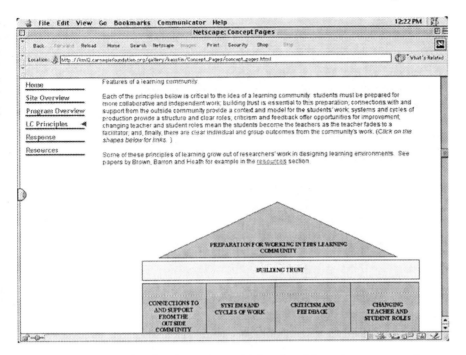

Figure 7.3 Principles for designing a high school learning community.

homepage of the Creating a Community of Learners Project. This is a good example of authentic learning in a high school context that is based on real-life problem solving by working as a community and using technology. What is particularly interesting is that it has a web page that outlines the theoretical basis for the establishment of their learning community with a collective of principles, as shown in Figure 7.3.

The educative principles that the community is based upon include: (1) independent and collaborative work; (2) building trust; (3) connections with the outside community; (4) systems and cycles of production; (5) criticism and seeking feedback for improvement; (6) changing teacher and student roles; and (7) clear individual and group outcomes. The web site also has examples of how students develop skills in journalism. The purpose of making this innovation public is to seek feedback on the idea of generating a community of practice in a high school setting and to make it available for use in other contexts. This is an example of a good teaching idea that can be adapted and used by teachers in other schools and in different subjects – and the web makes it accessible for others to copy.

Conclusion

The proliferation of online technologies over the last 10 years is creating new possibilities for teacher learning that should not be overlooked. This is not meant to imply that all professional learning should be done online, as any medium for learning has limitations as well as strengths. However, it is clear that Internet technologies can help establish conditions for teacher learning by providing flexibility as to when and where learning can occur, as well as creating new opportunities with emerging technologies. But there are some limitations. First, online learning cannot provide the type of interaction evident in face-to-face meetings. As such, it is harder for most people to get to know each other and build a sense of trust to promote the sharing of ideas and a sense of community. However, some people are more willing to share ideas online than they are face-to-face and perhaps a different type of trust is established when participating online for these people. A second limitation of online learning is that the introduction of new technologies could create more stress for teachers with the expectation that professional learning is always conducted online in your own time. In particular, many teachers do not want to spend their spare time at home using the World Wide Web for professional learning.

There are also problems associated with the design of some online learning environments. Schlager *et al.* (2002) suggest that many online communities fail because their designs are not based on a clear framework to support activities that are fundamental to a community. Accordingly, they are not used for meaningful activities because the technology cannot capture the to-and-fro informal interactions that are essential to establish a sense of collaboration and trust among the participants. Also, many teachers do not know how to use technologies effectively and so it is recommended that participants need to be familiar with how to use online tools *before* they participate in online activities. They suggest that online technologies should not be used as a replacement for face-to-face professional learning, as they have different purposes. Instead, a different mindset is needed to re-conceptualize professional learning from the ground up, taking into account the affordances of online learning.

But the benefits in using the Internet for professional learning are undeniable. First, the Internet is unequalled in its ability to provide teachers with professional learning in a flexible way and to overcome problems of geographical isolation. Further benefits are related to the extent of information that can be accessed on the web. This includes links to policy initiatives, school-based teacher networks and innovative professional learning projects via a technological infrastructure to support sharing of information and communication across different stakeholder groups. This idea was recently proposed by Willinsky (2001), who argued that the World Wide Web could be a vehicle to bring teachers and educational researchers together by making research knowledge more accessible. Exposing research knowledge for public debate would give it more value by providing a 'website portal strategy for public and professional engagement with the relevant research in the context of policy and practice' (Willinsky 2001: 7). Exposing research in this way not only makes it more accessible, but it can also be used as a platform for dialogue between teachers and researchers. In the context of a professional learning system, such a web site would be ideal for finding research relevant to teachers' interests as a *conceptual input* into their discussions. Another advantage in using Internet technology is that instead of 'just-in-case' assistance provided in conventional professional development programmes, online learning can provide 'just-in-time' assistance that can be accessed when it is most needed. Accessing ideas when it suits the user, such as downloading resources when they are needed, makes information more relevant for an immediate need.

The other major use of online technology is to create possibilities for professional learning to be scalable. The theoretical framework of a professional learning system, as proposed in Section 2, provides a powerful framework for long-term learning, but in most cases it operates on a small scale. Schlager *et al.* (2002) suggest that online technologies have the potential to assist in broader systemic reform. Although they admit that technology is only a small part of a large-scale effort for reform, it is the affordances of technology that can support large-scale teacher networks. But the choice of a medium for professional learning does not have to result in a dichotomy between face-to-face or online learning. Face-to-face opportunities may be integrated with online learning, taking into account the benefits of both mediums. The former plays an important role for developing trust and an understanding of each other's personal needs and contexts for learning. Online technologies, however, are useful for creating flexibility as to how teachers can access help or share ideas when and where it suits them. And no doubt some teachers prefer different mediums for different purposes. Developing trust with others to share ideas and build a sense of community may come from face-to-face meetings or a different type of trust may evolve for people who prefer to share ideas online with others who they do not know and do not feel threatened by. In short, opportunities for online learning should complement, not replace, face-to-face interactions, providing additional ways for conditions of teacher learning to interrelate as a system. As new technologies continue to develop, no doubt further opportunities will arise to create additional professional learning possibilities.

eight

Designing a professional learning system

So that a group of individuals can jointly stay at the edge of chaos relies first on the quality of the relationships that people in the group develop among themselves. In other words, it is not simply the extent of connectivity but the quality of the connections that causes the system to operate at the edge . . . The second way of containing anxiety without abandoning the edge of chaos is provided by the opportunity and capacity for honest self-reflection, that is, when members of a group jointly reflect upon and discuss the system they constitute.

(Stacey 1996: 162)

So far, complexity theory and systems thinking have mainly been used in the disciplines of science, mathematics and business. This book demonstrates that these mindsets are also useful in education because they provide a way of thinking that is more in tune with reality than a mechanistic paradigm. It is unrealistic to think about change by analysing the educational landscape into independent elements or factors, identifying those that are 'effective' and then try to plan and control change by manipulating them one at a time – the world does not work in this way! When educational change is viewed as a complex system, however, it suggests that change, or the lack of it, is influenced by multiple elements that interact with each other in dynamic, non-linear ways.

From the perspective of complexity theory, most schools are in a balanced equilibrium with tensions created from multiple systems. Some are micro-systems that are internal to the school, such as each classroom, where teachers and students interact with one another, as well as other staff and students in the school. Other influences are external and are part of larger macrosystems, such as government policies, community expectations and curriculum demands. Collectively, these influences act as interrelated systems with each one dynamically affecting the others. A complexity paradigm, therefore, explains why educational change is so difficult to predict and manage because of the number of microsystems and macrosystems interacting with each other. But these interrelated influences are not a chaotic system creating unpredictable and spontaneous change. Instead, when educational change is viewed as a complex system, it explains why schools are in a state of equilibrium and display an inertia to resist change or may self-organize for change in response to a combination of influences.

As this book has made clear, systems thinking is an approach or mindset focusing on interrelationships that helps us to understand how complex systems work. This focus not only helps us to understand the non-linear nature of the change process, but also provides insights into ways to manage it. This involves thinking about educational change from multiple perspectives and considering the dynamic interactions involved. This is a more realistic way of thinking about change than proposed by a step-by-step mechanistic world view, because change is rarely due to one influence alone. In respect to teacher learning, systems thinking also gives us a way of thought to draw together ideas from diverse theoretical perspectives as a basis for designing a framework for long-term teacher learning to support educational change. Accordingly, we can view sustained teacher learning as a result of a combination of interrelated personal, social and contextual conditions.

The best way for schools to manage change is to redesign themselves to become learning environments for their teachers. According to Sarason (1990), the quality of student learning in a school depends on the quality of teacher learning. Yet the organization of schools focuses almost exclusively on ways to enhance student learning, without consideration for structures to support teacher learning. When designing a learning environment for teachers, administrators need to think about the type of learning that they wish teachers to engage in. Current structures that use isolated one-off workshops or professional development days tend to reinforce existing practices and maintain the status quo. According to Sachs and Logan (1990), conventional inservice education does not empower teachers to generate their own knowledge:

> Rather than initiating programmes that are intellectually challenging and rigorous, inservice education, with some exceptions, has reproduced current practice by catering for teachers' preoccupation with 'practicality' and 'relevance.' One consequence is that teachers' professional knowledge is being controlled, devalued and deskilled.
>
> (Sachs and Logan 1990: 479)

Most existing professional development programmes do not challenge teachers to articulate why they teach the way they do or to encourage them to think 'outside the square they teach in' to become knowledge producers in their own workplace. In some ways, teachers have become conditioned to expect one-off workshops to deliver information to them as passive learners because this form of learning is all they have experienced in their careers (Moore and Shaw 2000).

In contrast, a professional learning system is an educative environment that empowers teachers to generate their own knowledge and products. When teachers understand this process, they can manage their own learning and set their own directions for change, rather than being slaves to the change agendas of those external to a school. As stated previously, a professional learning system is not a recipe to design successful teacher learning projects; rather, it is a framework to support change as a multidimensional process. Understanding the dynamics of this process provides support to cope with non-linear change and possibly ways to manage it. When thinking about designing a professional learning system, there are several key questions that need to be considered – but there are still no guarantees!

Considerations for designing a professional learning system

When we approach the task of designing a professional learning system (PLS) based on the beliefs of a complexity paradigm, there are certain questions that could be asked to increase the likelihood that change might occur. Addressing these questions provides guidelines to design a learning environment for teachers, because educational change is essentially about them learning to do something differently. I suggest how each question could be addressed and then provide a specific example for change in terms of supporting teachers to become designers of world wide web pages with the long-term outcome that their students also become designers.

What is the focus or content of the change effort?

Teachers need to decide upon a focus for their change effort to provide a real purpose. This is an important decision that should be negotiated with the staff, as change in any aspect of teaching will have an impact on other areas in the school. The extent of the proposed change will depend on its focus and how widespread it becomes in the school. Possible foci for change include implementing a new curriculum, developing new teaching strategies, teachers evaluating their own practice, designing a new assessment or reporting scheme and introducing innovations such as web-based designs. Perhaps schools could have groups of teachers who work on different but complementary projects. Of course, this is assuming that policy makers are not continually forcing mandatory change on teachers that gives them no flexibility in determining their own focus. It is also important that the content of the workshops or professional development days are not completely prescribed for teachers, but have a flexible agenda that provides opportunities for the staff to negotiate or determine the content and format. Deciding on a particular focus, however, does not guarantee that this will be the outcome, as directions may change in unintended ways. If teachers decide to embark on a project to design web pages, these could be used for displaying children's work, using a database for administration, collecting resources for different subjects, working on community projects or as a portfolio of student work throughout their school years.

What is the time frame?

Any attempts at significant educational change will have ripple effects within a school and so a time frame of one or two years or longer is not unrealistic. This would require staff being involved in ongoing professional learning experiences that may include a combination of after-school workshops, lunch-time meetings and professional learning days. But what is important here is that these are connected so that there is some continuity in the learning process. For example, for teachers to learn about designing web pages and to implement these skills into their regular classroom practice would need one to two years. This is because staff need to learn how to design web pages and then learn to integrate them in different ways into their regular classroom practice. Accordingly, flexibility needs to be incorporated into the project to give teachers options for deciding how they want to learn and use these newly acquired skills.

Is the PLS for an individual teacher, a small group or a whole school?

A PLS can be designed on several different levels as long as the participants understand how it works. At an individual level, a teacher can reflect on his or her own practice and connect with practitioners in other schools using an online community, as explained in Chapter 7, or participate in teacher research groups via the Internet. For instance, a teacher may want to develop a class web site and have the students display their work on the site. At a group level, teachers within a school need to nominate a regular meeting time, say once every two weeks. In a high school, this may occur within a subject department, as explained in Chapter 4, or with participants across subject departments. This group may also like to stay connected with each other as well as with teachers in other schools using online technologies. At a whole-school level, teachers need to allocate meeting times every second week and focus on whole-school issues or department-focused issues if they are in a secondary school. Preferably, a school could structure into its timetable a session for this process.

What conditions will help to establish a framework for long-term teacher learning?

Multiple conditions for teacher learning are needed to establish a framework to support teachers through the non-linear process of learning to design web pages. These include: personal conditions, such as reflection by keeping a journal on the ideas tried and thinking about the purposes of designing a web site to provide motivation; social conditions, such as group meetings to share ideas with others who may have a common purpose to provide ways to foster trust and collegiality; and contextual conditions, such as authentic class projects to develop a web-based prototype for a real purpose, to test it out and modify it. As many conditions for learning as possible need to be identified to give teachers options in their planning of the PLS. Teachers also need to share ideas as a community to discuss the different ways of teaching their students how to design their own web pages.

What are the relationships between the conditions for learning?

The key issue for making a PLS work is ensuring that there are interconnections to encourage dynamic interplay among personal, social and contextual conditions. It is this interplay that creates continuity in the learning process and enables a project to develop a 'critical mass' to sustain change. This is the central aspect of the PLS that makes it different from one-off workshops or professional development days that exist in isolation to other aspects of professional learning. For this reason, a series of workshops or professional learning days need to have some connection to web-based designs so there is continuity in the teacher learning experiences. Moreover, it is important that there are quality relationships established among the conditions as described by Stacey (1996), which means that the connections need to be personally meaningful for the teachers involved. Unless relationships between the conditions are ensured, a project is in danger of falling back into a mechanistic view of change with fragmented learning that lacks continuity to sustain the effort.

How can Internet technologies support professional learning?

It is undeniable that web-based technologies are creating new possibilities for teacher learning, as explained in Chapter 7. In particular, for teachers in isolated locations or who are professionally isolated within schools, online professional learning has a huge advantage in that teachers can connect with like-minded colleagues from any location to form teacher networks. I suggest that each new project for professional learning be accompanied by a web site designed to help teachers stay 'in the loop' with colleagues and researchers. With the example of designing web sites, this is a perfect opportunity to use existing sites to analyse their features and to ascertain if these can be modified to fit the purposes of an intended project. This site can be designed with a range of web-based tools to support different aspects of professional learning. Teachers can keep in touch through informal conversations via an asynchronous discussion forum or share their products publicly by displaying them on the web, as explained in Chapter 7. As this communication can be carried out anywhere and at any time, a web site aids in providing continuity to the teacher learning process and provides possibilities for larger-scale projects.

What conceptual inputs can be used?

Getting together on a regular basis and sharing ideas is what teachers value most about professional learning because they resonate with each other's experiences – empathy is a strong teacher learning characteristic. However, when any group of people share their practical knowledge, the ideas are constrained by the limitations of the experiences of the participants. Alternatively, conventional inservice programmes that only focus on the introduction of new ideas usually do not consider teachers' personal experiences and provide no context for learning. A PLS attempts to provide a happy medium, as it values teachers sharing their experiences as a community, but also addresses the need for alternative ideas to extend the collective knowledge of the group. However, discretion needs to be used for deciding how and when to introduce conceptual inputs. New ideas need to be introduced in context with teachers' experiences and in a form that they value and understand. Conceptual inputs can come from a variety of sources: educational research articles, the Internet, content specialists, and research conducted within a school setting in the form of teacher research or by collecting data from students, as explained in Chapter 4.

What is the role of the facilitator?

A facilitator can be a consultant external to the school or a teacher in the school who has a good understanding of how a professional learning system works. As discussed in Chapter 5, the main role of the facilitator is to support the interrelationships among the conditions so that they complement each other to provide continuity in the teacher learning process. Providing appropriate conceptual inputs is one of the main challenges for a facilitator. Such inputs may take the form of educational research or data collected from within the school itself. If teachers focus on a change effort, such as designing web sites, the role of the facilitator may be to

Figure 8.1   Overview for designing a professional learning system.

employ a content expert to get teachers started and then to encourage teachers to work in small groups on projects that they can trial with their classes.

Drawing a diagram that highlights the main elements of the PLS helps to conceptualize how the system works (see Figure 8.1). The example provided is a project to support teachers in designing their own web sites, the outcome being that they would teach their own students how to undertake such designs. The most important part of the system is the interrelationships among the conditions, as emphasized by the bold lines of the spider web; these always need to be the feature of the system rather than the elements in isolation.

The misconception of mastery in teaching

In this book, I have emphasized that long-term teacher learning results from a combination of conditions that interrelate as a framework to increase the likelihood that educational change will occur. Up until now, I have resisted saying that one condition for teacher learning is more important than another. But I cannot conclude this book without identifying what I think is the most important condition of all – how teachers think about their role, that is, their conception of teaching. Although multiple conditions are needed to sustain learning, teachers will be reluctant to participate in a long-term project in the first place if they do not perceive a need or desire to change. This is why it is important for teachers to recognize the ambiguities and uncertainties of their practice in the first place, because these are triggers for reflection, as explained by Dewey (1933) and Schön (1983, 1987, 1991). But being reflective is usually not a characteristic of teachers who have a conception of teaching as a craft, because they believe that over time they have 'mastered' their craft. In short, it is one thing to design a school-based learning environment for teachers, but it is another to have them want to engage in sustained professional learning over a period of several years.

In the introduction to this book, I spoke about my own conception of teaching as a high school science teacher for 14 years from 1976 to 1989. During this time, I perceived teaching to be a craft and believed that I had mastered it, because I knew my science knowledge and had developed many strategies to pass on this information to students. To me, student learning was a matter of them mastering the content that I presented, as this had worked for me in high school – I assumed that my students would learn in the same way as I did. I thought that my main role was to deliver to children the science knowledge in small chunks so that they could progressively acquire my knowledge. During this time, I mainly saw teaching as a one-way process – I organized the content and the learning experiences and expected the students to engage accordingly. When planning lessons, what was foremost in my mind was the sequence of knowledge concepts that I was trying to present; the ways in which the students would learn the concepts was a secondary issue. I certainly did not understand the complex nature of teaching and did not perceive teaching and learning as a dynamic relationship in a classroom system. Unfortunately, it was only after I finished my career as a high school science teacher that I realized that mastering subject matter is not the same as mastering teaching.

Upon reflection, I now realize where my original notion that teaching could be mastered came from. I believe that this conception is perpetuated by the educational community itself at many different levels. I see it at university in preservice courses where some professors portray themselves as 'experts' and preach about the importance of 'what research says', without

explaining its limitations and the contexts in which the research was generated. Also, it is rare at the preservice level to have debates on the applicability
of educational research or discussions about its utility in different contexts.
And when preservice teachers try out the ideas in classrooms, they often
claim that theory does not work in practice as expected. No wonder –
many theories are context specific and evolve from a narrowly based research
perspective. It reminds me of the well-known saying, 'to every complex
problem there is a simple solution that is always wrong'. Too often preservice
teacher education courses present research to students in discrete packages
as a 'given' without sufficient discussions about the ambiguities and complex nature of the context in real classrooms. And I believe that many
beginning teachers often develop a cynicism towards educational research
because they do not believe that 'theory' works in practice.

I also remember from my own teacher education experiences that different courses presented content in isolation to the other courses, as if no
others existed. Little effort was made to show me the relationships between
courses or to illuminate the complexities that exist in any classroom, at
university or at school. This notion of mastery in teaching is also promoted
in school districts, which often use the old world model of one-off 'how-to'
workshops, where teachers gather in groups and are addressed by an expert.
The not so hidden message is that teachers 'add to their mastery' if they
attend a few inservice courses each year. And I see mastery in teaching pro-
mulgated by policy makers who continually demand that standards for
teaching should be based on a mastery of technical skills and subject matter
knowledge. I do not deny that these are important aspects of teaching;
rather it is how, when and why skills and knowledge are applied that
requires professional judgement and is the heart and soul of teaching.

Conversely, how often is funding provided for small groups of teachers
to meet regularly and share ideas about what they already do and discuss
the complexities of their work? These meetings encourage teachers to reflect,
share ideas and build on each other's insights in line with the notion of
'scholarship in teaching' (Shulman 1998). Ironically, this is what teachers
value most about professional learning, because it helps them to understand their own practice better when they hear about the experiences and
dilemmas of other teachers in similar situations. When teachers resonate
with the experiences of others, they are more likely to pay attention to
suggestions for change in their own thinking and practice. If educational
theory was presented to teachers with the caveat that much of it is context
specific and is not intended to be an 'all-purpose recipe', perhaps more
teachers would appreciate its value. Some practitioners may even engage in
their own teacher research (Cochran-Smith and Lytle 1993; Mills 2000) or
conduct a self-study in their own classroom (Loughran and Northfield 1998;
Mitchell and Weber 1999). And it is often when teachers become researchers

in their own classroom that they become more aware of the complexity of this setting. Also, if their colleagues become teacher researchers as well, they can share their insights and it is in a genre that can be understood and valued by other teachers.

The obvious and not so obvious signals sent out by many researchers, teachers, policy makers and administrators is that teaching is a craft to be mastered and this message permeates the culture of teaching. I believe that this is one reason why many teachers will not talk publicly about their practice and acknowledge the uncertainties and ambiguities of what they do. They are afraid that acknowledging their weaknesses is a sign that they have not 'mastered' teaching and that they may be seen as professionally incompetent. Brookfield (1995) suggested that there are three cultural barriers that discourage teachers from being critically reflective or actively seeking alternative perspectives on their practice:

1 *The culture of silence.* Teachers soon learn on the job not to talk too much about how they teach and so it is rare to discuss their practice in public. Instead, Brookfield (1995) argues that teachers should 'talk about the dynamics and rhythms of classroom processes and the daily struggle to confront what we know are unsolvable dilemmas and contradictory demands . . . talk about meaning that teaching has in our lives; the way we draw strength from it or suffer humiliations in doing it' (p. 247).

2 *The culture of individualism.* Teachers at all levels usually work in isolation and do not collaborate with others. Perhaps this is reinforced by scarce resources or promotion procedures that encourage competition rather than collaboration and reward teachers for showing that they are better than others.

3 *The culture of secrecy.* Self-disclosure will only occur if teachers are comfortable with people they can trust and disclosure will not be seen as a sign of weakness. Administrators need to model the declarations of error and the willingness to seek alternative perspectives and 'learn from mistakes'.

Unfortunately, a climate that promotes 'a willingness to make public one's private dilemmas, uncertainties, and frustrations' (Brookfield 1995: 250) is not common in schools. Maintaining the masquerade that teaching can be mastered, therefore, fails to acknowledge the complex nature of teaching and sustains a culture of 'pseudo-mastery'.

Conclusion

It is clearly time that the educational community gave up on a mechanistic paradigm that views teaching, educational change and learning in simplistic, one-dimensional ways. This paradigm is naive and denies the complexity and uncertainty of everyday classroom practice. I believe that teachers at all levels should 'come clean' and acknowledge publicly the dilemmas, complexities and uncertainties of their work. We all need to declare that there are always dilemmas in teaching, because classroom reality is complex and teaching is by nature, uncertain and problematic. I believe that this fundamental misunderstanding of the nature of teaching is at the heart of why many teachers are unwilling to make their beliefs and practices public.

Perhaps even the language we use to describe the uncertainties of teaching supports the culture of not sharing ideas. Bass (1999) suggests that we should consider changing the meaning of the word 'problem' because it is acceptable to have a problem in research that needs to be solved, but a problem in teaching is often perceived to be a sign of weakness. He contends that the common assumption that teaching can be done 'right ... has strangulated the development of teaching as an intellectual enterprise and analytic subject' (Bass 1999: 5). Instead, he suggests we should consider the notion of 'changing the status of the *problem* in teaching from terminal remediation to ongoing investigation' (p. 1; emphasis in original). Similarly, Cuban (1992) contends that the word 'problem' is too simplistic for teaching, because it suggests a technical approach focusing on independent skills and knowledge and implies that there is an answer or solution:

> What I want to argue is that we seldom examine these below-the-surface conflicts even though we cope with them continually in our work. We call them pesky problems or brush them aside as peripheral to our core business of getting the job done. What many practitioners, policymakers, and researchers call problems, I contend, are really fundamental dilemmas. The distinction between problems and dilemmas is worth making on intellectual and moral grounds.
>
> (Cuban 1992: 6)

Cuban (1992) prefers to use the word 'dilemma' in discussions about teaching, suggesting that we should focus our conversations on managing dilemmas rather than solving problems.

In sum, we need to reculture teaching with a paradigm based on complexity theory. We need to debate publicly what is a conception of teaching based on an understanding of the dynamic relationships that occur in all classrooms. Moreover, we need to redefine what it means to be a professional and acknowledge the art of teaching as central to that meaning. Hargreaves and Goodson (1996) argue that debates about standards in teaching have emphasized the importance of technical skills and subject matter knowledge, but have neglected to consider what a professional needs to do in the context of an increasingly complex society. They identified seven principles of what they called 'postmodern professionalism' that are required for teachers to work in an increasingly changing age:

- increased opportunity and responsibility to exercise *discretionary judgement* over the issues of teaching, curriculum and care that affects one's students;
- opportunities and expectations to engage with the *moral and social purposes* and value of what teachers teach, along with major curriculum and assessment matters in which these purposes are embedded;
- commitment to working with colleagues in *collaborative cultures* of help and support as a way of using shared expertise to solve the ongoing problems of professional practice, rather than engaging in joint work as a motivational device to implement the external mandate of others;
- occupational *heteronomy* rather than self-protective *autonomy*, where teachers work authoritatively yet openly and collaboratively with other partners in the wider community (especially parents and students themselves), who have a significant stake in the students' learning;
- a commitment to active *care* and not just anodyne *service* for students. Professionalism must in this sense acknowledge and embrace the emotional as well as the cognitive dimensions of teaching, and also recognise the skills and dispositions that are essential to committed and effective caring;
- a self-directed search and struggle for *continuous learning* related to one's expertise and standards of practice, rather than compliance with the enervating obligations of *endless change* demanded by others (often under the guise of continuous learning or improvement);
- the creation and recognition of high task *complexity*, with levels of status and reward appropriate to such complexity.

  (Hargreaves and Goodson 1996: 20–1; emphasis in original)

I would like to add an eighth principle – that, as professionals, we declare publicly to our colleagues and students the dilemmas and ambiguities of our everyday practice and justify why we teach the way we do. In particular, teacher educators need to make these issues public to their preservice students by making explicit real classroom complexities and proposing ways to manage these tensions, similarly to Loughran's (1996) notion of modelling reflective practice. Too often teacher educators portray themselves as experts and neglect to focus on the most important aspect of teacher education – understanding the nature of teaching.

Hutchings and Shulman (1999) argue that there is an important difference between 'excellence in teaching' and 'scholarship in teaching'. Whereas 'excellence in teaching' suggests a degree of expertise or mastery, 'scholarship' suggests an ongoing inquiry into the dilemmas of teaching. And it is the recognition that dilemmas always exist that is at the heart of scholarship in teaching. Similarly, Shulman (1999) contended that teachers should 'profess' their beliefs in the name of scholarship by making their work public, seeking critique and accepting it as community property that others can use. A hallmark of teaching as an art or profession, then, is an acknowledgement that it cannot be 'mastered':

> At the core of any field that we call a profession is an inherent and inescapable uncertainty. Professions deal with those parts of the world that are characterized by unpredictability. Teachers can teach in the same manner to three classes in a row and experience different consequences each time. Professions (like teaching) deal with that part of the universe where design and chance collide. One cannot resolve that uncertainty by writing new rules. The way forward is to make that collision, that unpredictability in our fields, itself an object of individual and collective investigation. We can never fully remove the uncertainty from teaching any more than we can from such other professions as clinical medicine, architecture, economic planning, or clinical social work. But as a profession, we can grow much wiser about how to anticipate and deal with uncertainty.
>
> (Shulman 1999: 15)

I want to conclude this book with a suggestion that *how* we became 'much wiser' to deal with uncertainty is by embracing the paradigm of complexity theory, because this view is a closer approximation to how the world works than is a mechanistic paradigm. It is time for public discussions about the nature of teaching, teacher learning and educational change to be more consistent with the complex nature of reality. It is only when the discourse of teachers at all levels focuses on sharing the ordinary, everyday events in classrooms – the ups, downs, laughs, mistakes, disappointments, insights, emotions, dilemmas, tensions and achievements – that we have a *reason* to engage in professional learning and work together on the edge of chaos.

References

Acker, S. (1983) Women and teaching: the semi-detached sociology of a semi-profession, in L. Barton and S. Walker (eds) *Gender, Race and Schooling*. Lewes: Falmer Press.

Acker, S. (1995) Gender and teachers' work, in M. Apple (ed.) *Review of Research in Education*, Vol. 21. Washington, DC: American Educational Research Association.

Ackerman, M.S. and Palen, L. (1996) The zephyr help instance: promoting ongoing activity in a CSCW system. Paper presented to the CHI'96 Conference, New York, July.

Anderson, J.R., Reder, L.M. and Simon, H.A. (1996) Situated learning and education, *Educational Researcher*, 25(4): 5–11.

Anderson, J.R., Greeno, J.G., Reder, L.M. and Simon, H.E. (2000) Perspectives on learning, thinking and activity, *Educational Researcher*, 29(4): 11–13.

Argyris, C. (1993) *On Organizational Learning*. Cambridge, MA: Blackwell.

Argyris, C. and Schön, D.A. (1974) *Theory in Practice: Increasing Professional Effectiveness*. San Francisco, CA: Jossey-Bass.

Asayesh, G. (1993) Using systems thinking to create systems, *Journal of Staff Development*, 14(4): 8–13.

Atkin, J. (1999) *Understanding How We Learn*, ICT Cluster seminar notes, 12 April.

Atwood, R.K. and Howard, M.N. (1990) SCIS-II and the elementary teacher: a cognitive view, *Journal of Research in Science Teaching*, 27(9): 206–12.

Baird, J.R. (1992) Collaborative reflection, systematic enquiry, better teaching, in T. Russell and H. Munby (eds) *Teachers and Teaching: From Classroom to Reflection*. New York: Falmer Press.

Baird, J. and Mitchell, I.J. (eds) (1987) *Improving the Quality of Teaching and Learning: An Australian Case Study – the PEEL Project*. Melbourne: Monash University Printing Services.

Baird, J., Mitchell, I. and Northfield, J. (1987) Teachers as researchers: the rationale; the reality, *Research in Science Education*, 17: 129–38.

Baird, J.R., Fensham, P.J., Gunstone, R.F. and White, R.T. (1991) The importance of reflection in improving science teaching and learning, *Journal of Research in Science Teaching*, 28(2): 163–82.

Ball, S. (1997) *Micropolitics of the School*. London: Methuen/Routledge & Kegan Press.

Banathy, B.H. (1991) *Systems Design of Education: A Journey to Create the Future*. Englewood Cliffs, NJ: Educational Technology Publications.

Banathy, B.H. (1996) Systems inquiry and its application in education, in D.J. Jonassen (ed.) *Handbook of Research for Educational Communications and Technology*. New York: Macmillan.

Bandura, A. (1978) The self system in reciprocal determinism, *American Psychologist*, 33: 344–58.

Bandura, A. (1986) *Social Foundations of Thought and Action: A Social Cognitive Theory*. Englewood Cliffs, NJ: Prentice-Hall.

Barnes, D. (1992) The significance of teachers' frames for teaching, in T. Russell and H. Munby (eds) *Teachers and Teaching: From Classroom to Reflection*. London: Falmer Press.

Barth, R. (1990) *Improving Schools from Within: Teachers, Parents, and Principals Can Make a Difference*. San Francisco, CA: Jossey-Bass.

Bascia, N. and Hargreaves, A. (2000) Teaching and leading on the sharp edge of change, in N. Bascia and A. Hargreaves (eds) *The Sharp Edge of Change: Teaching, Leading and the Realities of Reform*. London: Routledge/Falmer.

Bass, R. (1999) The scholarship of teaching: what's the problem?, *Inventio*, 1(1): 1–6.

Bell, B. and Gilbert, J. (1994) Teacher development as professional, personal, and social development, *Teaching and Teacher Education*, 10(5): 483–97.

Bellah, R.N., Madsen, N., Sullivan, W.M., Swidler, A. and Tipson, S.M. (1985) *Habits of the Heart: Individualism and Commitment in American Life*. Berkeley, CA: University of California Press.

Bereiter, C. and Scardamalia, M. (1993) *Surpassing Ourselves: An Inquiry into the Nature and Implications of Expertise*. Chicago, IL: Open Court.

Berman, P. and McLaughlin, M.W. (1976) Implementation of educational innovation, *The Educational Forum*, 40(3): 345–70.

Berry, A. and Loughran, J.J. (2000) Developing an understanding of learning to teach in teacher education. Paper presented to the Third International Conference on Self-Study of Teacher Education Practices, Herstmonceux Castle, East Sussex, UK, August.

Betts, F. (1992) How systems thinking applies to education, *Educational Leadership*, 50(3): 38–41.

Bickel, W.E. and Hattrup, R.A. (1995) Teachers and researchers in collaboration: reflections on the process, *American Educational Research Journal*, 32(1): 35–62.

Biggs, J. (1993) From theory to practice: a cognitive systems approach, *Higher Education Research and Development*, 12(1): 73–85.

Biggs, J. (1999) *Teaching for Quality Learning at University: What the Student Does*. Buckingham: Open University Press.

Blase, J. (1998) The micropolitics of educational change, in A. Hargreaves, A. Lieberman, M. Fullan and D. Hopkins (eds) *International Handbook of Educational Change*, Vol. 1. Dordrecht: Kluwer Academic.

Boyer, E.L. (1990) *Scholarship Reconsidered: Priorities of the Professoriate.* Princeton, NJ: The Carnegie Foundation for the Advancement of Teaching.

Bredderman, T. (1983) Effects of activity-based elementary science on student outcomes: a quantitative synthesis, *Review of Educational Research*, 53(4): 499–513.

Brody, C. (1994) Using co-teaching to promote reflective practice, *Journal of Staff Development*, 15(3): 32–6.

Bronfenbrenner, U. (1979) *The Ecology of Human Development: Experiments by Nature and Design.* Cambridge, MA: Harvard University Press.

Brookfield, S. (1986) *Understanding and Facilitating Adult Learning.* San Francisco, CA: Jossey-Bass.

Brookfield, S. (1995) *Becoming a Critically Reflective Teacher.* San Francisco, CA: Jossey-Bass.

Brown, A.L. and Campione, J.C. (1994) Guided discovery in a community of learners, in K. McGilly (ed.) *Classroom Lessons: Integrating Cognitive Theory and Classroom Practice.* Cambridge, MA: MIT Press.

Brown, J.S. and Duguid, P. (1992) *Stolen Knowledge.* New York: Educational Technology Publications.

Brown, J.S., Collins, A. and Duguid, P. (1989) Situated cognition and the culture of learning, *Educational Researcher*, 18(1): 32–42.

Brown, S. and Eisenhardt, K. (1998) *Competing on the Edge.* Boston, MA: Harvard Business School Press.

Butts, D.P. (1973) *Teaching Science in the Elementary School.* New York: Macmillan.

Cain, S.E. and Evans, J.M. (1984) *Sciencing.* Columbus, OH: Merrill.

Caine, R. and Caine, G. (1997) *Education on the Edge of Possibility.* Alexandria, VA: ASCD.

Calhoun, E. and Joyce, B. (1998) 'Inside-out' and 'outside-in': learning from the past and present school improvement paradigms, in A. Hargreaves, A. Lieberman, M. Fullan and D. Hopkins (eds) *International Handbook of Educational Change*, Vol. 2. Dordrecht: Kluwer Academic.

Cambourne, B. (1988) *The Whole Story: Natural Learning and the Acquisition of Literacy in the Classroom.* Auckland, NZ: Ashton Scholastic.

Cambourne, B. (1991) Ideology and the literacy curriculum: the teaching of phonics. Paper presented to the Australian Reading Conference, Adelaide, SA, February.

Candy, P.C. (1991) *Self-direction for Lifelong Learning.* San Francisco, CA: Jossey-Bass.

Capra, F. (1982) *The Turning Point.* New York: Simon & Schuster.

Capra, F. (1988) *Uncommon Wisdom: Conversations with Remarkable People.* London: HarperCollins.

Capra, F. (1996) *The Web of Life: A New Scientific Understanding of Living Systems.* New York: Anchor Books.

Carnap, R. (1966) The scientific world view, in J.A. Mann and G.F. Kreyche (eds) *Perspectives on Reality.* New York: Harcourt, Brace & World.

Carr, W. and Kemmis, S. (1986) *Becoming Critical.* London: Falmer Press.

Clandinin, D.J. and Connelly, F.M. (1996) Teachers' professional knowledge landscapes: teacher stories–stories of teachers–school stories–stories of schools, *Educational Researcher*, 25(3): 24–30.

Clarke, C.J.S. (1996) *Reality Through the Looking-glass.* Edinburgh: Floris Books.

Cobb, P. (1994) Where is the mind? Constructivist and sociocultural perspectives on mathematical development, *Educational Researcher*, 23(7): 13–19.

Cobb, P. and Bowers, J. (1999) Cognitive and situated learning perspectives in theory and practice, *Educational Researcher*, 28(2): 4–15.

Cochran-Smith, M. (1994) The power of teacher research in teacher education, in S. Hollingsworth and H. Sockett (eds) *Teacher Research and Educational Reform*. Chicago, IL: University of Chicago Press.

Cochran-Smith, M. and Lytle, S. (1993) *Inside/Outside: Teacher Research and Knowledge*. New York: Teachers College Press.

Cole, A. and Knowles, G. (2000) *Researching Teaching: Exploring Teacher Development Through Reflexive Inquiry*. Needham Heights, MA: Allyn & Bacon.

Cole, M. and Engeström, Y. (1993) A cultural-historical approach to distributed cognition, in G. Salomon (ed.) *Distributed Cognitions: Psychological and Educational Considerations*. Cambridge: Cambridge University Press.

Coulter, D. (1999) The epic and the novel: dialogism and teacher research, *Educational Researcher*, 28(3): 4–13.

Cuban, L. (1990) Reforming again, again, and again, *Educational Researcher*, 19(1): 3–13.

Cuban, L. (1992) Managing dilemmas while building professional communities, *Educational Researcher*, 21(1): 4–11.

Cusins, P. (1995) Action learning revisited, *Industrial and Commercial Training*, 27(4): 3–10.

Darling-Hammond, L. (ed.) (1994) *Professional Development Schools: Schools for Developing a Profession*. New York: Teachers College Press.

Datnow, A. (2000) Gender politics in school reform, in N. Bascia and A. Hargreaves (eds) *The Sharp Edge of Educational Change: Teaching, Leading and the Realities of Reform*. London: Routledge/Falmer.

David, J.L. (1994) Realizing the promise of technology: a policy perspective, in B. Means (ed.) *Technology and Educational Reform: The Reality Behind the Promise*. San Francisco, CA: Jossey-Bass.

Day, C. (1999) *Developing Teachers: The Challenges of Lifelong Learning*. London: Falmer Press.

Dewey, J. (1897) *My Pedagogic Creed*. New York: E.L. Kellogg.

Dewey, J. (1901) *Psychology and Social Practice*. Chicago, IL: University of Chicago Press.

Dewey, J. ([1902] 1990) *The Child and the Curriculum*. Chicago, IL: University of Chicago Press.

Dewey, J. (1916) *Democracy and Education*. New York: Macmillan.

Dewey, J. (1933) *How We Think: A Restatement of the Relation of Reflective Thinking to the Educative Process*, 2nd edn. Boston, MA: Heath.

Dewey, J. (1938) *Experience and Education*. New York: Collier.

Diltz, R. (1996) 'The Belief Change Cycle', Santa Cruz (available online at: http://www.scruz.net/~rdilts/Articles/article3.htm).

Doll, W.E.J. (1986) Prigogine: a new sense of order, a new curriculum, *Theory into Practice*, 25(1): 10–16.

Doll, W.E.J. (1993) *A Post-modern Perspective on Curriculum*. New York: Teachers College Press.

Driver, R. and Oldham, V. (1986) A constructivist approach to curriculum development in science, *Studies in Science Education*, 13: 105–22.

Driver, R., Asoko, H., Leach, J., Mortimer, E. and Scott, P. (1994) Constructing scientific knowledge in the classroom, *Educational Researcher*, 23(7): 5–12.

Duffy, G. (1990) What counts in teacher education? Dilemmas in educating empowered teachers. Presidential Address to the National Reading Conference, Miami, FL, August.

Elias, D. (1979) Critique: andragogy revisited, *Adult Education*, 29: 252–5.

Erickson, G.L. (1979) Children's conceptions of heat and temperature, *Science Education*, 63(2): 221–30.

Eve, R.A., Horsefall, S. and Lee, M.E. (1997) *Chaos, Complexity and Sociology: Myths, Models and Theories*. Thousand Oaks, CA: Sage Publications.

Faire, J. and Cosgrove, M. (1988) *Teaching Primary Science*. Hamilton, NZ: Waikato Education Centre.

Fensham, P. (ed.) (1988) *Development and Dilemmas in Science Education*. Philadelphia, PA: Falmer Press.

Fenstermacher, G.D. (1994) The knower and the known: the nature of knowledge in research on teaching, in L. Darling-Hammond (ed.) *Review of Research in Education*. Washington, DC: American Educational Research Association.

Fink, D. (2000) *Good School/Real Schools: Why School Reform Doesn't Last*. New York: Teachers College Press.

Fink, D. and Stoll, L. (1998) Educational change: easier said than done, in A. Hargreaves, A. Lieberman, M. Fullan and D. Hopkins (eds) *International Handbook of Educational Change*, Vol. 1. Dordrecht: Kluwer Academic.

Flood, R.L. and Carson, E.R. (1988) *Dealing with Complexity: An Introduction to the Theory and Application of Systems Science*. London: Plenum Press.

Fullan, M. (1982) *The Meaning of Educational Change*. Toronto: Ontario Institute for Studies in Education.

Fullan, M. (1992) *Successful School Improvement*. Buckingham: Open University Press.

Fullan, M. (1993) *Change Forces: Probing the Depths of Educational Reform*. London: Falmer Press.

Fullan, M. (1999) *Change Forces: The Sequel*. London: Falmer Press.

Fuller, F.F. (1969) Concerns of teachers: a developmental conceptualization, *American Educational Research Journal*, 6(2): 207–26.

Gleick, J. (1987) *Chaos: Making a New Science*. New York: Penguin.

Goodlad, J.I. (1975) *The Dynamics of Educational Change: Toward Responsive Schools*. New York: McGraw-Hill.

Goodson, I. (2001a) Social histories of educational change, *Journal of Educational Change*, 2(1): 45–63.

Goodson, I.F. (2001b) Educational change and professional biography. Paper presented to the Annual Meeting of the American Educational Research Association, Seattle, WA, April.

Goodson, I.F. and Hargreaves, A. (1996) *Teachers' Professional Lives*. London: Falmer Press.

Greeno, J.G. (1997) On claims that answer the wrong question, *Educational Researcher*, 26(1): 5–17.

Grimmett, P.P. and Erickson, G.L. (eds) (1988) *Reflection in Teacher Education*. New York: Teachers College Press.

Grossman, P. and Wineburg, S. (2000) *What Makes Teacher Community Different from a Gathering of Teachers?* Washington, DC: Center for the Study of Teaching and Policy, University of Washington.

Gunstone, R.F. (1990) Children's science: a decade of developments in constructivist views of science teaching and learning, *Australian Science Teachers Journal*, 36(4): 9–19.

Guskey, T.R. (1986) Staff development and the process of teacher change, *Educational Researcher*, 15(5): 5–12.

Hall, G.E. (1978) Concerns-based inservice teacher training: an overview of concepts, research and practice. Paper presented to the Conference on School-focused Inservice Training, Bournemouth, UK, 2–3 March.

Hannay, L. (1994) Strategies for facilitating reflective practice: the role of staff developers, *Journal of Staff Development*, 15(3): 22–6.

Hargreaves, A. (1994) *Changing Teachers, Changing Times: Teachers' Work and Culture in a Postmodern Age*. London: Cassell.

Hargreaves, A. (1998) Pushing the boundaries of educational change, in A. Hargreaves, A. Lieberman, M. Fullan and D. Hopkins (eds) *International Handbook of Educational Change*, Vol. 1. Dordrecht: Kluwer Academic.

Hargreaves, A. and Goodson, I. (1996) Teachers' professional lives: aspirations and actualities, in I.F. Goodson and A. Hargreaves (eds) *Teachers' Professional Lives*. London: Falmer Press.

Hargreaves, A., Shaw, P. and Fink, D. (1997) *Change Frames: The Creation of Learning Communities*. International Centre for Educational Change, Toronto, ON: OISE/University of Toronto.

Heckenberg, K., McKenzie, P. and Turbill, J. (1994) Towards the development of a grounded theory for the initial implementation stage of an innovation in a change process. Unpublished honours thesis, University of Wollongong, NSW.

Hoban, G.F. (1992) An intervention program to facilitate the teaching of enquiry-based science in one-teacher schools. Unpublished master of education thesis, Charles Sturt University, Wagga Wagga, NSW.

Hoban, G.F. (1996) A professional development model based on interrelated principles of teacher learning. Unpublished doctoral dissertation, The University of British Columbia, Vancouver, BC.

Hoban, G.F. (1999) The role of community in action learning: a Deweyian perspective on sharing experiences, in J.A. Retallick, K. Coombe and B. Cochlin (eds) *Learning Communities in Context: Issues and Contexts*. London: Routledge.

Hoban, G.F. (2000a) Making practice problematic: listening to student interviews as a catalyst for teacher reflection, *Asia–Pacific Journal of Teacher Education*, 28(2): 133–47.

Hoban, G.F. (2000b) Using a reflective framework to study teaching–learning relationships, *Reflective Practice*, 1(2): 165–83.

Hoban, G., Hastings, G., Luccarda, C. and Lloyd, D. (1997) Faculty based professional development as an action learning community, *Australian Science Teachers Journal*, 43(3): 49–54.

Holmes, M. (1998) Change in tradition in education: the loss of community, in A. Hargreaves, A. Lieberman, M. Fullan and D. Hopkins (eds) *International Handbook of Educational Change*, Vol. 1. Dordrecht: Kluwer Academic.

Hord, S.M. and Boyd, V. (1994) Professional development fuels a culture of continuous improvement, *Journal of Staff Development*, 16(1): 10–15.

Huberman, M. (1993) The model of the independent artisan in teachers' professional relations, in J.W. Little and M.W. McLaughlin (eds) *Teachers' Work: Individuals, Colleagues and Contexts*. New York: Teachers College Press.

Huberman, M. (1995) Networks that alter teaching, *Teaching and Teaching: Theory and Practice*, 1(2): 193–221.

Hutchings, P. and Shulman, L.S. (1999) The scholarship of teaching: new elaborations, new developments, *Change*, 31(5): 10–15.

James, R.K. and Hord, S.M. (1988) Implementing elementary school science programs, *School Science and Mathematics*, 88(4): 315–34.

Knapp, C. (1992) *Lasting Lessons: A Teacher's Guide to Reflecting on Experience*. Charleston, WV: Eric Clearinghouse on Rural Education and Small Schools.

Knowles, M. (1968) Andragogy, not pedagogy. *Adult Leadership*, 16(10): 350–2.

Knowles, M. (1980) *The Modern Practice of Adult Education: From Pedagogy to Andragogy*, 2nd edn. New York: Cambridge Books.

Knowles, M. and Associates (1984) *Andragogy in Action: Applying Modern Principles of Adult Learning*. San Francisco, CA: Jossey-Bass.

Kolb, D.A. (1984) *Experiential Learning: Experience as the Source of Learning*. Englewood Cliffs, NJ: Prentice-Hall.

Kollock, P. and Smith, M. (1996) Managing the virtual commons: cooperation and conflict in computer communities, in S. Herring (ed.) *Computer-mediated Communication: Linguistic, Social, and Cross-cultural Perspectives*. Amsterdam: Benjamins.

Kozma, R. and Schank, P. (1998) Connecting with the 21st century: technology in support of educational reform, in D. Palumbo and C. Dede (eds) *Learning and Technology*. New York: Association for Supervision and Curriculum Development.

Kuhn, T.S. (1970) *The Structure of Scientific Revolutions*. Chicago, IL: University of Chicago Press.

Lagemann, E.C. (2000) *An Elusive Science: The Troubling History of Educational Research*. Chicago, IL: University of Chicago Press.

Lave, J. (1988a) *Cognition in Practice*. Boston, MA: Cambridge.

Lave, J. (1988b) *The Culture of Acquisition and the Practice of Understanding*, IRL Report 88-00087. Palo Alto, CA: Institute for Research on Learning.

Lave, J. and Wenger, E. (1991) *Situated Learning: Legitimate Peripheral Participation*. Cambridge: Cambridge University Press.

Lawler, E. (1992) *The Ultimate Advantage: Creating the High-involvement Organisation*. San Francisco, CA: Jossey-Bass.

Lazear, D. (1994) *Seven Ways of Teaching – The Artistry of Teaching with Multiple Intelligences*. Melbourne: Hawker Brownlow Education.

Leary, J. (1983) The effectiveness of concern-based staff development in facilitating curriculum implementation. Paper presented to the Annual Conference of the American Educational Research Association, Montreal, Quebec, April.

Leithwood, K.A. (1992) The move toward transformational leadership, *Educational Leadership*, 49(5): 8–12.

Leithwood, K., Jantzi, D. and Steinbach, R. (1999) *Changing Leadership for Changing Times*. Buckingham: Open University Press.

Lewin, K. (1946) Action research and minority problems, *Journal of Social Issues*, 2(4): 34–46.

Lieberman, A. (1996) Creating intentional learning communities, *Educational Leadership*, 54(3): 51–5.

Lortie, D. (1975) *Schoolteacher: A Sociological Study*. Chicago, IL: University of Chicago Press.

Loucks, S.F. (1977) Concerns expressed by elementary school teachers about the implementation of the SCIS curriculum. Paper presented to the Annual Meeting of the Association for the Education of Teachers of Science, Cincinnati, OH, April.

Loughran, J.J. (1996) *Developing Reflective Practice: Learning about Teaching and Learning Through Modelling*. London: Falmer Press.

Loughran, J. and Northfield, J. (1998) A framework for the development of self-study practices, in M.L. Hamilton (ed.) *Reconceptualizing Teaching Practices: Self-study in Teacher Education*. London: Falmer Press.

Mainzer, K. (1994) *Thinking in Complexity: The Complex Dynamics of Matter, Mind, and Mankind*. Berlin: Springer-Verlag.

Marion, R. (1999) *The Edge of Organization: Chaos and Complexity Theories of Formal Social Systems*. Thousand Oaks, CA: Sage.

McKenzie, J. (1997) The question is the answer – creating research programs for an age of information, *Now On web site*, October 1997 (available online at: http://emifyes.iserver.net/fromnow/oct97/question.html).

McLaughlin, M. (1993) What matters most in teachers' workplace context, in J.W. Little and M.W. McLaughlin (eds) *Teachers' Work: Individuals, Colleagues and Contexts*. New York: Teachers College Press.

Means, B. and Olson, K. (1994) Tomorrow's schools: technology and reform in partnership, in B. Means (ed.) *Technology and Educational Reform: The Reality Behind the Promise*. San Francisco, CA: Jossey-Bass.

Merriam, S.B. and Caffarella, R.S. (1999) *Learning in Adulthood: A Comprehensive Guide*, 2nd edn. San Francisco, CA: Jossey-Bass.

Mills, G.E. (2000) *Action Research: A Guide for the Teacher Researcher*. Columbus, OH: Merrill.

Minick, N. (1989) *L.S. Vygotsky and Soviet Activity Theory: Perspectives on the Relationship Between Mind and Society* (Vol. Literacies Institute, Special Monograph Series No. 1). Newton, MA: Educational Development Center.

Minnes Brandes, G. and Erickson, G. (1998) Developing and sustaining a community of inquiry among teachers and teacher educators, *Alberta Journal of Educational Research*, 64(1): 38–52.

Mitchell, C. and Weber, S. (1999) *Reinventing Ourselves as Teachers: Beyond Nostalgia*. London: Falmer Press.

Mitchell, I. and Erickson, G. (1995) Initiating school–university collaborations. Paper presented to the Annual Meeting of the American Educational Research Association, San Francisco, CA, April.

Moore, S. and Shaw, P. (2000) The professional learning needs and perceptions of secondary school teachers: implications for professional learning community.

Paper presented to the Annual Meeting of the American Educational Research Association, New Orleans, LA, April.

Mortimer, P. (1998) The vital hours: reflecting on research on schools and their effects, in A. Hargreaves, A. Lieberman, M. Fullan and D. Hopkins (eds) *International Handbook of Educational Change*, Vol. 1. Dordrecht: Kluwer Academic.

Munby, H. and Russell, T. (1992) Frames of reflection: an introduction, in H. Munby and T. Russell (eds) *Teachers and Teaching: From Classroom to Reflection*. New York: Falmer Press.

Munby, H. and Russell, T. (1994) The authority of experience in learning to teach: messages from a physics method class, *Journal of Teacher Education*, 45(2): 86–95.

Munsterberg, H. (1914) *Psychology: General and Applied*. New York: Appleton.

Negroponte, N. (1998) Beyond Digital, *Wired*, 6(12): 288.

Nicolis, G. and Prigogine, I. (1989) *Exploring Complexity: An Introduction*. New York: W.H. Freeman.

Osborne, R. and Freyberg, P. (1985) *Learning in Science: The Implications of Children's Science*. Auckland, NZ: Heinemann.

Osborne, R. and Wittrock, M.C. (1983) Learning science: a generative process, *Science Education*, 67(4): 489–508.

Pea, R. (1993) Practices of distributed intelligence and designs for education, in G. Salomon (ed.) *Distributed Cognitions: Psychological and Educational Considerations*. New York: Cambridge University Press.

Piaget, J. (1950) *The Psychology of Intelligence*. London: Routledge & Kegan Paul.

Placier, P. and Hamilton, M.L. (1994) Schools as context: a complex relationship, in V. Richardson (ed.) *A Theory of Teacher Change and the Process of Staff Development: A Case of Reading Instruction*. New York: Teachers College Press.

Polanyi, M. (1966) *The Tacit Dimension*. New York: Doubleday.

Pouravood, R.G. (1997) Chaos, complexity, and learning community: what do they mean for education?, *School Community Journal*, 7(2): 57–64.

Pratt, D. (1993) Andragogy after twenty-five years, in S.B. Merriam (ed.) *An Update on Adult Learning*. San Francisco, CA: Jossey-Bass.

Prawat, R.S. (1999) Dewey, Pierce, and the learning Paradox, *American Educational Research Journal*, 36(1): 47–76.

Putnam, R.T. and Borko, H. (1997) Teacher learning: implications of new views of cognition, in B.J. Biddle (ed.) *International Handbook of Teachers and Teaching*. Dordrecht: Kluwer Academic.

Putnam, R. and Borko, H. (2000) What do new views of knowledge and thinking have to say about research on teacher learning?, *Educational Researcher*, 29(1): 4–15.

Quartz, K.H. (1995) Sustaining new educational communities: toward a new culture of school reform, in J. Oakes and K. Hunter (eds) *Creating New Educational Communities*. Chicago, IL: University of Chicago Press.

Resnick, L. (1987) Learning in school and out, *Educational Researcher*, 16(9): 13–20.

Retallick, J. and Fink, D. (2000) Framing leadership: contributions and impediments to educational change. Paper presented to the Annual Meeting of the American Educational Research Association, New Orleans, LA, April.

Richardson, V. (1992) The agenda-setting dilemma in a constructivist staff development process, *Teaching and Teacher Education*, 8(3): 287–300.

Richardson, V. (ed.) (1994) *A Theory of Change and the Staff Development Process*. New York: Teachers College Press.

Rorty, R. (1991) *Objectivity, Relativism, and Truth: Philosophical Papers*. Cambridge: Cambridge University Press.

Ross, J. and Regan, I. (1993) Sharing professional experience: impact of professional development, *Teaching and Teacher Education*, 9(1): 91–106.

Rudman, H.C. (1978) Science teaching in the '80s: a case of benign neglect, *Science and Children*, 16(2): 7–8.

Saban, J., Killion, J. and Green, C. (1994) The centric reflection mode: a kaleidoscope for staff developers, *Journal of Staff Development*, 15(3): 16–21.

Sachs, J. and Logan, L. (1990) Control or development? A study of inservice education, *Journal of Curriculum Studies*, 22(5): 473–81.

Salomon, G. (1993) No distribution with individuals' cognition: a dynamic interactional view, in G. Salomon (ed.) *Distributed Cognitions: Psychological and Educational Considerations*. Cambridge: Cambridge University Press.

Salomon, G. (2000) It's not just the tool, but the educational rationale that counts. Keynote address to the EDMEDIA World Conference on Educational Multimedia, Hypermedia and Telecommunications, Montreal, July.

Salomon, G. and Perkins, D.N. (1998) Individual and social aspects of learning, in P.D. Pearson and A. Iran-Nejad (eds) *Review of Research in Education*, Vol. 23. Washington, DC: American Educational Research Association.

Sarason, S. (1971) *The Culture of School and the Problem of Change*. Boston, MA: Allyn & Bacon.

Sarason, S. (1981) *Psychology Misdirected*. New York: Free Press.

Sarason, S. (1990) *The Predictable Failure of Educational Reform: Can We Change Course Before it is Too Late?* San Francisco, CA: Jossey-Bass.

Saxe, G.B. (1988) Candy selling and math learning, *Educational Researcher*, 17: 14–21.

Schlager, M., Fusco, J. and Schank, P. (1998) Cornerstone for an on-line community of educational professions, *IEEE Technology and Society Magazine*, 17(4): 15–21.

Schlager, M., Fusco, J. and Schank, P. (2002) Evolution of an on-line education community of practice, in K.A. Renninger and W. Shumar (eds) *Building Virtual Communities: Learning and Change in Cyberspace*. New York: Cambridge University Press.

Schoenfeld, A.H. (1999) Looking toward the 21st century: challenges of educational theory and practice, *Educational Researcher*, 28(7): 4–14.

Schön, D.A. (1983) *The Reflective Practitioner: How Professionals Think in Action*. New York: Basic Books.

Schön, D.A. (1987) *Educating the Reflective Practitioner: Toward a New Design for Teaching and Learning*. San Francisco, CA: Jossey-Bass.

Schön, D.A. (ed.) (1991) *The Reflective Turn*. New York: Teachers College Press.

Schwier, R.A. (1999) Turning learning environments into learning communities: expanding the notion of interaction in multimedia. Paper presented to the World

Conference on Educational Multimedia, Hypermedia and Telecommunications, Seattle, WA, July.

Seashore Louis, K., Toole, J. and Hargreaves, A. (1999) Rethinking school improvement, in J. Murphy and K.S. Louis (eds) *Handbook of Research on Educational Administration*, 2nd edn. San Francisco, CA: Jossey-Bass.

Senge, P. (1990) *The Fifth Discipline: The Art and Practice of the Learning Organization*. New York: Doubleday.

Sergiovanni, T.J. (1994) *Building Community in Schools*. San Francisco, CA: Jossey-Bass.

Sfard, A. (1998) On two metaphors for learning and the dangers of choosing just one, *Educational Researcher*, 27(2): 4–13.

Shrigley, R.G. (1983) Persuade, mandate and reward: a paradigm for changing the science attitudes and behaviours of teachers, *School Science and Mathematics*, 83(3): 204–15.

Shulman, L. (1988) The dangers of dichotomous thinking in education, in P. Grimmett and G.L. Erickson (eds) *Reflection in Teacher Education*. New York: Teachers College Press.

Shulman, L. (1998) Course anatomy: the dissection and analysis of knowledge through teaching, *The Course Portfolio: How Faculty can Examine their Teaching to Advance Practice and Improve Student Learning*, 2: 5–12.

Shulman, L.S. (1999) Taking learning seriously, *Change*, 31(4): 11–17.

Sikes, P. (1985) The life cycles of the teacher, in S. Ball and I. Goodson (eds) *Teachers' Lives and Careers*. London: Falmer Press.

Sirotnik, K.A. (1998) Ecological images of change: limits and possibilities, in A. Hargreaves, A. Lieberman, M. Fullan and D. Hopkins (eds) *International Handbook of Educational Change*, Vol. 1. Dordrecht: Kluwer Academic.

Smylie, M.A. (1995) Teacher learning in the workplace: implications for school reform, in T.R. Guskey and M. Huberman (eds) *Professional Development in Education: New Paradigms and Practices*. New York: Teachers College Press.

Smyth, J. (1992) Teachers' work and the politics of reflection, *American Educational Research Journal*, 29(2): 267–300.

Solomon, J. (1994) The rise and fall of constructivism, *Studies in Science Education*, 23: 1–19.

Sparkes, A.C. (1991) The culture of teaching, critical reflection and change: possibilities and problems, *Educational Management and Administration*, 19(1): 4–19.

Sparks, D. and Loucks-Horsley, S. (1990) Models of staff development, in W.R. Houston (ed.) *Handbook of Research on Teacher Education*. New York: Macmillan.

Stacey, R.D. (1996) *Complexity and Creativity in Organizations*. San Francisco, CA: Berrett-Koehler.

Stoll, L. and Fink, D. (1996) *Changing Our Schools: Linking School Effectiveness and School Improvement*. Buckingham: Open University Press.

Stuckey, B. and Hedberg, J. (2000) Building on-line community: the way forward for professional development. Paper presented to the 17th Annual Conference of the Australasian Society for Computers in Learning in Tertiary Education, Coffs Harbour, NSW, December.

Sullivan, T.J. (1993) System metamorphosis: an examination of chaos theory applied to a system of school organization undergoing policy implementation. Unpublished doctoral thesis, University of New England, Armidale.

Swain, L.J. (1994) A naturalistic study investigating teachers' perceptions of the new English K-6 syllabus in relation to reading in one primary school. Unpublished honours thesis, University of Wollongong, NSW.

Tapscott, D. (1999) Educating the net generation, *Educational Leadership*, 56(5): 6–11 (available online at: http://www.ascd.org/readingroom/edlead/abstracts/feb99.html).

Thorndike, E.L. (1903) *Educational Psychology*. New York: Science Press.

Tolstoy, L. (1967) On teaching the rudiments, in L. Weiner (ed.) *Tolstoy on Education*. Chicago, IL: University of Chicago Press.

Turbill, J. (1994) From a personal theory to a grounded theory in staff development. Unpublished doctoral thesis, University of Wollongong, NSW.

Turbill, J., Butler, A., Cambourne, B. with Langton, G. (1991, 1993) *Frameworks: A Whole Language Staff Development Program 3–8*. Stanley, NY: Wayne Finger Lakes Board of Cooperative Services.

von Bertalanffy, L. (1933) *Modern Theories of Development*. London: Oxford University Press.

von Bertalanffy, L. (1968) *General System Theory: Foundations, Development, Applications*. New York: Penguin.

von Glasersfeld, E. (1984) An introduction to radical constructivism, in P. Watzlawick (ed.) *The Invented Reality*. New York: Norton.

von Glasersfeld, E. (1987) Learning as constructive activity, in C. Janvire (ed.) *Problems of Representation in the Teaching and Learning of Mathematics*. Hillsdale, NJ: Lawrence Erlbaum Associates.

von Glasersfeld, E. (1989) Constructivism, in T. Husen and T.N. Postlewaite (eds) *The International Encyclopedia of Education*. Oxford: Pergamon Press.

Vygotsky, L.S. (1978) *Mind in Society*. Cambridge, MA: Harvard University Press.

Waldrop, M.M. (1992) *Complexity: The Emerging Science at the Edge of Order and Chaos*. New York: Simon & Schuster.

Wenger, E. (1998) *Communities of Practice: Learning, Meaning and Identity*. Cambridge: Cambridge University Press.

Wertsch, J.V. (1991) A sociocultural approach to socially shared cognitions, in L.B. Resnick, J.M. Levine, and S.D. Teasley (eds) *Perspectives on Socially Shared Cognition*. Washington, DC: American Psychological Association.

Willinsky, J. (2001) The strategic education research program and the public value of research, *Educational Researcher*, 30(1): 5–14.

Wilson, K.G. and Daviss, B. (1995) *Redesigning Education*. New York: Henry Holt.

Wise, A.E., Darling-Hammond, L., McLaughlin, M.W. and Bernstein, H.T. (1984) *Teacher Evaluation: A Study of Effective Practice*. Santa Monica, CA: Rand Corporation.

Wundt, W. (1921) *Elements of Folk Psychology*. London: Allen & Unwin.

Zalles, R.D. (2001) Web-based professional development: defining the territory and putting it in perspective. Paper presented to the Annual Meeting of the American Educational Research Association, Seattle, WA, July.

Index